THE CUSHION IN THE ROAD

THE CUSHION IN THE ROAD

Meditation and Wandering
as the Whole World Awakens
to Being in Harm's Way

ALICE WALKER

THE NEW PRESS
NEW YORK

Requests for permission to reproduce selections from this book should be
mailed to: Permissions Department, The New Press, 38 Greene Street,
New York, NY 10013.

Published in the United States by The New Press, New York, 2013
Distributed by Perseus Distribution

LIBRARY OF CONGRESS CATALOGING-IN-PUBLICATION DATA

Walker, Alice, 1944–
    [Essays. Selections]
    The cushion in the road : meditation and wandering as the whole world
awakens to being in harm's way / Alice Walker.
        pages cm
    ISBN 978-1-59558-872-2 (hardcover) — ISBN 978-1-59558-886-9 (e-book)
    I. Title.
    PS3573.A425C87 2013
    814'.54—dc23

                                                        2012041852

The New Press publishes books that promote and enrich public discussion and
understanding of the issues vital to our democracy and to a more equitable
world. These books are made possible by the enthusiasm of our readers; the
support of a committed group of donors, large and small; the collaboration of
our many partners in the independent media and the not-for-profit sector;
booksellers, who often hand-sell New Press books; librarians; and above all by
our authors.

www.thenewpress.com

Book design by Lovedog Studio
Composition by Westchester Book Composition
This book was set in Monotype Sabon

Printed in the United States of America

10   9   8   7   6   5   4   3   2   1

In honor of the lives of

Celia Sánchez Manduley and Fidel Castro Ruz—

revolutionaries, teachers, and spiritual guides who were,

as well, one of the most inspiring power couples

of the twentieth century.

CONTENTS

MEDITATION

The Settled Mind

"This Is What You Shall Do"

WANDERING

SOLIDARITY

Letters

On Palestine

Onward

ACKNOWLEDGMENTS

I thank Amy Goodman of *Democracy Now!* for being a fine leader in these challenging times. I thank Howard Zinn for being a mentor and inspiration especially to my teenage self; *I miss you Howie.* I thank Jack Kornfield, Pema Chodron, the Dalai Lama, and Amma for being models of mindfulness, courage, soulfulness, and persistence. You make the Universe a brighter place; it sings with you.

I thank my daughter, Rebecca Walker, for teaching me my own strength. I thank G. Kaleo Larson for loving our life together. I thank Charlie and Surprise and Miles, Ziggy, Otis, and Misty for showing me the delight and comfort of becoming a simpler part of the web of life. I also thank Emily Z.

I thank Julie Enzer, Julie McCarroll, Marc Favreau, and Maury Botton of The New Press for their care in preparing this book to reach its place in the world. With our words and work we are building a different and hopefully better world, guided by the belief that this is possible.

I thank my agent of forty years, Wendy Weil, who transitioned recently, for reading and loving this book and for finding a proper home for it. *It is your voice, Wendy; that has not gone anywhere. I hear it still.*

I thank Mexico and its people for reviving me, body and soul, time and time again. You are the best, regardless of *Las Noticias.*

THE CUSHION IN THE ROAD

INTRODUCTION

I HAVE LEARNED MUCH FROM TAOIST THOUGHT; it has been a comfort to me since I read my first Taoist poem: *Sitting quietly, doing nothing, spring comes, and the grass grows by itself.* By Bashō, I believe. But there is also, from that tradition, this thought: *A wanderer's home is in the road.* This has proved very true in my life, much to my surprise. Surprise because I am such a homebody. I love being home with my plants, animals, sunrises and sunsets, the moon! It is all glorious to me. And so, when I turned sixty, I was prepared to bring all of my wandering self home to sit on my cushion, in a meditation room I had prepared long ago, and never really leave.

It so happened that I was in South Korea that year, and South Koreans agreed with me. In fact, in that culture it is understood that when we turn sixty we become "eggy" (it sounds like "eggy," though perhaps this is not how Koreans spell it) and this means we are free to become once again like a child. We are to rid ourselves of our cares, especially those we have collected in the world, and to turn inward to a life of ease, of leisure, of joy. I loved hearing this. What an affirmation of a feeling I was already beginning to have: enough of the world! Where's the grandchild? Where's the cushion?

And so I began to prepare myself to withdraw from the worldly fray.

There I sat, finally, on a cushion in Mexico, with a splendid view of a homemade stone fountain, with its softly falling water a perfect, soothing backdrop to what I thought would be the next, and perhaps final, twenty years of my life.

And then, a miracle seemed to be happening. America was about to elect or not elect a person of color as its president. What? My cushion shifted minutely. Then too an unsuspecting guest left the radio on and I learned bombs were falling on the people of Gaza. A mother, unconscious herself, had lost five of her daughters. Didn't I have a daughter? Would I have wanted to lose her in this way? Wasn't I a mother—even if reportedly imperfect in that role? Well! My cushion began to wobble.

I had friends who became "eggy" and managed to stay "eggy." I envied them. For me, the years following my sixtieth birthday seemed to be about teaching me something else: that, yes, I could become like a child again and enjoy all the pleasures of wonder a child experiences, but I would have to attempt to maintain this joy in the vicissitudes of the actual world, as opposed to the meditative Universe I had created, with its calming, ever flowing, fountain.

My travels would take me to the celebrations in Washington, D.C., where our new president, Barack Obama, would be inaugurated; they would carry me the morning after those festivities to far away Burma (Myanmar), which would lead to much writing about Aung San Suu Kyi. They would take me to Thailand, for a lovely trip up a long river, where I could wave happily at the people who smiled back when smiled upon! They would take me to Gaza, yes. And much writing about the Palestine/Israel impasse. To the West Bank, to India. To all kinds of amazing places. Like, for instance, Petra, in Jordan. Who knew? I would find myself raising a nation of chickens in between travels and visits to holy people in Kerala, Oakland, Woodacre, and Dharamsala. My cushion, the fountain, the peace, because of my attention to some of the deep suffering in the world, sometimes seemed far away.

I felt torn. A condition I do not like and do not recommend.

And then, in a dream, it came to me. There was a long asphalt highway, like the one that passed by my grandparents' place when I lived with them as an eight- and nine-year-old. My grandfather and I would sit on the porch in the still Georgia heat and count the cars as they whizzed by. He'd choose red cars, I would choose blue or black. It was a sitting on cushions of sorts, I suppose, for the two of us, because hours could go by and we were perfectly content. Perhaps that is why, in the dream, the solution to my quandary was available. There, in the middle of the long, perfectly straight highway with its slightly faded yellow centerline, that I had known and loved as a child, sat my rose-colored meditation cushion. Directly on the yellow line, right in the middle of the road.

So what do I believe? That I was born to wander and I was born to sit. To love home with a sometimes almost unbearable affection, but to be lured out into the world to see how it is doing, as my beloved larger home and paradise.

WITNESS

On Barack Obama

LEST WE FORGET:
AN OPEN LETTER TO MY
SISTERS WHO ARE BRAVE

MARCH 27, 2008

I HAVE COME HOME FROM a long stay in Mexico to find—because of the presidential campaign, and especially because of the Obama/ Clinton race for the Democratic nomination—a new country existing alongside the old. On any given day, we collectively become the Goddess of the Three Directions, and can look back into the past, look at ourselves just where we are, and take a glance, as well, into the future. It is a space with which I am familiar.

When I was born in 1944 my parents lived on a Middle Georgia plantation that was owned by a distant white relative, Miss May Montgomery. (During my childhood it was necessary to address all white girls as Miss when they reached the age of twelve.) She would never admit to this relationship, of course, except to mock it. Told by my parents that several of their children would not eat chicken skin, she responded that of course they would not; no Montgomerys would.

My parents and older siblings did everything imaginable for Miss May. They planted and raised her cotton and corn, fed and killed and processed her cattle and hogs, painted her house, patched her roof, and ran her dairy. Among countless other duties and responsibilities, my father was her chauffeur, taking her anywhere she wanted to go at any hour of the day or night. She lived in a large white house with green shutters and a green, luxuriant lawn: not quite as large as Tara of *Gone With the Wind* fame, but in the same style.

We lived in a shack without electricity or running water, under a rusty tin roof that let in wind and rain. Miss May went to school as a girl. The school my parents and their neighbors built for us was burned to the ground by local racists who wanted to keep ignorant their competitors in tenant farming. During the Depression, desperate to feed his hardworking family, my father asked for a raise from ten dollars a month to twelve. Miss May responded that she would not pay that amount to a white man and she certainly wouldn't pay it to a nigger; that before she'd pay a nigger that much money she'd milk the dairy cows herself.

When I look back, this is part of what I see. I see the school bus carrying white children, boys and girls, right past me and my brothers as we trudge on foot five miles to school. Later, I see my parents struggling to build a school out of discarded army barracks while white students, girls and boys, enjoy a building made of brick. We had no books; we inherited the cast-off books that Jane and Dick had previously used in the all-white school that we were not, as black children, permitted to enter.

The year I turned fifty, one of my relatives told me she had started reading my books for children in the library in my hometown. I had had no idea that such a place existed—so kept from black people it had been. To this day, knowing my presence was not wanted in the public library when I was a child, I am highly uncomfortable in libraries and will rarely, unless I am there to help build, repair, refurbish, or raise money to keep them open, enter their doors.

When I joined the freedom movement in Mississippi in my early twenties, it was to come to the aid of sharecroppers, like my parents, who had been thrown off the land they'd always known—the plantations—because they attempted to exercise their democratic right to vote. I wish I could say white women treated me and other black people a lot better than the men did, but I cannot. It seemed to me then and it seems to me now that white women have copied, all too often, the behavior of their fathers and their brothers, and in the South, especially in Mississippi, and before that, when I worked to register voters in Georgia, the broken bottles thrown at my head were gender-free.

I made my first white women friends in college; they were women who loved me and were loyal to our friendship, but I understood, as they did, that they were white women and that whiteness mattered. For instance, at Sarah Lawrence, where I was speedily inducted into the board of trustees—practically as soon as I graduated—I made my way to the campus for meetings by train, subway, and on foot, while the other trustees, women and men, all white, made their way by limo. Because, in our country, with its painful history of unspeakable inequality, this is part of what whiteness means. I loved my school for trying to make me feel I mattered to it, but because of my relative poverty I knew I could not.

I am a supporter of Obama because I believe he is the right person to lead the country at this time. He offers a rare opportunity for the country and the world to start over, and to do better. It is a deep sadness to me that many of my feminist white women friends cannot see him; cannot see what he carries in his being; cannot hear the fresh choices toward movement he offers. That they can believe that millions of Americans—black, white, yellow, red, and brown—choose Obama over Clinton only because he is a man, and black, feels tragic to me.

When I have supported white people, men and women, it was because I thought them the best possible people to do whatever the job required. Nothing else would have occurred to me. If Obama were in any sense mediocre, he would be forgotten by now. He is, in fact, a remarkable human being, not perfect but humanly stunning, like King was and like Mandela is. We look at him, as we looked at them, and are glad to be of our species. He is the change America has been trying desperately and for centuries to hide, ignore, kill—the change America must have if we are to convince the rest of the world that we care about people other than our (white) selves.

True to my inner Goddess of the Three Directions, however, this does not mean I agree with everything Obama stands for. We differ on important points probably because I am older than he is, I am a woman and person of three colors (African, Native American, European), I was born and raised in the American South, and when I look at Earth's people, after sixty-four years of life, there is not one person I wish to see suffer, no matter what they have done to me or to anyone else, though I understand quite well the place of suffering, often, in human growth.

I want a grown-up attitude toward Cuba, for instance, a country and a people I love; I want an end to the embargo that has harmed my friends and their children, children who, when I visit Cuba, trustingly turn their faces up for me to kiss. I agree with a teacher of mine, Howard

Zinn, that war is as objectionable as cannibalism and slavery; it is beyond obsolete as a means of improving life. I want an end to the ongoing war immediately and I want the soldiers to be encouraged to destroy their weapons and to drive themselves out of Iraq.

I want the Israeli government to be made accountable for its behavior toward the Palestinians, and I want the people of the United States to cease acting like they don't understand what is going on. All colonization, all occupation, all repression basically looks the same, whoever is doing it. Our heads cannot remain stuck in the sand; our future depends on our ability to study, to learn, to understand what is in the records and what is before our eyes. But most of all I want someone with the self-confidence to talk to anyone, enemy or friend, and this Obama has shown he can do. It is difficult to understand how one could vote for a person who is afraid to sit and talk to another human being. When you vote you are making someone a proxy for yourself; they are to speak when, and in places, you cannot. But if they find it impossible to talk to someone else, who looks just like them—human—then what good is your vote?

It is hard to relate what it feels like to see Mrs. Clinton (I wish she felt self-assured enough to use her own name) referred to as a woman while Barack Obama is always referred to as a black man. One would think she is just any woman, colorless, raceless, pastless, but she is not. She carries all the history of white womanhood in America in her person; it would be a miracle if we, and the world, did not react to this fact. How dishonest it is to attempt to make her innocent of her racial inheritance.

I can easily imagine Obama sitting down and talking, person to person, with any leader, with any woman, man, or child in the world, with no baggage of past servitude or race supremacy to mar their talks. I cannot see the same scenario with Mrs. Clinton, who would drag into twenty-first-century American leadership the same white privilege and distance from the reality of other lives that have so marred our country's contacts with the rest of the world.

And yes, I would adore having a woman president of the United States. My choice would be Representative Barbara Lee, who alone voted in Congress five years ago not to make war on Iraq. That to me is leadership, morality, and courage; if she had been white I would have cheered just as hard. But she is not running for the highest office in the

land, Mrs. Clinton is. And because Mrs. Clinton is a woman and because she may be very good at what she does, many people, including
some younger women in my own family, originally favored her over
Obama. I understand this, almost. It is because, in my own nieces' case,
there is little memory, apparently, of the foundational inequities that
still plague people of color and poor whites in this country. Why, even
though our family has been here longer than most North American
families—and only partly due to the fact that we have Native American genes—it was only very recently, in my lifetime, that we secured
the right to vote, and only after numbers of people suffered and died
for it.

When I offered the word Womanism many years ago, it was to give
us a tool to use, as feminist women of color, in times like these. These
are the moments we can see clearly, and must honor devotedly, our singular path as women of color in the United States. We are not white
women and this truth has been ground into us for centuries, often in
brutal ways. But neither are we inclined to follow a black person, man
or woman, unless they demonstrate considerable courage, intelligence,
compassion, and substance. I am delighted that so many women of
color support Barack Obama and genuinely proud of the many young
and old white women and men who do.

Imagine: if he wins the presidency we will have not one but three
black women in the White House—one tall, two somewhat shorter,
none of them carrying the washing in and out of the back door. The
bottom line for most of us is: with whom do we have a better chance
of surviving the madness and fear we are presently enduring, and with
whom do we wish to set off on a journey of new possibility? In other
words, as the Hopi elders would say: who do we want in the boat with
us as we head for the rapids? Who is likely to know how best to share
the meager garden produce and water? We are advised by the Hopi
elders to celebrate this time, whatever its adversities.

We have come a long way, Sisters, and we are up to the challenges of
our time, one of which is to build alliances based not on race, ethnicity,
color, nationality, sexual preference, or gender, but on truth. Celebrate
our journey. Enjoy the miracle we are witnessing. Do not stress over its
outcome. Even if Obama becomes president, our country is in such
ruin it may well be beyond his power to lead us toward rehabilitation.
If he is elected, however, we must, individually and collectively, as

citizens of the planet, insist on helping him do the best job that can be done; more, we must insist that he demand this of us. It is a blessing that our mothers taught us not to fear hard work. Know, as the Hopi elders declare: The river has its destination. And remember, as poet June Jordan and Sweet Honey in the Rock never tired of telling us: We are the ones we have been waiting for.

Namasté.

And with all my love,

AW

WHAT I WANT: COMPASSION AS A VALUE

SEPTEMBER 9, 2008
MY FATHER'S BIRTHDAY

I REMEMBER SEEING A PICTURE of Fidel Castro in a parade with lots of other Cubans. It was during the emergency years, the "special period" when Cuba's relationship with the Soviet Union had collapsed and there was little gas or oil or fertilizer; people were struggling to find enough to eat. It was perhaps Cuba's nadir, as a small Caribbean island nation considered a dangerous threat by its nearest neighbor, the United States, which, during this period, tightened its embargo against it. Fidel, tall, haggard, his clothes hanging more loosely than usual from his gaunt frame, walked soberly along, surrounded by thousands of likewise downhearted, fearful people—he, like them, waving a tiny red, white, and blue Cuban flag. This photograph made me weep, not only because I love Fidel and the Cuban people, but also because I was envious.

However poor the Cubans might be, I realized, they cared about each other and they had a leader who loved them. A leader who loved them. Imagine. A leader not afraid to be out in the streets with them, a leader not contemptuous of their fear and impoverishment, a leader not ashamed to show himself as troubled and humbled as they were. A leader who would not leave them to wonder and worry alone, but would stand with them, walk with them, celebrate with them—whatever the parade might be.

This is what I want for our country, more than anything. I want a leader who can love us. It is hard to say this because this is not what we usually say, or think, when we are trying to choose a leader. People like to talk about "experience" and war and the economy and whether a potential leader will make Americans look good again. I care about all these things. But when the lights are out and I'm left with just the stars in a super-dark sky and I feel the new intense chill that seems to be the underbreath of even the hottest day, when I know that global warming may send our planet into a deep freeze even before my remaining years run out, then I think about what it is that truly matters to me. Not just as a human, but as an American.

I want a leader who can love us. And, truthfully, by our collective behavior, we have made it hard to demand this. We are as we are, imperfect to the max, racist and sexist and greedy above all; still, I feel we deserve that our leader(s) love us. We will not survive more of what we have had: leaders who love nothing, not even themselves. We know they don't love themselves because if they did they would feel compassion for us, so often lost, floundering, reeling from one bad thought, one horrid act, to another; killing, under order, folks we don't know; abusing children of whose existence we hadn't heard; maiming and murdering animals that have done us no harm; eating beings that are more intelligent and thoughtful than we are. Our teachers. We might well be the only species that routinely gobbles up its messengers of instruction.

I would say that, in my lifetime, it was only the Kennedys, in national leadership, who seemed even to know what compassion meant; certainly John, and then Bobby, were unafraid to grow an informed and open heart. (After he left the White House President Carter blossomed into a sheltering tree of peace quite admirably.) I was a student at a segregated college in Georgia when John Kennedy was assassinated. His was a moral voice, a voice of someone who had suffered, someone who, when looking at us in the South, so vulnerable, so poor, so outnumbered by the violent racists surrounding us, could join his suffering to ours. The rocking chair in which he sat reminded us that he was somehow like us: feeling pain on a daily basis and living a full-tilt life in spite of it. And Bobby Kennedy, whom a mentor, Marian Wright (later Edelman), brought to Mississippi, years later. He had not believed there were starving children in the United States. Marian took him to visit the Delta. Kneeling before these hungry children in the

Mississippi dirt and heat, he wept. We were so happy to have those tears; they made such a difference to us. Never before had we witnessed compassion in anyone sent out to lead us.

The present administration and too many others before it have shown the most clear and unapologetic hatred for the American people—a contempt for our minds, our bodies, and our souls that is so breathtaking most Americans have numbed themselves not to feel it. How can they do this or that awful unthinkable thing, we ask ourselves and each other, knowing no one in power will ever be bothered to answer us. I'm sure we, the American people, are the object of laughter and the butt of jokes by those in power, our suffering not making a dent in their pursuit of goals that almost always bring more tragedy and degradation to our already fragile, disintegrating republic. Sometimes, reading a blog, which I do infrequently, I see that generations of Americans have been willfully crippled and can no longer spell or write a sentence. The money for their education has gone to blow off someone else's intelligent and beautiful head. Visiting a hospital I see sick and frightened people who have no clue whether they will get the care they need or whether it will be fifteen minutes of an incompetent physician's opinion. If we were loved there would be a doctor free of charge on every block with time to listen to us. Visiting the lunchrooms of our schools I see no one has seriously thought about teaching Americans what to eat, just as no one at the national helm insists that we take sex education seriously and begin to unencumber our planet Earth of the projected hordes (Earth's view) of coming generations She can no longer tolerate. Our taxes are collected without fail, with no input from us; sometimes, because we lack jobs, paid with money we have to borrow. Our children are sent places they never dreamed of visiting, to harm and make enemies of people who, prior to their arrival, had thought well of them. Kind, smart, freedom-loving Americans.

When we are offered a John McCain, who is too old for the job (and I cherish old age and old men but not to lead the world when it is ailing), or a George Bush, or a Sarah Palin, how unloved we are as Americans becomes painfully plain. McCain talks of war with the nostalgia and forgetfulness of the very elderly; she talks of forcing the young to have offspring they neither want nor can sustain; both of them feel at ease, apparently, with the game in which their candidacy becomes

more of a topic of discussion than whether the planet has a future
under their leadership.

Where does this leave us average Americans who feel the chill of
global warming, the devastation of war, the terror of the food crisis,
the horror of advancing diseases? Hopefully with a sense of awakening: that we have had few opportunities to be led by those who have
the capacity to care for us, to love us, and that we, in our lack of love
for ourselves, have, too often, not chosen them. Perhaps with the certainty that though we are as we are and sorely imperfect, we still deserve someone in leadership who "gets" us, and that this self-defeating
habit of accepting our leaders' contempt is one we need not continue.
Maybe with the realization that we, the people, are truly the leaders
and that we are the ones we have been waiting for.

MAY WHATEVER
WE HAVE GAINED,
NOT BE LOST

I HAVE SENT OUT A REQUEST that Senator Barack Obama, or Michelle Obama, get in touch with me. While waiting for a response (and imagining how busy they must be), I decided to write down my thoughts. After watching the debates between Obama and McCain, something has leapt out at me. It has now leapt out twice, and I would like to avoid having it appear a third time. It is Obama's statement that, when he is president, he (the United States) will pursue Al Qaeda in the hills of Pakistan, find Osama bin Laden, and "kill" him. Though I understand that Obama wishes to show himself as "strong," even "tough," this is problematic on ethical, moral, and practical levels. It might also cost him the election.

For many this may seem farfetched. I don't think so. I am also not saying the same thing John McCain is saying about walking and speaking softly and carrying a big stick. We know that during McCain's service to the country countless people were assassinated, bombed, disappeared, and in other ways destroyed, if not by him directly, then by the system of government that he serves. No, this is about something else: the language we use in leading, and why.

Each time Obama has said, "We will kill" Osama bin Laden, I have felt a testing of my confidence in his moral leadership. And I support him and have demonstrated that support to the very limits of my finances and my strength. Could it be that, like millions of children around the globe who are taught "Thou shalt not kill," I am reacting with disappointment and shock to someone blatantly declaring their intention to kill a specific person? This could be it. In a Christian nation, this is what most of us learn. And even if we cease to call ourselves Christians, the notion of not killing is hardwired in us. We are not likely to accept the "killer" (even if the killing is done in our defense) with the same openheartedness and lack of fear we might have for someone who has not declared for murder. This is why John McCain coyly smiles each time Obama makes this statement.

We live in a country with a not-too-distant custom of lynching, particularly in the South. For those of us who are forever aware of this reality, something rises in us whenever there is a manhunt (in my case, even an animal hunt) to demand decent treatment of whoever is captured and a fair trial. To the surprise of both McCain and Obama, apparently, millions of people in the world don't believe Osama bin Laden bombed the World Trade towers and the Pentagon. But even laying such disbelief aside, we have to think of what we are teaching the youth of the planet. And it is through language that we can help them grow into the responsible world citizens of our dreams. Obama quite often says, "We'll 'take out' Osama bin Laden," and this is far better than saying "We will kill him." It is a metaphor. The very, very young will not even get it, hopefully. But to announce, "We will kill him," leaves no doubt. Unfortunately this conjures up nightmares of murderous possibilities in old and young alike: not a good thing to have on one's mind and conscience when entering the voting booth. Of course there are "tough" guys and gals for whom the spectacle of bin Laden's destruction (and all the women, children, and old folks who are bound to be living around him and his nurses because somebody has to handle his dialysis machine) will be an entertainment. But for most people, and especially for the women and the young who are Obama's most ardent supporters, this will not be the case. Our hearts will feel divided at best. Not because we're "bleeding-heart liberals," but because we remember another way of saying, "I'll get my man"; it is "Justice will be done."

There is also the black man factor. For many, finally getting to know a black man in all his glory is the high point of their education as American citizens. However, there lingers in the collective psyche a very carefully planted fear: that he is vicious, that he is mean, that he is . . . a killer. This, I think, is not to be shrugged off, even if, by now, much of the planet knows who most of the serious killers are. There is the danger of linking in the public mind one's self to a behavior one might personally abhor, and, in the public imagination, drawing to one's self the behavioral possibility one describes, sometimes identified as the boomerang effect. Even if everyone in North America is as careful as can be, this will still be a dangerous presidency; making it more so by using language without nuance and metaphor, when nuance and metaphor would help, does not serve us.

I admire Barack Obama for many reasons. His courage alone to take on this deeply dysfunctional, falling-apart, fantasy-addicted country is breathtaking. When I look at him and Michelle Obama and their daughters I have to stifle an impulse to scream, "Run!" Not for the presidency, but for a sane life for you and your family. What they are preparing to sacrifice for a country that hasn't yet learned the meaning of gratitude is enough to make us weep; and yet, they are brave enough to stand up for all of us and for this land that is so beautiful and so abused. Fundamental goodness shines in them. So no, this is not exactly a criticism. It is a caution. About the power of language. One writer reminding another.

FINALLY IT IS HERE:
ELECTION DAY

November 4, 2008

FINALLY IT IS HERE, NOVEMBER 4, election morning. This election will change the face of the planet, if Barack Obama wins the presidency. All last week I was thinking of my father, and of Christmas. When I was a child Christmas was the most exciting event of the year, and that is what these last weeks have felt like, getting ready for Christmas. We didn't know it then, but all the shoeboxes from the shoes my parents bought us at Easter had been carefully saved and stored somewhere. The weekend before Christmas morning, my father had gone into town and bought our Christmas gifts. We had all gone into the woods together to find our perfect tree. We had decorated it together, using lots of red and white crepe paper for the streamers, and for the ornaments and star, tin foil.

The anticipation leading up to Christmas morning was intense. We knew it would be good, and it always was. In each child's shoebox would be a stick of peppermint candy, raisins, a scattering of brazil nuts, a bunch of grapes, and the most wondrous thing of all, an orange. The smell alone sent one into ecstasy. Because I had been feeling this sensation of "Christmas gift" (which is what neighbors called out as they visited our yard on Christmas day), I thought I would not have been able, last night, to sleep. I did, though. Soundly, and well. We have, all of us, done all that we can peacefully do, to bring about this present shift in the consciousness of the world, and therefore deserve our rest.

As do the Obamas, who have fought the good fight, with courage and class.

It is only now, entering my sixty-fifth year, that I begin to realize how little I understood anything while I was growing up. A child's job is simply to be, perhaps to observe, certainly to play. But now, watching this election, I think of how little I grasped—there was no way I could—my father's quiet heroism. Who knew what monsters he encountered buying those oranges and those grapes, walking in the town's streets, where he was not really welcome? And his constant faith that he and my mother, out of almost nothing in today's terms, could nonetheless create a Christmas that would make every member of their large family happy.

My father was one of the people who trusted this day would come: I think of him laughing now at the sheer wonder of it. A man of shining dark skin, in a white work shirt and blue bibbed overalls, his large brown eyes filled with . . . the quiet peace of completion. He probably thought it was impossible, but at the same time, he was waiting for this day if only to give his children, who are still living, a feeling they had almost forgotten: hope for the blessing that is change, when it is fueled by devotion, generosity, courage, and love.

DEAR BROTHER
PRESIDENT (ELECT)

NOVEMBER 5, 2008

Dear Brother President (Elect),

You have no idea, really, of how profound this moment is for us—us being the black people of the Southern United States. You think you know because you are thoughtful and you have studied our history. But seeing you delivering the torch so many others carried, year after year, decade after decade, century after century, only to be brought down before igniting the flame of justice and of law, is almost more than the heart can bear. And yet, this observation is not intended to burden you, for you are of a different time, and, indeed, because of all the relay runners before you, North America is a different place. It is really only to say: well done. We knew, through all the generations, that you were with us, in us, the best of the spirit of Africa and of the Americas. Knowing this, that you would actually appear, someday, was part of our strength. Seeing you take your rightful place, based solely on your wisdom, stamina, and character, is a balm for the weary warriors of hope, previously only sung about.

I would advise you to remember that you did not create the disaster that the world is experiencing, and you alone are not responsible for bringing the world back to balance. A primary responsibility that you do have, however, is to cultivate happiness in your own life. To make a schedule that permits sufficient time of rest and play with your gorgeous wife and lovely daughters. Not to mention your brave and precious grandmother.* And so on. One gathers that your family is large. We are used to seeing men in the White House soon become juiceless and as white-haired as the building; we notice their wives and children looking strained and stressed. They soon have smiles so lacking in joy that they remind us of scissors. This is no way to lead. Nor does your family deserve this fate. One way of thinking about all this is: it is so bad now that there is no excuse not to relax. From your happy, relaxed state, you can model real success, which is only what so many people in the world really want. They may buy endless cars and houses and furs and gobble up all the attention and space they can manage, or barely manage, but this is because it is not clear to them yet that success is truly an inside job; that it is within the reach of almost everyone.

I would further advise you not to take on other people's enemies. Most damage that others do us is out of fear, humiliation, and pain. Those feelings occur in all of us, not just in those of us who profess a certain religious or racial devotion. We must all of us learn not to have enemies, but only confused adversaries who are ourselves in disguise. It is understood by all that you are commander-in-chief of the United States and are sworn to protect our beloved country; this we understand completely. However, as my mother used to say, quoting a Bible with which I often fought, "Hate the sin, but love the sinner." There must be no more crushing of whole communities, no more torture, no more dehumanizing as a means of ruling a people's spirit. This has already happened to people of color, poor people, women, children. We see where this leads, where it has led.

A good model of how to work with the enemy internally is presented by the Dalai Lama in his endless caretaking of his soul as he confronts the Chinese government that invaded Tibet. Because, finally, it is the soul that must be preserved if one is to remain a credible leader. All else might be lost, but when the soul dies, the connection to Earth, to people, to animals, to rivers, to mountain ranges purple and majestic also dies. And your smile, with which we watch you do gracious battle with unjust characterizations, distortions, and lies, is the

*Obama's "brave and precious" grandmother made her return to the Great Source a day before her grandson's historic turn of the historical wheel. We imagine her flying, smiling, free. Well done, Grandmother. Those of us who intuit your greatness send our thanks.

expression of healthy self-worth, spirit, and soul that, kept happy and free and relaxed, can find an answering smile in all of us, lighting our way and brightening the world.

We are the ones we have been waiting for.

In Peace and Joy,
Alice Walker

WHAT DO I EXPECT
FROM THIS TURN OF
THE HISTORICAL WHEEL:

*Barack Obama's Election to the Presidency
of the United States of America*

FEBRUARY 5, 2009

MANY YEARS AGO I WROTE A POEM that began: *Expect nothing. Live frugally on surprise.*

It was to remind myself of a difference between expectation, which is often unfulfilled, and openness, which holds a space for what is not only unexpected but almost unimagined. Boldly I open myself to the possibility of an increase in meaning for American culture and for the world at large, and a decrease in our common suffering.

How is this likely to happen? It can happen in areas too numerous to count if each of us embraces the opportunity to meet the challenge of living in a changed world, a world in which global warming is just as astonishing, with as much necessity to rise to the new occasion, as having a black president; but for me, what comes to mind with a certain relentlessness is the necessity for all those who are held unjustly in prisons around the country to be freed. It is disturbing that so many of us are celebrating a sensation of feeling newly liberated from long years of political repression and societal hopelessness while countless others sit in what has become a colossal gulag that should be an embarrassment to anyone who longs to think of America as a place of justice. I have visited women in prison, some of them incarcerated for two and three lifetimes, as if that were even possible, for having been involved in their husbands' or boyfriends' drug deals. Their children are growing up without them, wounded and alienated, awaiting their turn to explode into rage that will send them also into prison or jail. We can do better than this, and besides: we need all of our people who are not violent—and the majority of drug offenders are not—outside the prisons with us, working to bring about the changes, life-enhancing changes, of this brand new day. (Read Van Jones's *The Green Collar Economy* for how some of this might be done.)

There are also the political prisoners for whose release I, and others, have struggled (writing, rallying, speaking, marching) over decades: Leonard Peltier, the Native American activist who was accused of a crime he almost certainly did not commit, but who was imprisoned for life, regardless, as a lesson to the Native American people; and Mumia Abu-Jamal, a journalist and human being of such grandeur it is a grief that he is not outside the prison with us but is rather locked up, and has been, for over twenty-five years. Then there are the prisoners from Cuba, who should have been received as our guests: Gerardo Hernández, Antonio Guerrero, Ramón Labañino, Fernando González, and René González, also known as the Cuban Five. These husbands of wives and fathers of families came to the United States ten years ago to monitor terrorist groups in Miami that were infiltrating Cuba and harming Cuba's fledgling tourist industry, killing or endangering innocent people in the process. Information they discovered they turned over to the FBI only to be arrested and imprisoned for their troubles. They have been behind bars all this time since their arrest, their wives and families denied access to them. Who are we to treat anyone in this way? And how naïve or perhaps simply uncaring to assume only Cubans suffer from the imprisonment of these men.

There is little meaning in a society that does not venerate justice and the peace that comes because a society, at the very least, aims to be fair. There is no end to suffering in a society, or a world, that finds the anguished pleas for justice and balance, respect and a proper hearing, ignored.

While contemplating Barack Obama's election and the administration he is gathering around him, I have looked closely at each person being attracted to America's urgent cause: that of steering us into a wildly uncertain future. Mostly I have seen people of good faces, people with an open look of humanity in their eyes. It certainly does seem possible, as it did not during the Bush years, that we could change our penal system in ways that honor the people we hope we can be. Only time will answer whether the Obama team will have the courage and compassion to hear our cries for justice and simple mercy for our brothers and sisters dying slow and unjust deaths behind prison walls. Our cries for their release will not cease, any more than will their challenges in prison stop: the daily dangers, frustrations, humiliations, and fears. It would be a delightful relief to discover that our new leaders have humanity not only in their hearts and eyes, but also in their ears.

A LETTER TO PRESIDENT OBAMA ABOUT TORTURE

JULY 15, 2009

Amnesty International is sending ten letters to President Obama about torture; this is one of them.

From the Ten Against Torture campaign.

To President Barack Obama
The White House
Washington, D.C.

From Alice Walker
Temple Jook House
Mendocino, CA

June 27, 2009

Dear President Obama,
If word reached me that you were being tortured, I would instantly feel tortured myself, because I would be. Torture is something an entire society feels, whether we are within earshot of the screaming or not. People don't like to believe this, but there is no way human beings can remain unaffected by what is done to other human beings, or even to animals who are not human. If I heard this about you, I would do ev-

erything in my power to come to your aid, not simply because I know you to be rare and necessary to our planetary survival, but because you are simply a person, with feelings, aspirations, sorrows, and dreams. And you have children. If I were a child and knew my parent was being tortured, day after day, what would I myself become?

It has already been recognized that confessions obtained by torture are useless. It is easy to see why. If someone is waterboarding you and you think you will never see your little ones again, you would say anything. So would I. It is only in movies, I think, where the hero tells the torturer nothing as various body parts are cut, burned, frozen, electroshocked, or pulled out.

If one keeps company with cruel people, one loses, bit by bit, one's own compassion. This is one of the reasons living in Washington, in the White House, as leader of the United States, is so treacherous. And why I said to you when we met briefly prior to my introducing you to my community in San Francisco that failure to win the presidency had not insignificant value: you could have a fine life living as a writer, doing and saying what you want, and traveling the world incognito and free. Leadership has its downside, and one of them is who one has to associate with in order to get things done. When we look at the destruction, around the globe, caused by prior leaders of our country, and the terrible choices of how to behave, and we look at the White House today and see some of those folks still coming and going, what can I say? It gives us pause.

Ringing in my ears is something I thought I heard you say: America does not torture. And if this is true, now, under your watch, this letter is unnecessary. I also thought I heard you say Indefinite Detention Without Charge was gone with the wind of George Bush's administration. Was I wrong? Writers, and especially poets, don't always keep their ears to the political ground, and so we are likely to miss the daily dramas that keep others informed. I hope you are holding steady on these points, because if you are, you are right. The cruelty and injustice of holding anyone indefinitely without charge will not lead to carefree days and guilt-free nights for you or for any citizen of the United States, and we want those days and nights in order to convince the youth of the world that there are basic human laws protecting their right to grow up without fear of endless detention.

I think about people in prison, being tortured, being frightened and starved and humiliated, every single day. Voting for you was one way I felt I could reach out to them, fiction and poetry writing, even protests and arrests, having their limitations. You are the world's hope for a better, a fairer, day. You have what few leaders of this country ever had: genuine affection and love from the people who elected you. We are good people, too, for the most part. And even if we weren't, we can be improved by a leadership of compassion, a leadership whose basic human instincts of fairness and decency we can trust to look at the whole story, the entire state of affairs, and not close off any portion of it. A leadership unafraid to hold accountable those responsible for torture and abuse. This is our only hope, actually, to begin to soothe a little of the sorrow in the world. It isn't a desire for vengeance, because we know vengeance, a karma, is created by itself; it is instead a need to make right, to make whole again, by demonstrating to an injured and insulted world that we, as Americans, care about the harm other Americans, in our name, have done. We must show above all that we wish to understand our own madness in order not to continue growing and exporting it.

We know your plate is full. And I am always happy to hear of you and Michelle going off somewhere out of town for dinner. (No pun!) Any complaint about the cost is ridiculous: what your time away from your desk does for the world is priceless. You are a Leo/Ox and only someone with your combination of strengths could handle the presidency, which you do with grace. (What can I say? I love astrology!) Even so, it's too much for one person, or two; I myself favor a council for leading the country, but that is far in the future. Maybe not too far! So, delegate. We need the world to know we don't accept the behavior as usual of American presidents and others who do horrible things to people, and then retire, wealthy, into memoir writing and golf, as if the disasters inflicted on a vulnerable world never happened. I applaud and deeply appreciate all the good work you are, in fact, doing. It is huge. And beautiful, which I personally resonate with in world leadership. It has a beat. It has a heart.

In closing, I send this poem about torture that I wrote a few weeks ago and posted on my blog, alicewalkersgarden.com.

———

DYING
For those who with our taxes die of torture.

What is it like
Dying?
Is it like

Sinking
Into a bath
Of warm
Milk?

Is it like
Lying naked
In the
Sun
Those first
Truly
Warm

Days
Of Spring
After
A winter
That
Froze
Your teeth?

Dying
I think
Can be
Like that.

Above all,
It
Is yours.

It is
A safe
Place.

They may
Be
Electrocuting
Your

Toes
At
The time
Or
Pulling out

Your
Finger
Nails
Or
Causing
Your terrified

Heart to stop
In
Other
Ingenious
Ways.

But
Dying
You
Escape
Them

Into
Peace.

They will
Never
Know

Something
Only
You
Can have.

Dying
Is yours.

Precious
Human being;
Whatever you
Have done.

Dying
Is
Your secret.

With loving kindness, and
despite the gravity of the
subject, Joy,

Alice Walker

UNDERSTANDING
HEALTH CARE

AUGUST 24, 2009

I HAVEN'T BEEN FOLLOWING the debate on health care because it is obvious we don't have that much: caring about health, that is. And to be honest, I've been raising chickens and they have taken all of my attention; even so, I've lost two: one to a careless human and another to a predator, possibly a bobcat. But what is there to debate? Healthy debate has the power to transform society, as the beloved and essential film *The Great Debaters* reminds us. So chicken shepherding distraction is probably not a good excuse. For a relatively prosperous country, our population is riddled with the kind of ill health people in much poorer countries—with more attention to what they eat and how they exercise, how they rest and how they play—avoid.

We can do better.

People are falling sick and dying all around us and when, and if, we go to the hospital most of us hope we don't, from lack of care, die there. How bizarre it is that President Obama, this thoughtful, kind, smart being we've at long last been graced with as a leader, has to spend so much energy trying to get Americans to accept what we so desperately need: a system of health care that means we don't have to be terrorized by the thought of getting sick. We would laugh, except it's really sad. And self-defeating. Even the well-heeled people who hate this man will benefit from the sense of security real health care reform will provide. Their children, though well provided for through wills and trust funds and who knows, overseas stashes of cash, may yet fall on hard times and need care. They will not be happy to realize what most of us have always known: that being sick in America, without insurance or a substantial amount of money, brings one at last to the level of all the other minorities. People in pain. People with a grievance. This could be an enlightening experience, of course, and that would be wonderful. But it could be sordid and dark and horrid, with nothing but suffering and despair to recommend it.

Why risk it?

I never had an assistant until I was in my forties. My business as a writer was so small I could, with a bit of struggle, handle it myself. When my fortunes changed and a deluge of mail and other stuff arrived at my house and I couldn't handle it, I simply threw it into a room and closed the door. This worked for a few months. Finally someone arrived who opened the door, took out all the crazy-making demands, requests, complaints, etc., and began to make sense of them. It was an amazing experience for me that such organization was even possible. Lucky for me, I knew what I had in my new assistant: I gratefully referred to her as St. Joan* and we lived happily in each other's appreciation for a decade.

The key to running a successful enterprise is to attract the very best people to help run it. This is part of what I learned from working year in and year out with St. Joan. She soon proved she knew exactly what she was doing, and could do it just fine, even when I didn't remember or had forgot. It is the same with electing a president. Part of the reason I voted for Barack Obama is that I believe in him as a human being. That he's decent and caring and wants the best for every single person in our country. That he's really sharp in his thinking and cool in his behavior; that we're in good hands as long as we don't overtax him with work and blame him for the mess the country's in when he just, in a sense, got here. I know he's doing his best and that's all I ask of him, or of anyone. Dismissing the guidance of the very person you've elected to lead you is an absurdity we can't afford.

The latest I heard is that he and Michelle Obama and the girls have gone on vacation. This is excellent news. Who knows, maybe it's somewhere out of reach of media, fax, BlackBerry, and phone. Of course it won't be, but those of us who truly understand health care, caring about health, can hope.

*Joan Miura

WELL DONE—
OBAMA AND
THE NOBEL PRIZE

October 9, 2009

WHEN I THINK OF OBAMA winning the Nobel Peace Prize, for which, after all, he didn't audition, I think about that photograph of him with his feet up on a desk, and there's a hole in one very worn shoe. This is someone who has stood up for himself and for the good of the human group for a long time, even though he's still relatively young. I personally think all prizes are risky; they often come with strings, even if a string is just other people's freedom to tell you how much you didn't deserve to win. But this one is a timely confirmation of Obama's dogged faith in humanity and, more particularly, in Americans: that if talked to as if we have sense, we will, possibly, act sensibly. The Prize recognizes that we are at long last being guided by someone who deeply cares for us, wants us to have peace (though how to achieve it will take everyone's best behavior and thought and a bit less blaming of the recently elected commander), and who is, as he has stated, not naïve about the politics of the world we live in and the frightening war machinery he has inherited.

It's healthy, I think, to face the reality that, having built so much war technology, our military may well be unable as well as disinclined to refrain from using it. War is big business, and, as one of our former presidents put it: the business of America is business. Still, the Nobel Peace Prize is confirmation that one's peaceful intentions have been noted, and, as well, in Obama's case, of the deep inner peace that appears to be his very nature.

FOR WHAT IT'S WORTH: SOME THOUGHTS ON WAR, DISAPPOINTMENT, AND ANGER

March 5, 2010

I DO NOT BELIEVE IN WAR AT ALL, although I am as capable of anger as anyone. To me war is something to be outgrown, recognized as immature, wasteful, and so destructive to life that human beings should shun it as they shun swine flu, or HIV/AIDS, or as they once shunned bubonic plague. If our species survives, and it may well not, it will be because we learn not to fight to kill each other, though some of us may continue to fight as an expression of our not yet controllable nature. It is painful to feel the war machine continuing in Iraq and Afghanistan and in all the other parts of the globe not covered by our media. It isn't that I thought one man, a new president, could stop it overnight or in one year—it has been acceptable behavior for millennia—but it was my hope that there would be, out of Washington, an entirely new and different approach to what is essentially the failure of human beings to listen to each other, to teach and guide and share with one another. To see the best, even in "the enemy." And where no "best" is discernable, to understand how what might have been good has become horribly twisted or destroyed. To think of small children who have no alternative, often, to growing up imprisoned in poisonous ideologies; there they stand in our missile sights, "terrorists" who never really had a chance.

Is there no way to reach our enemies other than by killing them? Do we "win" in this way? I cannot believe it. Rather, I believe killing other human beings is not about winning but about failure. Winning would be to begin to train our military to do what it also does wonderfully well: look after the inhabitants of the planet. It has been such a relief to see our soldiers stepping in to help earthquake victims in Haiti and elsewhere; to see their self-assurance and can-do spirit as they tackle the problems of crumbled buildings, trapped children, pain-crazed persons who, having lost homes and possessions, have nowhere to go. This is when I have felt most proud of our military. And it has been easy to see that this is where our soldiers have felt most proud of themselves.

There is much anger at our president from the community of paci-fists and antiwar activists to which I belong. There is much disappoint-ment and rage. I share some of this; what I mostly feel, however, is not anger or rage, but grief. Eisenhower was right to warn us about the burgeoning power of the military-industrial complex, as he termed it. That it was quite capable of taking over the country, and the president with it. That we are in the hands of a war machine that doesn't really care who is elected to run the country; its aim is plunder, destruction, conquest, and exploitation. Taking whatever its creators want by force. All in the name of "defense." Looking in our own families we can see how we are connected to this machine: the jobs, the pensions, the chance to learn a trade or go to school. Many people's fear is that if the military stopped its machinations around the globe millions of people would have no place, and no work.

And that is why what we must insist on, I believe, is transformation of the military. Though what use can be found for our obsolete mis-siles and weapons of mass destruction I cannot, myself, imagine. But my faith is that someone can imagine this; that we can make some-thing useful out of things like old fighter planes and bomb casings. The way the Earth is shaking so many of us out of bed in the middle of the night with no shelter left to our names, perhaps we should put our architects and builders to the task of designing and creating housing out of them. Humans are very clever, as we know. No more clever hu-mans exist—along with some who are abysmally not clever—than in the United States.

In these times it is easy to see why war is obsolete. Nature has taken it on herself to show us how destructive unanticipated and uncontrol-lable violence is. And that nothing humans can ever do on the battle-field is a match for her power. After an earthquake, especially after earthquakes like the recent ones in Haiti and Chile, how can humanity permit our governments to cause similar devastation, with our money, deliberately?

Recently I was in Cairo, attempting to cross into Gaza with the courageous women of CODEPINK. This organization had worked for nearly a year to collect about two million dollars' worth of aid for the people of Gaza. They had also invited fourteen hundred people from around the world to join in a freedom march inside Gaza, in protest of the imprisonment of 1.5 million Palestinians, in Gaza, by the Israeli government. The Egyptian government, apparently under the control of Israel and the United States, refused to permit us entry. Perhaps its leader feared losing the large amount of aid the United States gives Egypt every year.

In any case, on my third day in Cairo I found myself traveling with Jodie Evans, co-founder of CODEPINK, to pay a visit to the Red Crescent, similar to the Red Cross. We were escorted into the office of a large, kindly man who seemed to want to help us. Jodie Evans, wearing a lot of pink, had come armed with her cell phone and her computer. At each point of questioning from the kindly but cautious Egyptian, she used these tools to connect with her base of information. There was not a single question put to her that she did not, sitting there in all her glorious pink, answer politely, firmly, and conclusively. She explained about the 1,400 citizens from around the world who were outside, some camping in front of embassies, some battling police in the Cairo streets. She talked about the two million dollars' worth of aid. Milk and cheese and bread and beans. Water. Chocolate. School supplies. Medicine.

I had arrived in Cairo ill; speaking brought on a spell of coughing. I was sorry to be of so little help. However, I did have one question:

"Have you ever been to Gaza?" I asked our host, when Jodie Evans took a moment to catch her breath.

"No," he said. "But I hear it's better than when you were there last year."

More people dead? I wondered. Or did he mean more rubble cleared?

But then Jodie Evans was back on the case. To every question, she found an answer.

At last, the kindly man, someone's uncle or father or brother or son, allowed the possibility of sixty-five people being allowed entry into

Gaza. sixty-five out of fourteen hundred. Jodie Evans tried to increase
the number, speaking again of the hardship many had suffered to be
able to come so far. Maybe two buses? And what of the aid? There was
now given to us a long list of all that could not be carried into Gaza.
Milk was out, for starters. It was a liquid.

This haggling went on for some time. As people who had visited
Gaza a year ago, both she and I would be denied entry this time.

And so forth.

But here is what the feeling was: we were begging to be allowed to
help desperate people, many of them slowly starving to death. Begging. I will not forget this feeling as long as I live, because it was not
right. And yes, I longed to have a government behind me that would
have made it unnecessary for us to beg; I yearned for a government
whose leaders would go with us into Gaza. Shoulder to shoulder with
us. Because until our leaders go with us to try to understand and right
the wrongs our nations have caused, what chance as a planet do we
have? And yet, ironically, this encounter, where we felt we had nothing
officially supportive at our backs, is where I saw the Goddess in Jodie
Evans. Even though this was begging, she never lost her dignity, her resolve, her commitment to the people of Gaza who are suffering. I witnessed something I never expected to experience that day: that to beg
for the good of others is noble. I saw this nobility, very strong, in her.
That moment was worth the trip.

When the disastrous earthquake hit Haiti, even Israel sent a shipment of aid. But why not send such a shipment to Gaza, where Israel
has done the damage? Looking at the photo of a collapsed school in
Port-au-Prince, I thought it seemed almost identical to the American
School in Palestine in whose rubble, a year ago, I spent part of a morning. America sent aid, but why had it not helped the Haitians (over decades) as their capsized boats, filled with impoverished people headed
toward survival in the United States, floundered and were drowned by
the waves? Not to mention the atrocious colonial treatment of Haiti
for centuries.

I have said many times that my caring for Barack Obama and his
family is unconditional; this is the only kind of caring that makes sense
to me. Within that caring, held just as unshakably, is my disagreement
with some of his choices. War cannot be stopped by killing more people;
there has to be another way. What is it? Nuclear power is treacherous;

is there no faith that Americans can consume less of everything, especially the rapaciously pursued "energy"?

And so on.

Talking some of this over with a friend, I asked her to make a list of all the good things Barack Obama has done in his first year. Within minutes she had a list of about a hundred things. This was a great relief, because sometimes the rhetoric against his leadership is so condemning it is as if he's done nothing at all. What is the blindness and anger that causes this unfairness? How can it become more balanced? Not for Obama's sake—he seems to be weathering his storms as well as one could—but for the sake of those of us who like to think of ourselves as people of ethics, fairness, balance. Some of us call ourselves "spiritual progressives."

At the end of some of the more virulent blasts against Obama there is the threat of punishment: wait until the next election! Can we learn to disagree with someone without instantly attempting to punish them? What is this but a stirring up of one's inner war? War without a military, but violence just the same. And who do we have in mind as a replacement? With our luck we will find ourselves stuck with another Bush, or worse, though our dream might be Dennis Kucinich, whose belief that the United States should have a Department of Peace is one with which most of us resonate. Anger makes us lose our ability to think clearly, to strategize, to plan. It is useless at this point in humanity's distress. We are headed over a cliff of our own making; blaming anyone without at the same time blaming ourselves is a waste of the time we could at least spend dancing.

Can we learn to care about our leaders in ways that support their ability to move forward as we would wish them to? Is our only mode of behavior instant rage and blame if someone cannot deconstruct in one year what has taken five hundred years to build? Can we sit with ourselves and the truth of our crisis as humans long enough to see where we ourselves must lead and change?

Before traveling to Cairo I spent a few days in Dharamsala calling on the spiritual and political leaders of Tibet in Exile. These are people who obviously know a thing or two about life, about conflict, about inner discipline and care of the personal and the planetary soul. At a dinner with the political head of Tibet in Exile, Professor Samdhong Rinpoche, along with six cabinet ministers, we found ourselves talking about what it feels like to be up against opponents who might be a billion times larger than you. Which is pretty much the case of China vs. Tibet. Talking together we soon realized that everyone in the room was working hard for the same things: feeding and clothing and teaching and healing our people and our communities. Finally, in the face of all attempts to stop us from doing what we feel we must, someone raised a glass to toast "our friends the enemy." In Buddhist thought one's enemy is likely to teach so much we otherwise would not learn, is so helpful in strengthening us in ways we might never have imagined, and is so likely to be a primary reason for our growth, that it is wise to recognize him or her as a friend. This is a teaching I have found profoundly useful in my own life, so much so I rarely am capable of seeing anyone as an enemy, but rather as someone who is heartbreakingly confused. I first heard "my friends the enemy" used by the Dalai Lama when he was speaking about the Chinese government. He shares this concept with Burmese spiritual warrior Aung San Suu Kyi, who speaks of the possibility of becoming friends, literally, with the dictators who have held her imprisoned for years.

Inwardly bowing to Aung San Suu Kyi and His Holiness, I raised my glass in response to the toast. Thank you, I said: "They (our friends the enemy) have their job and we have ours."

That is also how I feel about every U.S. administration I have ever read about or known, all of them our friends the enemy to our parents and grandparents and very often to us, none of them as morally intelligent and responsive to regular Americans as the one we have now, for all its limitations. They have their job, whatever it might be. But I have mine. Mine is to work for the world that I want, in the belief that it can only be just, fair, balanced, and dedicated to peace if I am.

WHY WAR IS NEVER
A GOOD IDEA

WHEN I WROTE *Why War Is Never a Good Idea* I was thinking about children who play "war" long before they have any understanding of its meaning. Their parents buy toys for them that are miniature rifles, tanks, and bombs. Small babies are dressed in military print. They lie in their cribs grinning up at the adults of the world, without a clue that they are being set up to fight other young people, in not so many years, who would more sensibly be their playmates. I wanted to write a book for small children that would begin to counter the entrenched belief that it is all right for small children to think positively about war. It isn't all right, and the adults of the world must say so.

We've all heard of "the good war," presumably a war that is righteous and just. However, seen from the perspective of my children's book, there is no such thing as a "good" war because war of any kind is immoral in its behavior. It lands heavily on the good and the not good with equal impact. It kills humans and other animals and destroys crops. It ignites and decimates forests and it pollutes rivers. It obliterates beauty, whether in landscape, species, or field. It leaves poison in its wake. Grief. Suffering. When war enters the scene, no clean water anywhere is safe. No fresh air can survive. War attacks not just people, "the other," or "enemy"; it attacks Life itself: everything that humans and other species hold sacred and dear. A war on a people anywhere is a war on the Life of the planet everywhere. It doesn't matter what the politics are, because though politics might divide us, the air and the water do not. We are all equally connected to the life support system of planet Earth, and war is notorious for destroying this fragile system.

Our only hope of maintaining a livable planet lies in teaching our children to honor nonviolence, especially when it comes to caring for Nature, which keeps us going with such grace and faithfulness. *Why War Is Never a Good Idea* doesn't take sides because we are ultimately on the same side: the side of keeping our home, Earth, safe from attack. We cannot live healthy lives without a healthy Earth ever supporting and inspiring us, in all her unspoiled radiant generosity.

WITNESS
The Road of Life

HUMAN SUNRISE

A Letter to the Graduating Class
of Naropa University

June 2009

Someone told me once

that Earth is

the only planet that has
mornings.

The only planet that has mornings!
   This is an intriguing thought: and, how would they know? The poet
in me loves it, however, because it sees the metaphor of new beginnings,
optimism, rising to the occasion (in Mexico a friend calls sunset "the
occasion"), and getting on with the new day. I also appreciate the notion
of our specialness, as a planet, whether it is accurate or not.

Dear Graduating Class of Naropa,
I have been thinking of you for many months. Wanting to share your
day with something useful from my experience of Life. It is wonderful
to see you; to know you have worked and studied and played hard.
That you have meditated much. That you have struck out on your own
through these perilous times to be of benefit to yourselves and to the
world. You are children of this cosmos, this galaxy, of your no doubt
innocent Earthling parents who brought you into this existence, and

also children of the Buddha, which is to say, Beings who continue to grow into people who treasure wisdom, joyfulness, and peace. In fact, you are practically adults. We recall that to the Cherokee, as to other people who have noticed how long it sometimes takes for humans to develop fully, adulthood comes—if it is coming at all—at the age of fifty-two.

I salute you and your parents for the accomplishment your graduation represents today, in this most beautiful and inspiring place where, I am told, there is sunshine three hundred days of the year, and the mountains near enough to cause a continual raising of the eyes and rising of the spirit.

What have I learned that might be useful to you?

One thing I have learned is that just as we are lucky enough to live on a planet that has mornings, there is such a thing as a Human Sunrise.

Decades ago when I traveled to Mississippi to work in the Civil Rights Movement, which eventually gained voting rights for African Americans, I encountered this Human Sunrise for the first time. I met black people and a few of their white sisters and brothers who were attempting to dismantle a system of oppression that had been in place for centuries. White supremacy, fascism, the most virulent racism, were the order of the day. Black people, and the whites who supported them, lived in a state of terror. There were lynchings, bombings, assassinations, humiliations, jailings, on a regular and predictable basis. And yet, the people not only were determined to be free of these things, they were determined, as well, to free their oppressors—the racists and white supremacists of the world—of their need to oppress. It was in Mississippi that I witnessed, as an adult, the full implementation of the compassion for others that I, and most black people of the South, had been taught at home. And, of course, in our church.

With just their songs, their chants, their good and noble hearts, their marching feet, the black people of Mississippi met, with soul force, the violence of a system that had traditionally ground them into dust. "We shall not, we shall not be moved. We shall not, we shall not be moved," they sang: "Just like a tree that's planted by the water, we shall not be moved."

Their daughters and sons were raped and murdered. Martin Luther King Jr., one of the world's great teachers, was killed. They continued to sing, and to believe in their right to have a voice in the running of America and in the protection of what was most precious to them: freedom to explore the universe unfettered by anyone else's power to condemn, discredit, or dismiss them.

They knew they were the ones they had been waiting for, and took responsibility for shifting the direction of Life in Mississippi so that their children would not have to.

And we today, all of us on this Earth, are exactly who we have been waiting for. It is for us to change the direction of the planet and we must not lose our belief that we can do so.

We are rising all over the globe now, in this most terrible of times for Earthlings and for our home planet. People everywhere are moving, joining each other, plotting and planning how we may protect and provide for the challenges of the age. Still, there are, and will be, days of incredible depression and distress as we encounter the hard truths of the suffering of the Earth and her creatures. There are abominations occurring on our planet that I'm convinced would have been unimaginable in the Buddha's lifetime. They are unimaginable even in my own lifetime—and I have actually encountered some of them. The horrible genocide, the incessant war and war mongering, the dropping of bombs on the poor, the starving, deliberately, of children. The greed. The mutilation, cannibalism, and enslavement forced on people who are at the mercy of weaponry and force wielded by people they've never even seen.

And I say to that: when it is all too much, when the news is so bad meditation itself feels useless, and a single life feels too small a stone to offer on the altar of peace, find a Human Sunrise. Find those people who are committed to changing our scary reality. Human Sunrises are happening all over the Earth, at every moment. People gathering, people working to change the intolerable, people coming in their robes and sandals or in their rags and bare feet, and they are singing, or not, and they are chanting, or not. But they are working to bring peace, light, compassion, to the infinitely frightening downhill slide of human life.

You will find those of the Human Sunrise movement speaking with heart about the suffering of animals, and also the necessity of preparing, in a good way, for death.

There was a recent article in *Rolling Stone* magazine about the treatment and slaughter, each year, of 27 million hogs in, I believe, Virginia.

By one company. This is as many beings as the population of several large cities. Beings who are treated with such disrespect and cruelty that it is amazing that any of us can bear knowing what is going on. This must be the same blind heart and unseeing gaze that was turned on the slave trade, during its four horrendous centuries, when black people coming to America on slave ships were treated as cruelly as these hogs, their lives often eaten up by forced labor within as little as seven years. What have we turned off in ourselves to be able to bear the mistreatment of the precious other animals that inhabit the planet with us? The carnage, in this one case, is so bad that the countryside around the facility is completely, densely polluted, and the people who live there are sick. The freeing of animals, the returning of land and habitat to them, must become part of what it means to be human. Part of what it means to be animal. Without the other animals the land is dead in spirit, as it is dead in spirit when indigenous human life is removed from it.

Find the Human Sunrise that love of animals draws you to, and stay close to it, for that is the way of a future without self-deception and shame.

Always remember that there is nothing too small any of us can learn to do to help us out of our predicament, and that learning to extend the range of our compassion is activity and work available to all.

If we are open to it, we will be taught by masters.

Many years ago I visited Oaxaca during Day of the Dead. A local acquaintance took my friend and me to a cemetery far in the countryside outside the city of Oaxaca. It was astonishing, magical, to see the people gathered in the middle of the night in this cemetery, brightly lit by thousands of candles. People were actively being with their deceased loved ones: sitting on and around their graves, talking, eating, playing guitars, playing cards. It was a giant party, filled with love and celebration. I was mesmerized and filled with joy.

Far in the distance we heard singing, beautiful, incredible singing. Mournful and loving and intense. It drew us to the back of the cemetery. And there, in the ruins of what had once been a church, many men and women were singing with a solemnity and passion so moving it was almost impossible to endure it. *Who are these people and what are they singing?* we asked, already weeping, though we understood not a word of what they sang.

These are the people who come each year to sing to those whom no one comes to visit.

I had already loved Oaxaca and the people of Oaxaca. This made me understand that love.

When the tragedy at Virginia Tech occurred, and I listened to the news that thirty-two people had been killed, and we were encouraged, rightly, to mourn the loss of their beautiful lives, I thought of the singers in the cemetery. And of their compassion. We know it was not only thirty-two people who lost their lives, but thirty-three. And we must allow ourselves to feel compassion for the person who killed the other thirty-two before killing himself. This thought—that compassion does not stop at who was right or wrong, does not stop at feeling loving kindness for the miserable and oppressed, does not stop at feeling the pain of the victim while ignoring the pain of the victimizer—is a human expression of warmth, a human sunrise, our world desperately needs. This way of seeing the world, and the calamities now afflicting us, can be uniquely carried by meditators and contemplatives such as you. If human beings are not taught to feel compassion for the Hitlers, Mussolinis, and Stalins of the world, if Saddam Hussein is so demonized no one bothers to remember how cruelly he was beaten as a little boy, if our own leaders are ridiculed and called names that even in childhood must have frightened and scarred them, how are we ever to see these same shadowy parts of ourselves and do the real work of change that survival on our Earth requires?

The extraordinary teacher Pema Chodron taught me, via cassette tape, Tonglen practice. Knowing how to do this ancient practice of taking in pain and suffering and sending out peace and light has been a wonderful gift to the medicine bundle I carry in my life. One of the slogans in the lojong teachings that accompany Tonglen is: Be grateful to everyone. Be grateful to everyone. How beautiful is that! Because everyone is a teacher. Everyone brings us something of value, even if it seems totally negative to us at the time we receive it. I would add to that, and the Buddha of course already did so: Be compassionate to everyone. Don't just search for whatever it is that annoys and frightens you; see beyond those things to the basic human being. Especially see the child in the man or woman. Even if they are destroying you, allow a moment to see how lost in their own delusion and suffering they are. It is only this insight into brutality and any form of meanness and cruelty that lessens the pain of being oppressed and, in so many cases on this planet, senselessly annihilated.

I thought long and hard about exploring this next area with you: preparing to die. Graduation day is, after all, something like a wedding celebration: you are marrying your future. And perhaps all thought should be happy, cheerful thought. On the other hand, you chose to invite me to speak to you today, and what has come up continually when I have queried Spirit about what to say to you is: talk to them about preparing to leave this plane.

I have thought about my own death a great deal in my life; I thought of it on a daily and almost moment to moment basis while I was experiencing the Human Sunrise in Mississippi. It could have come at any moment; it did come for many people that we knew. Over time I realized it is not death itself that frightens me, and in fact I suspect that being dead will be a delight. Such freedom, such spaciousness! And hasn't everything in life, up to that point, been pretty mind-blowing?

What I recommend is much sitting with the thought of dying. Of the moments when you will be leaving your present consciousness. How would you like to transition? After much contemplation, I settled on the idea that if only I could die touching some shred or scrap of the Earth, a bit of grass, a trunk or root of a tree, a twig or stone, I would be content. If I could see some small corner of the sky, some leaf being blown by the wind. Smell the earth, whether flowers or straw—that would be enough. But later on, reading the news, listening to the heavy footsteps of death rumbling the planet, I refined this. I sat long enough to realize I might have to deeply know that a flaming plastic plane seat is also Earth. That a classroom filled with desks and computers is also Earth. That prison cells with their sadistic guards and cement floors are also Earth. That, in fact, all dying is returning to the Earth. And that, because I love Earth, I can be content to feel myself returning to Her in whatever is Her form. That Her elements are also mine. Since of course I am made of Her. This was very helpful to me.

Incorporating deep thought about how we might leave our present incarnation can make us stronger, like preparing for a challenging test rather than relying on guesswork can make us stronger. It will be a major moment of our lives, and filled with meaning—meaning that only we can give it. Instead of dissolving into panic or fear, it will be good to understand beforehand that, before transition, however unexpected it might be, you could just possibly be granted a moment of centeredness, mindfulness, even a split second of real peace. Peace that comes from gratitude for whatever life you have lived on this astounding Earth. If there is a moment to have the presence of mind to kiss Her, what a joy that would be. Imagine it! A kiss good-bye. A kiss hello. For you cannot ever really leave this Mother. She is all there is.

Which reminds me of something I recently learned about Mother Teresa. I had always thought Mother Teresa was only focused on endings. Poor people dying and her helping them die with dignity and peace. However, recently, in a very useful book by Lynne Twist called *The Soul of Money* (in which she discusses how we can use money to improve the world instead of using it, as many of us do, to make things worse), I discovered that at the same ashram where the dying were cared for, women often dropped off their unwanted newborns. Lynne Twist herself arrived at the door of the ashram and found a tiny baby on the doorstep wrapped in old newspapers. Mother Teresa's nuns took the child, cooing happily at it, washed and fed it, and added it to the nursery full of newborns they were already tending. Who knew?

That's how close it is, I think. We are always going and always coming again.

And we are made so beautifully, with a wonderful inner moral compass to guide us. Our inner light. The personal Human Sunrise we all carry which flames into a larger warmth when we join ourselves with others. The poor, humble, radiantly beautiful black people of Mississippi, and their maligned and harassed and sometimes beaten and murdered white allies, taught me this, and I am forever in gratitude to them for doing so. May they always know peace.

You have chosen well, I think, to come to a place that teaches meditation and contemplation and peace. A place founded by Chögyam Trungpa Rinpoche, who was apparently quite a free and very large spirit. A person who dared to dream a dream spacious enough to change the direction of a macho, frequently compassionless, America. I am so grateful for all the good things, and especially the wisdom, that has come to us from Tibet. I think I love it even more because it feels deeply familiar, just as the Dalai Lama reminds me of one of my mother's brothers. My uncle Willie. But I also love it because I see how beautifully it connects with, joins, African American Southern soul. If and when black people in the South begin to investigate Buddhism, a large part of their suffering will decrease and a large part of their peace of mind, which they have valued so highly, and with such persistence, will be enlarged. They will not fail to recognize the gift.

I am forever offering thanks for the wonderful presence among us of Bernice Johnson Reagon and Sweet Honey in the Rock. They are our African American nuns and monks and priests and priestesses traveling the world with our vision of what is justice and freedom, compassion and peace. In their songs they share the wisdom and compassion of African American ancestors just as devotedly as the Lamas and Rinpoches of Tibet share the worldview and beliefs of their lineages. It is good to understand that we in America have a culture and tradition of right thought, right speech, right livelihood, right action, and it is expressed in the mantras that are these black women's collection of songs. As in this one, with which I will close:

OUR HANDS ARE CLEAN

Our hands were clean
While you painted white walls in our streets
We kept our hands clean
While you tried to erase our past and our
Blood
Our clean hands survived
While you whitewashed our slogans
Our blood
Our dreams

We have not killed anyone
We have not tortured anyone

We have not taken work from the people
We have not starved and sold the children
We have not brought our country to ruin
Our hands are clean

Our hands are clean

Generals of death and of hunger
Let it be known to those who hear this
Song
Let it be known
The wearing thin

Of
Our patience.

Like these great women of Sweet Honey in the Rock, who have helped to inspire and carry many of us morally for a good many decades, we too are the ones we have been waiting for; carrying our own inner light in this time of darkness. We shall not, we shall not be moved. We shall not, we shall not be moved. Just like a tree that's planted by the water, we shall not be moved.

We are the Human Sunrise, brightest when we shine together, that will make sure morning continues to come, and be a grand "occasion" on our planet Earth.

INTRODUCING THE
OJIBWA WARRIOR

The First Time I Saw
Dennis Banks

MOLOKAI, HAWAII, SPRING 2008

THE FIRST TIME I SAW DENNIS BANKS I was struck by how merry he seemed. It was at Evergreen State University in Washington in the early seventies; I was there to read poetry and talk about my life in the Southern freedom movement in Mississippi, and I suppose he was on campus talking about the creation of the American Indian Movement, AIM, of which he was a founder. I remember being struck by his lightness of spirit, believing as I do that happiness is already victory. I don't recall everything he was wearing, but the effect was of someone blessedly returned to the clothing and hairstyle that suited him. Jeans, a fawn-colored ribbon shirt, a robe perhaps made from a Pendleton blanket. Wrapped around the coils of hair that made up his long, dark braid, the reddest of red thread signaled to the world that, yes indeed, here is an Indian and he is incredibly hip and alive. Seeing him there, in a landscape scrubbed clean of Indian presence, was a tonic to my spirit. I smiled, asking the young woman guiding me about campus who he might be. She knew his name and nothing else. I went back to Mississippi, where black people—many of them part Choctaw and Cherokee—heroically struggled to free themselves from the death grip of slavery and segregation, holding the treasure that was Dennis's vibrant survival as an Indian close to my heart.

Many years later, after moving to the West Coast, I became involved in the American Indian Movement: reading poetry with John Trudell; hosting fund-raisers with Nilak Butler, Bill Wahpepah, and his sculptor wife, Carol; celebrating UnThanksgiving Day at Alcatraz Island; praying on top of Black Mesa in Arizona; and joining demonstrations and vigils for Native American rights whenever I could. However, it wasn't until a decade had passed that I once again saw Dennis, this time handcuffed, on trial for a list of crimes designated by the court, having voluntarily returned to face sentencing after leading the FBI on a chase that lasted eleven years.

I have told the story of that meeting, in Custer, South Dakota, many times. It is worth telling again, however, in this context. I would like the people who read the history Dennis Banks has written of his life to witness one of the ways healing happens to us when we keep faith with our ideals and with each other.

And, in fact, with the ancestral spirits we recognize ourselves, reincarnated, to be. My own connection to Indians and Indian affairs has always felt natural. When I was a child my father took us to view Eagle Rock, a huge pile of stones in the shape of an eagle, left by an ancient native people in Putnam County, Georgia, where I was born. He felt a reverence for these stones that flowed directly to the hearts of his children. We were told in all seriousness that these Native people, who had existed in Georgia before the white people came, would someday return. This is what we desperately hoped, as years of poverty and racism stole my father's vitality and his optimism, and the civil rights movement, coming as it did just as he had completely lost his health—to diabetes and heart disease—must have seemed to him to signal only more disappointment and racial repression. Indeed, in the early days of the movement, the hatred unleashed against black people in the South brought an unending stream of bad news: lynchings, beatings, bombings, floggings—things he would have hoped were forever behind him.

Whenever I hear the story of how Tibetan lamas are determined (a small child is shown objects that he* used in a previous life and he recognizes them, chooses them, over whatever else might be offered) I am

---

*It is a bit fishy that these lama children are always male.

reminded of a time in grade school when we were given the cast-off textbooks sent over to us from the white children's school. In one of these, there was a drawing of an African, an Indian, and a white person, all stereotyped, of course. The African and the Indian were "heathens" of the most objectionable sort.

The Indian woman was seated, however, next to one of her beautifully decorated pots, and it seemed to be mine. The recognition I experienced was intense. I experienced the design as something I already understood and knew. This was my spiritual, my soul, connection to Native creativity. Native beauty. It would be years before I could grasp the importance of the fact that my mother's grandmother, Tallulah (Basket maker), was African and Cherokee.

And so, when I saw Dennis Banks, and later when I worked for Indian sovereignty alongside Nilak Butler, John Trudell, Bill and Carol Wahpepah and their sons, and later when Wilma Mankiller, principal chief of the Cherokee, became a treasured confidant, it was soul reaching out to soul over centuries and over years. I carried this sensibility into all interactions with Native people, even when it was obvious that most of them had no idea of the history of suffering and awareness of each other's tribulations and triumphs we had previously shared. I discovered that whenever I was with Native people, whether in the United States, Canada, New Zealand, or Australia, I felt at home. I used to "charge" Bill Wahpepah, a large, handsome man with two long braids, a modest fee for some of the events he managed to get me to participate in: a few minutes pounding on the big drum that always appeared at Native gatherings, around which six young male warriors always sat, a drum that seemed mine as well.

So this is to say it hurt a lot to know Dennis Banks had been forced into exile because he had gone to defend Native people on the Pine Ridge reservation. As had Leonard Peltier and Russell Means, and many other men and women who answered the call to claim their Indian identity by fighting, alongside their elders and their children, to preserve it.

At the time, I was very ill with Lyme disease and so debilitated I could barely walk. I would lie on my couch some days wondering if I could muster the energy to reach the table or the stove and whether I could make myself and my young daughter enough cooked food to eat. This many-years-long fatigue was, as well, extremely taxing to my spirit, and when I learned Dennis was to be tried in South Dakota, and tried in Custer, of "Custer died for your sins" fame, and that the attorney general of South Dakota had said the best thing for Dennis Banks would be a bullet through his head, I decided to go to Dennis's trial—to attempt to protect him, and all Indian people, with the blanket of my witness as shredded and tattered as one of the woolen blankets in a Curtis photograph of "vanishing Indians." It was impossible, of course, sick as I was, and that was incentive enough to attempt it. I learned that if I did not speak I could conserve enough power to actually move. I went, using energy that seemed to come just enough minute by minute to get me to the airport, to the plane, and finally to Custer, South Dakota. There I lay on the ground surrounded by dogs, children, and a couple of Buddhist nuns who calmly and resolutely pounded, throughout the trial, on handheld drums.

Eventually, I was lifted up and snuck into the courtroom by Bill Wahpepah, who placed a shawl over my head and stood me in the line of Native elders who were permitted to enter the courtroom. I saw Dennis's wife, Kamook, and their young children. I heard the elders, with so much love and humility in their voices, plead for Dennis's freedom and life. I saw Dennis, dressed in a flowing robe with his red cloth through his hair and, because he is a runner, running shoes on his feet. He stood with dignity. And bore the verdict of the court with grace.

I was able to slip a copy of *The Color Purple* to him before I returned to California. Years later, when we reconnected in Cuba, where we had gone to deliver medicines and to meet with Fidel Castro, who seemed to know as much about Indian concerns as we did, Dennis told me how he had read the novel and passed it around the prison to other inmates until the pages were like onionskin. Years later, over dinner at my house, he would laugh as he told me how the men in the prison always returned the book, but that when it was shared with the women in the prison, it disappeared for good.

There we were, a couple of decades after his sentencing, and after the amazing and sometimes horrific events described in this incredibly important book, laughing. He had experienced a healing from my work, and I had experienced what seemed to me a miracle: from the moment I left South Dakota, having given all that I had in the way of spiritual energy to Dennis's well-being, my own health began to improve. My recovery was dramatic, and unmistakably connected to making the journey to Custer. At the time that I had Lyme disease it did not have a diagnosis or a name. I recognized my symptoms as information appeared in the media about this mysterious affliction—an autoimmune disease—caused by a tick bite. I learned that one way to heal it is to give the immune system a chore that is impossible to accomplish. The insistence on an impossible act startles the system into a response. This is what I believe happened to me. And I have Dennis to thank.

When I was a child I read books for entertainment and information; I now think of books as lifeboats. Each book that comes rushing down the stream of my life is checked for its relevance to our survival and prospering as a species. For the use to which Earthlings, and all beings, might put our incredible intelligence to save our tiny, sinkable, ship. Thinking about Dennis's book in this way, I sat with its story for several months, waiting to see what was for me its most important bit of news. I believe it is this: that we must revive our capacity to intuit what is happening to us and around us. This seems to be a faculty almost completely lost. It was a shock to read of the government-paid informants who infiltrated the American Indian Movement almost from its inception. Although I was aware, from my own involvement in movements for change, that agents of the state were always shadowing any progressive political thought and work, it had not occurred to me how easily and smoothly this might be done. I also realize that, when we used to smile at the ubiquitous camera people who materialized to cover every march and demonstration, we were in a sense acknowledging our awareness that we were being spied upon and that there was little we could do about it. In Dennis's story we see how much harm is done by our own acceptance of people who claim to be our friends but who instead are working hard, with the backing of the U.S. government, to ensure our destruction. What to do?

The spiritual path that Dennis takes as he moves along in the American Indian Movement is the one with the most juice, as he discovers. It is in meditating, in sweats, in the Sun Dance, and in prayer that we sharpen our emotional and relational intelligence. It is easier to discern who one's friends are after a long quiet time with nature and with our own souls than it is when we are throwing Molotov cocktails and firing guns—behavior that provocateurs the world over tend to encourage.

It is also crucial to listen to women. Those you are married to, those you are sleeping with, and those who are giving birth to, protecting, and feeding the warriors, and taking care of the elders and the children. It is also necessary to listen to the Feminine within one's self, whatever one's sex. When the Feminine suspects the lifeboat has been infiltrated with someone who wishes to sink it, it is time to put aside whatever vanity of all-knowingness one might have, and to listen. It is enough to make us weep, worldwide, to contemplate the amount of suffering that might have been avoided had the Feminine, whose hallmark is not only fierceness and compassion but also intuition, been listened to.

What finally sinks in, when one is of African Amerindian or Native American descent, is that our battle for our lives is real. It is not a game. It has never ended, since the moment Christopher Columbus landed on our shores, commenting as he studied us how friendly, generous, and good-natured we were. But this awareness of our uphill struggle need not make us gloomy. In fact, when I consider my own bloodlines—African, Native American, European (from the British Isles, no less)—I am filled with an almost frisky sense of curiosity. How will this unusual drama unfold? Who are Americans eventually to be? How is it that my own small being encompasses such a large and often tragic portion of my nation's history? And what of the vast sense of love I so frequently feel that must have come down to me from the lovers among the bloodlines who defied everything and everyone around them, especially the government and the church, in order to send down to their descendant a sense of oneness that easily enfolds distant galaxies and the stars? Perhaps we are still as we always were, generous, gentle, and unashamed, as Columbus found us; but we, having temporarily lost our intuitive knowledge of our essence, have forgotten this.

Indians and Africans and free whites laughing. Being merry. Wearing red ribbons in our hair. And so we go on, in every moment honoring who we were and are; in every moment, being.

Perhaps it is enough to affirm the goodness of Life, as our ancestors did, whatever our struggles or suffering. To know that though much has been taken from us, Wonder remains. Joy of connection with the Universe. Inner calm in the face of massive assault, as we begin to see quite clearly that our victors have lost everything in attempting to conquer us. There is, finally, nothing to envy or to honor them for. To know, as my father did, that the Indians of the world, those who have attempted to care for Mother Earth, always return to Her, and that in our deepest heart, we never leave. Nor would we even dream of it.

Dennis Banks's book, Ojibwa Warrior, *was published in 2004,* before this essay (2008).

A WEDDING CEREMONY: MARRYING GOOD MEN

November 3, 2008

A MONTH AGO, I MARRIED TWO GOOD MEN. To each other. You can imagine how this must have shocked my grandparents, with whom I continue to have a close relationship, though they died half a century ago. Two good white men, at that. Which must have made my grandparents, and parents, also deceased, incredulous, to say the least. In their time, living black in the Deep South, there were no good white men, except Jesus and Santa Claus. One of my favorite things about being me (though this isn't about me) is that I had both my parents while I was growing up, loving them, fighting with them, and orchestrating my little high school affairs without their knowledge, and so on. I also had both grandparents, who lived near enough to be run away to. There they sat, implacable in the face of life's challenges, their tiny shack completely hidden from the world, their lives also. Nothing seemed to faze them; besides, everything was so far away. Still, in my lifetime, I've managed to rattle them a bit. I've enjoyed doing it because I know they actually enjoy a good shock to their placid systems, and are, like most Southerners, entertained by whatever's odd about any situation; just as I am delighted by their swift recovery time. These folks are hip, I always think.

And the way they sound.

I love hearing them say, time and time again: *Baby Alice done what?*

So there we all were, about a hundred of us, at the beautiful Bel-Air Hotel in Los Angeles, down by the lake that is home to several swans. One groom-to-be's mother had already been ushered to her seat by a best man; the other groom-to-be's father had been brought forth by another. I was waiting at the altar, having been specially ordained to perform the service. I had explained to the *New York Times*, where notice of the event would run, that no, I was not a clergywoman or a minister, but a priestess. A priestess is like a minister or clergyperson, but is of the pagan persuasion, or, more baldly, a worshiper of Nature and especially the Earth. They were having none of it. In fifty years, of course, this usage, even in the *Times*, will be routine. This is how Aquarians think. Anyway, coming toward me were Scott and Brad, handsome and vulnerable, strong of heart and very sweet. My hands went out automatically to touch theirs, reaffirming the reality that we are all in this together. New territory, new conviction, new lifeways, and that it is as exciting as anything.

How did this happen?

I met Scott Sanders when he came to my house to ask if he could produce a musical of my novel, *The Color Purple*. I said I didn't think so. I liked him, though, and over time he won me over. We worked closely together for eight years to bring this story—in which I got to hang out a lot, in imagination, with parents and grandparents—to the public, first in a showing in Atlanta, Georgia, and then to New York City and Broadway. At each of these events I ran into Scott's mother, Leona, and she would comment on the beauty and power of the play, and I would comment on the upstanding character of her son. Never once in all that time did Scott ever let me, and the ancestors, down. He carried the story like the fragile and nourishing egg it is, with reverence and respect. For this, he became one of the family the story created. Which was one reason I knew my grandparents and parents might roll over once or twice in their heavenly naps as they contemplated the wedding, but would soon see all was well with my marrying Scott to the man he loved, and go back to sleep.

I liked Brad as soon as I met him. Others before him had had their charms, but I knew right away that Brad was the right man for Scott. The son of a Quaker minister, and someone who's known the suffering of substance enthralldom, Brad has become a bodhisattva who goes back into the perils he left behind to show others, entire families, the way out. I could see Harriet Tubman and Sojourner Truth in the work that he does, and this endeared him to me. I also saw that, unlike certain earlier suitors, he properly appreciated in Scott the good man with whom he was associating.

So one predawn day on a talk show stage somewhere, maybe in Cleveland or Chicago, as Scott and I were preparing to pitch our play to the early-rising viewers, I said to Scott, just before the cameras rolled: You know, Scott, Brad's really the right one for you; and if you ever want to marry him, I'll marry you. Where did this audacity come from? I hadn't the faintest notion what I'd have to do to accomplish this. Scott's jaw dropped. It would be two years before Brad popped the question, and Scott would say yes. Of course, they thought about asking Brad's dad, a minister, to marry them, but in the end, Scott and Brad asked me. I was terrified and thrilled, which I think I like.

The ceremony, designed to the last flower by Scott's best friend and best woman, Susan, was beautiful in its totality, but if I tell you everything that happened, it will be too long. I will just say that, with Scott and Brad beside me at the altar, I was able to welcome the community that came out to witness their marriage. Reminding them that we were lucky to be in the safest place of all: a place where love and freedom were honored. For, ultimately, that is the only safe place to be. I then recited the following poems: the first one for Scott, the second for Brad.

NEW FACE

I have learned
Not to worry
About love:
But to honor
Its coming
With all my heart.

To examine the dark mysteries
Of the blood
With headless heed
And swirl,

To know the rush
Of feelings
Swift
And flowing
As Water.

The source
Appears to be
Some inexhaustible
Spring
Within
Our twin
And triple
Selves.

The new face
I turn up
To you
No one else
On Earth
Has ever
Seen.

WHILE LOVE IS UNFASHIONABLE

While love
Is unfashionable
Let us live

Unfashionably.
Seeing the world
A complex ball
In small hands;
Love
Our blackest
Garment.

Let us be poor
In all but truth
And courage
Handed
Down
By the old spirits.

Let us be intimate
With ancestral
Ghosts
And music
Of
The undead.
While love
Is dangerous
Let us walk
Bareheaded
Beside
The great
River.

Let us gather
Blossoms
Under
Fire.

I wrote these poems out of the love I felt for my own nonblack husband, a good man I married in 1967, a time when our marriage was illegal in the American South where I was born.

Then, after Brad and Scott exchanged exquisite vows to each other and received their rings, came the words that I felt privileged to offer them in this beautiful, changing, and challenging time we are living in: By the power vested in me by the state of California (loud cheering) and a loving universe, I now pronounce you husband and husband. You may kiss the groom.

Once upon a time, long ago, when I knew no gay people as friends, I still found it reassuring to see two men kiss, which men used to do all the time in the Castro, in San Francisco, instead of fighting and shooting each other. I wrote about this wonder in an essay called "All the Bearded Irises of Life," which is how such men kissing each other struck me. Like flowers, and, like the iris, some have beards. Now, years later, witnessing my two friends kissing each other, I, like so many others in the gathering, wanted to cry, because we were experiencing collectively something that is spiritually as well as physically profound: that love is always holy. Only I found I couldn't cry; I was too happy.

COMING TO MISSISSIPPI

*From The Third Annual Gathering
of Veterans of the Mississippi Civil
Rights Movement, 2008*

October 9, 2008

I CAME TO MISSISSIPPI in 1966. Forty-two years ago. I came alone. It was a time of blessed upheaval in the United States of America, as people of my parents' generation, especially those of poor and working-class backgrounds, held almost no hope that America could be anything but hostile to and oppressive of people of color. I came to join the Mississippi freedom movement to honor the dignity and tenacity of my sharecropper parents and grandparents, and even my great-grandparents who had been enslaved to work on the same plantation where I was born. I came especially to honor a legendary 4-great-grandmother, Mrs. Mary Poole, who lived to be 125 years old, and walked in a slave coffle from Virginia to Georgia, carrying two children. It is because of her that I kept the name assigned me at birth: Walker.

Almost immediately, across a table at Steven's Kitchen, in the black section of Jackson, I met my future husband, a handsome Jewish law student. We were not supposed even to entertain the thought of living together, much less of marrying each other. We did get married, though, in 1967, defying the segregationist law that banned "miscegenation," becoming the first legally married interracial inhabitants of Mississippi. Day and night my brave and brilliant husband handled the legal cases that dismantled Southern Jim Crow in Mississippi, specializing in integration of schools. His battered movement car had a bullet hole in the windshield, but he never let up. My role was to serve the children of Mississippi by joining Friends of the Children of Mississippi and by writing relevant history booklets for their teachers to use in the schools we set up. I was also writing a novel that explored the impact of brutal exploitation—the sharecropping system that replaced slavery—on the human beings who endured it: *The Third Life of Grange Copeland*. I also wrote *Meridian*, whose focus was the black Southern movement itself and the people who—faithful and flawed, loving and tortured— brought it into flower. And, inevitably, perhaps, into decline.

I had come to Mississippi to offer whatever skills I had been educated to claim. Education in my rural community was highly prized; it was also hoped by the community that it would return some benefit to those who sacrificed for its attainment. The Children's Defense Fund's Marian Wright Edelman, for whom my future husband, Mel Leventhal, worked, gave me the opportunity to immediately put my own writing skills to use for the most dispossessed of the people; Leventhal and I headed directly into the Delta, to Greenwood, Mississippi, to take depositions from sharecroppers who, exactly like my own parents of a generation earlier, had been thrown off the plantations for attempting to exercise their "democratic" right to vote. In the process of gathering these depositions our own lives were placed in danger, a danger averted only by the watchful eyes of local black Mississippians who placed their own bodies between us and those who would do us harm.

It was my joy to also teach at both Tougaloo College and Jackson State, the latter of which invited me to take over the class of the amazing poet Margaret Walker, author of *Jubilee* and "For My People," when she took a leave of absence. At Tougaloo I taught literature and writing to students so brave and wise our class occasionally read each other's poetry through tears. One of my students demonstrated for justice in Jackson in the morning, was jailed in the afternoon, terribly beaten and tortured during the night, and then returned to class two days later, bruised, battered, but with new poetry and no less enthusiasm for the struggle. His name was David Nall. Sometimes when I am very tired and I see the tattered state of our struggle for peace and justice globally, I think of him, and am refreshed.

I saw the best of human beings in Mississippi. They were black and they were white. They were young and they were old. They were women and they were men. They were children who sacrificed childhood so

that future generations might enjoy it. Mississippi, in its vanguard position of struggle in the Southern black freedom movement, was a
fierce, challenging, loving, rageful mother and father to my spirit. My
debt for what I learned of human courage and possibility can never be
paid with less than my understanding that I must never, given our
people's beauty, endurance, trust in each other, and grace, give up.

SAYING GOOD-BYE
TO MY FRIEND
HOWARD ZINN

January 29, 2010

We have lost a gift, which, having received it, all of us might become.

On hearing the news of his death.
Me: Howie, Where did you go?
Howie: What do you mean, Where did I go? As soon as I died, I went back to Boston.

I MET HOWARD ZINN in 1961, my first year at Spelman College in Atlanta, Georgia. He was the tall, rangy, good-looking professor that many of the girls at Spelman swooned over. My African roommate and I got a good look at him every day when he came for his mail in the post office just beneath our dormitory window. He was always in motion, but would stop frequently to talk to the many students and administrators and total strangers that seemed attracted to his energy of nonhesitation to engage. We met formally when some members of my class were being honored and I was among them. I don't remember what we were being honored for, but Howard and I ended up sitting next to each other. He remembered this later; I did not. He was the first white person I'd sat next to; we talked. He claimed I was "ironic." I was surprised he did not feel white.

© JEAN WEISINGER 1992

I knew nothing of immigrants (which his parents were) or of Jews. Nothing of his father's and his own working-class background. Nothing of his awareness of poverty and slums. Nothing of why a white person could exist in America and not feel white: i.e., heavy, oppressive, threatening, and almost inevitably insensitive to the feelings of a person of color. The whole of Georgia was segregated at that time, and in coming to Spelman I had had a run-in with the Greyhound bus driver (white as described above) who had forced me to sit in the back of the bus. This moment had changed my life, though how that would play out was of course uncertain to a seventeen-year-old.

One way it did play out was that the very next summer I was on my way to the Soviet Union to see how white those folks were and to tell as many of them as I could, even if they were white, that I did not agree to my country's notions of bombing them. I didn't see a lot of generals, but children and women and men and old people of both sexes were everywhere. They were usually smiling and offering flowers or vodka. There was no "iron curtain" between us, as I'd been told to expect by

Georgia media. I love to tell the story of how I was so ignorant at the time I didn't have a clue who folks were queuing up to see in Lenin's tomb; nor did I even know what "the Kremlin" was. I also didn't speak a word of Russian.

Coming back to Spelman, I discovered Howard Zinn was teaching a course on Russian history and literature and a little of the language. I signed up for it, though I was only a sophomore and the course was for juniors (as I recall). I had loved Russian literature since I discovered Tolstoy and Dostoyevsky back in the school library in Putnam County, Georgia. As for the Russian language, as with any language, I most wanted to learn to say: hello, good-bye, please, and thank you.

Howard Zinn was magical as a teacher. Witty, irreverent, and wise, he loved what he was teaching and clearly wanted his students to love it also. We did. My mother, who earned seventeen dollars a week working twelve-hour days as a maid, had somehow managed to buy a typewriter for me and I had learned typing in school. I said hardly a word in class (as Howie would later recall), but inspired by his warm and brilliant ability to communicate ideas and conundrums and passions of the characters and complexities of Russian life in the nineteenth century, I flew back to my room after class and wrote my response to what I was learning about these writers and their stories that I adored. He was proud of my paper, and, in his enthusiastic fashion, waved it about. I learned later there were those among other professors at the school who thought that I could not possibly have written it. His rejoinder: "Why, there's nobody else in Atlanta who could have written it!"

It would be hard not to love anyone who stood in one's corner like this.

Under the direction of SNCC (Student Nonviolent Coordinating Committee) many students at Spelman joined the effort to desegregate Atlanta. Naturally, I joined this movement. Howie, taller than most of us, was constantly in our midst, and usually somewhere in front. Because I was at Spelman on scholarship, a scholarship that would be revoked if I were jailed, my participation caused me a good bit of anxiety. Still, knowing that Howard and other professors—the amazingly courageous and generous Staughton Lynd, for instance, my other history teacher—supported the students in our struggle made it possible to carry on. But then, while he and his family were away from campus for the summer, Howard Zinn was fired. He was fired for "insubordination."

Yes, he would later say, with a classic Howie shrug, I was guilty.

For me, and for many poorer students in my position, students on scholarship who also worked in the movement to free us of centuries of white supremacy and second-class citizenship, it was a disaster. I wrote a letter to the administration that was published in the school paper pointing out the error of their decision. I wrote it through tears of anger and frustration. It was these tears, which appeared unannounced whenever I thought of this injustice to Howard and his family—who I had met and also loved—that were observed by Staughton Lynd, who realized instantly that (a) there was every chance I was headed toward a breakdown; and (b) the administration would quickly find a reason to expel me from school. Added to the stress, and which nobody knew about, was the fact that I was working for a well-respected older man who, knowing I had to work in order to pay for everything I needed as a young woman in school, was regularly molesting me. Lucky for me he was very old, and his imagination was stronger than his grasp. As a farm girl and no stranger to manual labor, I could type his papers with one hand while holding him off with the other. What rankled so much, then as now, is how much others respected, even venerated him.

Perhaps this was one of many births of my feminism. A feminism/Womanism that never seemed odd to Howard Zinn, who encouraged his Spelman students, all of them women, to name and challenge oppression of any sort. This encouragement would come in handy when, years later, writing my second novel, *Meridian*, I could explore the misuse of gender-based power from the perspective of having experienced it.

With Staughton Lynd's help, and after he had consulted with Howie (I did not know this), I was accepted to finish my college education at Sarah Lawrence College, a place of which I had never heard. I went off in the middle of winter, without a warm coat or warm shoes, and ice and snow greeted me. But also Staughton's mother, Helen Lynd, who immediately provided money for the coat and shoes I needed, as well as a blanket that had been her son's. In my solitary room, and knowing no one on campus, I hunkered down to write. Letters to the Zinns, first of all. To inform them I had been liberated from Spelman, as they had been, and had landed.

I was Howard's student for only a semester, but in fact, I have learned from him all my life. His way with resistance: steady, persistent, impersonal, often with humor, is a teaching I cherish. Whenever I've been arrested, I've thought of him. I see policemen as victims of the very system they're hired to defend, as I know he did. I see soldiers in the same way. In some ways, Howie was an extension of my father, whom he never met. My father was also an activist as a young man and was one of the first black men unconnected to white ancestry or power to vote in our backwoods county; he had to pass by three white men holding shotguns in order to do this. By the time I went off to college, the last of eight children, he was exhausted and broken. But these men were connected in ways clearer to me now as I've become older than my father was when he died. They each saw injustice as something to be acknowledged, confronted, and changed if at all possible. And they looked for signs of humanity in their opponents and spoke to that. They both possessed a sense of humor and love of a good story that made them charismatic teachers. I recently discovered, and it amuses me, that their birth dates are remarkably close, though my father was thirteen years older.

Howie and I planned to rendezvous in Berkeley in March, when he came out to spend a few weeks with his grandchildren. In April, we planned to be on a panel with Gloria Steinem and Bernice Reagon at an event in New Orleans for Amnesty International. I had decided not to go, but Howie said if I didn't come he would "sorely miss" me. I wrote back that in that case I would certainly be there as "soreness of any sort" was not to be tolerated.

Over the years I've been in the habit of sending freshly written poems to Roz and Howie. After her death, I continued to send the occasional poem to Howie. Last week, after the Supreme Court's decision to let corporations offer unlimited funding to political candidates, I wrote a poem about what I would do if I were president, called: "If I Was President: 'Were' for Those Who Prefer It." My first act as president, given that corporations may well buy all elections in America from now on, would be to free Mumia Abu-Jamal and Leonard Peltier, both men accused of murders I've felt they did not commit, both men in prison for sadistically long periods of time.

Howie's response, and the last word he communicated to me, was "Wonderful." I imagined him hurriedly typing it, then flying, even at eighty-seven, out the door.

The question remains: where do our friends and loved ones go when they die?

They can't all go back to Boston, or wherever they've lived their most intense life.

I fell asleep, after leaking tears for Howie most of the day: my sweetheart's shirt was luckily absorbent and available to me, and after tossing and turning almost all night, I had the following dream: We (someone and I) were looking for the place we go to when we die. After quite a long walk, we encountered it. What we saw was this astonishingly gigantic collection of people and creatures: birds and foxes, butterflies and dogs, cats and beings I've never seen awake, and they were moving toward us in total joy at our coming. We were happy too. But there was nothing to support any of us: no land, no water, nothing. We ourselves were all of it: our own Earth. And I woke up knowing that this is where we go when we die. We go back to where we came from: inside all of us.

Good-bye, Howie. Beloved. Hello.

Note: This piece ran Sunday, January 31, in the Boston Globe. *A few days after I wrote this remembrance a friend sent me a video about an orangutan and a hound dog. They had discovered each other and formed a bond. I realized the orangutan, whom (I prefer whom to that) I had never seen animated with joy, as shown in the video, was the principal being coming to welcome us in the dream. I was struck especially by the comment of the orangutan's human caregivers that sharing to the orangutan comes naturally: that if given anything he or she breaks it in half immediately and offers the other half back to the giver. This ancestral behavior is wonderful to know.*

ON *THE HELP*

September 2, 2011

I Blogged the following piece *about* The Help *several months ago under "Turning Madness into Flowers," a category I've created for those expressions in the culture that embrace and transform whatever is most difficult. I understand much of the controversy about the novel* The Help *and especially about the movie to be motivated by unalleviated pain stemming from our history of outrageous physical and psychic abuse. Abuse that has wounded us all. The pain, a constant feeling of inconsolable grief, when not addressed, has not been sufficiently acknowledged, worked through, and integrated. We still hurt from the theft of our mothers. But it is also useful to have it affirmed that the white children our mothers raised were often hurt by the loss of them also. Even this pains us, of course. Angers us. There is no escape, or healing, except through acceptance of the damage. Squaring off with the wound.*

I have recently seen the film made from the book and yes, it is like a cartoon compared to the book. But still helpful. For one thing, may it send its viewers to the book, for a careful reading. And may many readers opt for the audiobook of The Help, *in which the richness of the narrative is more apparent. There is nothing like hearing black women's voices telling their own story, no matter who gets credit for publishing it.*

What else can we learn?

Peter Bratt, *who wrote the scripts for* Follow Me Home *and* La Mission, *comes to mind as the kind of writer it would be safe to trust with this kind of material—if he were a Southerner and understood our nuances! Or Marsha Norman, who wrote the musical "book" for* The Color Purple. *I am not familiar with other work of the screenwriters of* The Help, *but I was embarrassed by the dumbing down of a story that, as a movie, isn't at all as disturbing as it should be. After all, we're looking at how coolly slavery continued well into the present time.*

Is the premise flawed? Of course. These women would not have spoken to Miss Skeeter about their trials under white female employment. She was one of the enemy. I lived in Jackson, Mississippi, during the sixties and taught women very much like the ones depicted in the novel. When they tried to vote, or organize schools for their children, when they raised their voices for anything beyond Yes m'am and No m'am, they were punished severely. Fired, slapped, beaten, run out of their houses, as a matter of course, and, in more extreme cases, raped and killed, sometimes thrown in the river. Just as men were; though, as Robin Morgan once wrote about: even black men considered crimes against black women in which rape was involved, to be sexual rather than political. They would have found it difficult to talk freely even to a person of color, one of the most tragic and remarkable things I discovered while teaching them.

But this is why fiction exists. To tell the story in the only way you can, given the reality of one's limitations. And I did not confuse the character Skeeter's obliviousness with the author's. I prefer to applaud Stockett's imagination rather than decry it.

For those who see the film, here is an example of a cheapening of black cultural experience: When we were little, growing up in the blessed company of parents and grandparents (if we were lucky! as some of us were) we always (most of us) wanted to drink coffee because our elders did. They knew coffee wasn't good for us and also it was expensive, since it was one of the few commodities our families could not grow. To keep us from asking for it, they said: coffee will make you black! Now, we were all black, but we also knew that wasn't supposed to be a good thing! Plus, and here's the depth of the exchange: while saying this to us, the grandparent or parent inevitably smiled slyly at us or laughed outright, sipping the delicious coffee

and smacking their lips right in front of our quizzical faces! You're
black, you're drinking coffee, you're. . . . What the heck are you say-
ing! Something really complicated, in fact. A teaching about many
kinds of love, including a love of being black. Enjoying it. Yum!

In the movie this is twisted when the black maid Abilene tells her
white charge, who asks why she's black, that she's black because she
drinks too much coffee. In this context, blackness can only be con-
strued as negative. Which goes against one of the most subtle teach-
ings from generations of black people who worked hard to keep our
souls intact.

That it is Minny's revenge that gets the most attention, and laugh-
ter, is another instance of cheapening; we are left thinking that some-
how this one grotesque act of rebellion (which most maids would
have been unable to perform because of Christian self-restraint)
makes up for centuries of unimaginable repression and degradation.

And so on.

The Help, by Kathryn Stockett.

Langston Hughes, who befriended me when I was very young, just beginning to write, exhibited a quality I also have: I deeply prefer to say
nothing about another's work if I dislike it. In fact, decades ago I wrote
a short review of another writer's work that hurt her feelings. Realizing this, I gave up writing reviews.

I put off listening to *The Help* thinking I wouldn't like it; that the
story would awaken pain (especially from my years as an activist living
in Jackson, Mississippi, the novel's setting) from which perhaps I had
not sufficiently recovered. My own mother and father and grandparents before them were "the help" to generations of racist white Southerners. My mother especially took on a job as maid and caretaker of a
white woman's house and children from seven in the morning to seven
at night, every day but Sunday. Leaving her own home and family be-
reft of her light-filled presence, attention, and love. A robbery of guidance and grace, a theft of security.

But when I began listening to *The Help*, I found myself seeing my
mother's sacrifice and love at an even greater depth than I had before.
By the time I finished the novel, late in the night, and after many tears
and some laughter, I felt immensely comforted by the reminder that

our mothers and fathers who basically re-enslaved themselves to feed, clothe, and educate their children, also did their best to love the children they were forced to tend, thus keeping themselves human in a situation in which the most self-destructive hatred might have developed. Destroying all our lives.

I used to wonder if any white child in the South who received the love of the great souls forced to tend them would ever develop enough soul of his or her own to rise in their defense. Or even to an understanding, however limited or imperfect, of their silenced, hidden sacrifice. Kathryn Stockett has done so.

I appreciate *The Help* for its healing response to a lifetime (really, lifetimes) of injustice and hurt. And for its teaching of solidarity with the intimately oppressed.

As a film, it too could move us forward into the necessary awareness humans must continue to develop: that it is our denial of ourselves as family, with one another, and with all of creation, that threatens our planetary existence.

The readers of this audiobook are brilliant, their voices delightfully true.

HONORING
CICELY TYSON

SEPTEMBER 19, 2011

CICELY TYSON PLAYS THE ROLE OF CONSTANTINE, the disappeared maid who raised Skeeter in the novel *The Help* by Kathryn
Stockett. She plays her as a very old woman, barely able to carry the
dish of peas and potatoes she's attempting to serve to the Daughters of
the Confederacy who've come to call on her mistress. In the novel Constantine isn't so old; the daughter who comes to visit during the disastrous luncheon that leads to Constantine's firing, not so rich in color. In
fact, in the novel the daughter—Rachel, I believe, is her name—is "light,
bright, almost white," and in fact, Skeeter's mother doesn't realize for
quite a while that she's entertaining a black woman in her living room.
When she does grasp this, and also realizes this well-educated daughter
of Constantine has no intention of acting like "the help"—which is
nearly the only role blacks in Mississippi have experienced having—she
becomes abusive and sends both mother and daughter packing.

The implication here, given our long history of the rape of black
women, especially of servants and maids, by the man of the house, is
that this "white-looking" daughter of Constantine's is possibly the
daughter of Skeeter's own father, who, in the film, is a passive "farmer";
though, with his vast acreage of cotton and his scores of black workers, he would more likely have been a typical plantation owner who
kept his house and farm in order by the same means his slave-owning
ancestors did: by violence.

If this line of the novel had been followed in the film we might have been encouraged to explore a whole Pandora's box of hidden relationships between blacks and whites and the ways in which they've shaped our culture. Leading, who knows, to some part of our collective racial enlightenment. (No pun.) But of course this is why discussion groups are born. We must educate ourselves about who we are if no one else ever feels the need. I thought of this as the case against Dominique Strauss Kahn—accused of sexually assaulting a hotel maid in New York City—was dismissed. Anyone who has stayed in a hotel and watched the behavior of maids, as they rush about cleaning up after the hordes they must encounter each day, would find it hard to imagine how one of them, almost middle-aged, overworked, probably not at all nimble, would manage to seduce a rich, white European, possibly the next president of France, and then run out of the room immediately after having sex with him, and, in very limited English, complain.

Rich white men, and some not so rich, in a society in which black women are considered less worthy than whites (our black First Lady notwithstanding) have rarely needed to worry. White men have been raping the black "help" for centuries, often leaving the most indelible proof of their misadventures—which reminds me of British writer Fanny Kemble's comment after visiting a Southern plantation in the 1800s. I paraphrase: Every white mistress likes to talk about all the light-skinned children on every other plantation than her own. It appears she thinks the mixed-race babies crawling in the dirt around her own place dropped from heaven.

For a useful understanding of this phenomenon—the confusion, the pain, the mental strain and sheer sadism of it—I recommend the novel *The Kitchen House* by Kathleen Grissom. This novel, like *The Help*, does important work: it factors in the experience not only of African Americans under enslavement, but of poor white Europeans, who, during the same period of American history, were often indentured. Neither black nor white people had any hope of being mentally healthy under the institution of slavery. Mental health, serenity, peace would have been impossible. The anguish of lives lived in corruption and deceit has been passed down. So that, for instance, within the last couple of months a gang of modern white "night riders" in Jackson, Mississippi, went on a hunt for a black person to torture and kill, as if this behavior, like so much of mental illness, has been inherited by unfortunate sufferers in the present. Finding their target, apparently the first black person they saw, they beat him savagely and murdered him by running over him with their truck. His name was James Anderson, a bespectacled middle-aged man, gay, and with a warm, wide smile. A smile lovingly recalled by his friends.

Ironically James Anderson could have been Emmett Till grown up (many people of color notice such resemblances; others might not). The same mixed-race characteristics: the curly or straight-ish hair, caramel to brown skin, and hazel or gray/green eyes. One always wonders (if one wonders about such things at all) how much unconscious anger, frustration, and hatred is unleashed when white racists attack blacks who are obviously related, racially, to themselves. If we had the kind of psychiatric curiosity we've always needed but never had in the United States, we'd have a way of helping people harmed by their own racism to see their projections, and to be more reflective about their racial responses to out of control emotions arising in themselves.

With such help, young Dedmon (who should have had an early name change, in my opinion) might have looked at his victim and thought about the why of Anderson's gray/green eyes. Or, if he knowingly wished to hurt someone who represented "racial impurity," as the state of Mississippi has always categorized the "crime" of race mixing, he could at least have taken a moment to consider why.

But I am thinking of Cicely Tyson.

What struck me about Tyson's performance in *The Help* is how much she was able to express without words. Suffering, indignation, hurt, outrage, as Skeeter's mother banishes her after a lifetime of service. I wanted to revisit at least two of Tyson's earlier films: *Sounder* and *The Autobiography of Miss Jane Pittman* (based on Ernest J. Gaines's great novel of the same name). Both films were released in the early seventies and, reviewing them all these years later, I am filled with gratitude for the integrity of Tyson's work. In fact, she is a wonder. Tiny, black, intense, she has a quality of authenticity that is rare in many of the "black" films that followed. What is it about Tyson? I was attempting to explain this to a visitor recently: it is that no matter what the white man in charge is saying, or the co-opted black man (or woman for that matter), she does not believe him. And her eyes tell us she does not. Her dignity. Her pride in what she knows is true. *Her experience.*

Her devotion to whatever she cares about is as fiercely expressed, with the same economy of emotional purity. One scene in *Sounder* has stayed with me all these years: it is when the wife realizes that, coming limping down the road toward their sharecropper's shack, is her husband Nathan. Nathan has been imprisoned (on the chain gang) for stealing meat to feed his starving family and is only allowed home after he's been badly injured. At first Tyson (Rebecca, in the film) can't believe her eyes. And when she does, she says just his name. And then, her whole being humming with long-suppressed worry and grief, and boundless relief and love, she begins to run toward Nathan, along the red dust road.

Here it is. This moment. What we need to remember. Our deep foundational love of each other. Our sacrifices. Our hidden-from-white-"civilization" joys. Our triumphs of spirit over disaster.

It is the same with *The Autobiography of Miss Jane Pittman*. (I read it decades ago as a miracle of a book.) Though compromised by the insertion of a white male journalist where none existed in the novel (unless memory isn't serving), Tyson perfectly carries this story of a black woman's life from her enslavement to her emancipation, to her involvement in the civil rights movement, with compassion and accurate fidelity to our collective struggle. Equally important, she models the love and faithfulness, in her private love affair with her husband, Joe Pittman, that is the fruit of the hard work required in hell to remain human.

Thank you, Cicely Tyson. For your beauty in all its forms: integrity of soul in your art, but also in your black skin, your big, dark eyes, your natural hair. Perhaps you know this already, but years ago you kept many of us going with your energy of respect for our real experience, and for our real selves.

WE ARE IN THIS PLACE
FOR A REASON

An Introduction to All Things Censored
by Mumia Abu-Jamal

November 28, 2008

This is why we became soldiers. This is why we remain soldiers. Because we want no more death and trickery for our people, because we want no more forgetting. The mountain told us to take up arms so we would have a voice. It told us to cover our faces so we would have a face. It told us to forget our names so we could be named. It told us to protect our past so we would have a future.

This is who we are. The Zapatista Liberation Army. The voice that arms itself to be heard, the face that hides itself to be seen, the name that hides itself to be named, the red star that calls out to humanity around the world to be heard, to be seen, to be named. The tomorrow that is harvested in the past.

—"What Made the Acteal Massacre Possible?"
All Things Censored

I WILL NOT WRITE ANY LONGER about Mumia Abu-Jamal's innocence. Millions of people around the world believe he is innocent. I will not write any longer about how he was framed: the evidence speaks for itself. I will not write any longer about the necessity of a new trial: that is obvious. The state intends to take Mumia's life for its own purposes; for all our love and work, it may succeed.

In every generation there is a case like Mumia's: a young black man is noted to be brilliant, radical, loving of his people, at war with injustice: often while he is still in his teens, as in the case of Mumia, the "authorities" decide to keep an eye on him. Indeed, they attempt to arrest his life by framing him for crimes he did not commit and incarcerating him in prison. There, they think of him as something conquered, a magnificent wild animal they have succeeded in capturing. They feel powerful in a way they could not feel if he were free. Imprisoning such a spirit prevents their knowing how much of the natural, instinctive, loving self they have lost, or have had stolen from them. Whether by abusive parents, horrendous schools, or grim economics. They do not know they have encaged their own masculine beauty, their own passionate soul.

This is immediately apparent when one enters the prison where Mumia is kept. The apprehensive, bored guards. And Mumia, in his orange prison uniform, alert to every spark of life on a visitor's face, seemingly interested in everything. His essays, many of them in this book, demonstrate his engaged attention to what is going on in the world, his identification with those who act against injustice and who suffer. His great love of truth and what is right. It is his integrity, in analyzing dozens of events, that makes it possible to sense he is not a murderer. Certainly not a liar. They will have to kill Mumia to silence him; he has lost his fear of death, having been threatened with it so many times; he is a free man, at last.

A man who is free, whose life has been signed away several times already, is a man I can listen to. What does such a man, unrepentant of his beliefs, have to say? And what places in the listener's soul are fed by his words? As we push off into the next thousand years, which I personally feel are going to be great, what is the fundamental voice we need to hear to start us on the journey? It is the voice of those, like the Zapatistas, like Mumia, whose love outweighs their fear.

So I will ask you to read at least one of Mumia's books, as a way to begin to feel your way into this new millennium. He has written and published books while on death row, an amazing feat, and of course he has been punished for doing so. I will encourage you to listen to his voice. Losing that voice would be like losing a color from the rainbow. I will tell you we have a reason for being here, in America, and that

Mumia reminds us what it is. It is to continue to delight in who we are, because who we are is beautiful. Who we are is powerful. Who we are is strong. Mumia is us, this amazing new tribe of people that being in America has produced. With plenty conciousness, plenty beauty, plenty intelligence, and plenty hair.

We are like the Zapatistas of southern Mexico in many ways: vastly outnumbered, many of us poor, humiliated on a daily basis by those in power, feeling ourselves unwanted, unseen, and unnamed. Mumia helps us know how deeply and devoutly we are wanted; how sharply and lovingly we are seen; how honorable is our much-maligned name. And like the Zapatistas, who are an indigenous people still trustful of Nature, we too can rejoice in knowing it is not too late to take direction from the Earth.

Therefore, the Ocean has told me to tell you this: As lovers of the life of Mumia Abu-Jamal, we must be prepared for three things: to see Mumia murdered by the state; to see him left to languish on death row indefinitely; to see him freed. What is our responsibility in the face of these things, all of them designed deliberately to cause great emotion in our hearts? Emotion that, in the past, has predictably sent us mad into the streets, our anger and frustration making us careless in our pain, set up, once more, to become victims of our grief.

If Mumia is left to languish in prison indefinitely, we must continue to try to get him out. But if he is murdered by the state or if he is set free by the state, there is something else we must do.

Ocean says: Bring his spirit and yours to me.

Therefore: on the afternoon of his release, whether into our waiting embraces, we his global family, or whether into the infinitely vast arms of the loving universe, let us prepare to welcome him into the place of honor his own life has created. Let us observe silence. This will be the hardest thing to do; but we can do it, and it will strengthen us. We can prepare to be silent, by making arrangements beforehand. Let us dress, if we can afford it, in white. White, because it is the color of potentiality, of emptiness, and also because, in America, it has so often been the color of our despair. Let us carry candles in all the colors of the rainbow, representing our multicolored family who have found such joy and inspiration in Mumia's life. Let us carry four stones, symbolic of Mumia's and all the ancestors' bones, and of the four directions. Let us carry sage, incense, flowers, and oranges. Let us carry, as well, a small paper photograph of Mumia and one of Judge Albert Sabo, who showed Mumia no mercy as he sentenced him to death, and another of Governor Thomas Ridge, who signed Mumia's death warrant almost the moment he took office. The fourth photograph should be of Mumia's lawyer, Leonard Weinglass, whose dedication to saving Mumia's life has been brave and unfaltering. These four men are linked for all eternity, and we should honor that. Let us, with our friends and family, and especially all the little children—each child entrusted with a flower and a single orange—make our way to the ocean. Any ocean. And if there is no ocean where you live, go to rivers, creeks, rivulets, and streams. These will eventually reach the ocean, just as you yourself will, someday.

Compose your altar there on the beach; Sabo's photograph to the left, reminding us never to forsake our hearts, and Governor Ridge's to the right, reminding us that force is not our way. Place Mumia's and Leonard's photographs in the center, to reassure us of the possibility of trust, friendship, and freedom. Use the rocks, the bones of the ancestors, to hold the photographs in place. Light your candles, place them on either side of the photographs. Light sage or incense and smudge each other. And now, in whatever way Spirit moves, facing Ocean, speak. Mother Ocean is so immense that she touches every shore; She can accept your tears, they are of her substance, and She can hold them.

After speaking, return to silence. Burn the photographs. Sabo's first, in gratitude for having been spared his life and his fate; Governor Ridge's next, in joy that your descendants will never need to remember you as someone who wished to kill, or who actually did kill, the Beloved. Then burn Mumia's and Leonard's photographs together, reminding us that those who work for justice are seldom without allies. Bless these ashes, all of which are made holy by your love and your restraint, and send them out to sea. Ask the children to let their flowers accompany them. When your ceremony is finished, hopefully at sunset, sit on the sand, facing the ocean, and share the oranges, symbolic of the sun that those in prison rarely see; a sun so generous in its nature that men have had to build prisons to hide other men away from it. Go home, gather around a good, light meal, no part of which was tortured or enslaved. Answer every child's questions thoroughly and with patience. Speak of Angelo Herndon, Hurricane Carter, Nelson Mandela, and Malcolm X. Read Mumia's censored radio commentaries aloud. Meditate together on whatever action you need to take. In re-membrance of our people, in their thousands, who are imprisoned: if there is anyone in your family who is in need, abandon judgment and commit yourself to helping them.

The meaning of our life is Life itself. As mysterious and as precious as That to which we belong.

Remember to look directly into each other's eyes throughout this long day. Embrace at every opportunity. Touch often.

Northern California, January 2008

LISTENING TO HOWIE: THE OPTIMISM OF UNCERTAINTY

November 4, 2011

FILMMAKER PRATIBHA PARMAR AND I ARE *in Cape Town, South Africa, where I am a juror at the Russell Tribunal on Palestine. Our first session begins today, November 4, in District Six—a place that used to be home to a mixture of all colors and kinds of people until the white supremacist government of South Africa bulldozed the houses.*

Turning a "black spot," as it was called, into a place for white-only settlement. What does this remind us of?

Well, it seemed to remind my computer to go back several years to this statement from Howard Zinn, who was one of my best friends and probably my best teacher, though I took a formal class with him for only one semester. He was actually writing to encourage me about something else entirely, but like Howie (to his friends) he managed to slip in this bright ray of light.

I share it with all of you sitting in and standing in and sleeping in around the world. In the cold and in the wet. Howie would have been so proud of you, so happy. He believed in you so much. In us.

The Optimism of Uncertainty

In this awful world where the efforts of caring people often pale in comparison to what is done by those who have power, how do I manage to stay involved and seemingly happy?

I am totally confident not that the world will get better, but that we should not give up the game before all the cards have been played. The metaphor is deliberate; life is a gamble. Not to play is to foreclose any chance of winning. To play, to act, is to create at least a possibility of changing the world.

There is a tendency to think that what we see in the present moment will continue. We forget how often we have been astonished by the sudden crumbling of institutions, by extraordinary changes in people's thoughts, by unexpected eruptions of rebellion against tyrannies, by the quick collapse of systems of power that seemed invincible.

What leaps out from the history of the past hundred years is its utter unpredictability. A revolution to overthrow the czar of Russia, in that most sluggish of semifeudal empires, not only startled the most advanced imperial powers but took Lenin himself by surprise and sent him rushing by train to Petrograd. Who would have predicted the bizarre shifts of World War II—the Nazi-Soviet pact (those embarrassing photos of von Ribbentrop and Molotov shaking hands), and the German army rolling through Russia, apparently invincible, causing colossal casualties, being turned back at the gates of Leningrad, on the western edge of Moscow, in the streets of Stalingrad, followed by the defeat of the German army, with Hitler huddled in his Berlin bunker, waiting to die?

And then the postwar world, taking a shape no one could have drawn in advance: the Chinese Communist revolution, the tumultuous and violent Cultural Revolution, and then another turnabout, with post-Mao China renouncing its most fervently held ideas and institutions, making overtures to the West, cuddling up to capitalist enterprise, perplexing everyone.

No one foresaw the disintegration of the old Western empires happening so quickly after the war, or the odd array of societies that would be created in the newly independent nations, from the benign village socialism of Nyerere's Tanzania to the madness of Idi Amin's adjacent Uganda. Spain became an astonishment. I recall a veteran of the Abraham Lincoln Brigade telling me that he could not imagine Spanish Fascism being overthrown without another bloody war. But after Franco was gone, a parliamentary democracy came into being, open to Socialists, Communists, anarchists, everyone.

The end of World War II left two superpowers with their respective spheres of influence and control, vying for military and political power. Yet they were unable to control events, even in those parts of the world considered to be their respective spheres of influence. The failure of the Soviet Union to have its way in Afghanistan, its decision to withdraw after almost a decade of ugly intervention, was the most striking evidence that even the possession of thermonuclear weapons does not guarantee domination over a determined population.

The United States has faced the same reality. It waged a full-scale war in Indochina, conducting the most brutal bombardment of a tiny peninsula in world history, and yet was forced to withdraw. In the headlines every day we see other instances of the failure of the presumably powerful over the presumably powerless, as in Brazil, where a grassroots movement of workers and the poor elected a new president pledged to fight destructive corporate power.

Looking at this catalogue of huge surprises, it's clear that the struggle for justice should never be abandoned because of the apparent overwhelming power of those who have the guns and the money and who seem invincible in their determination to hold on to it. That apparent power has, again and again, proved vulnerable to human qualities less measurable than bombs and dollars: moral fervor, determination, unity, organization, sacrifice, wit, ingenuity, courage, patience—whether by blacks in Alabama and South Africa, peasants in El Salvador, Nicaragua, and Vietnam, or workers and intellectuals in Poland, Hungary, and the Soviet Union itself. No cold calculation of the balance of power need deter people who are persuaded that their cause is just.

I have tried hard to match my friends in their pessimism about the world (is it just my friends?), but I keep encountering people who, in spite of all the evidence of terrible things happening everywhere, give me hope. Especially young people, in whom the future rests. Wherever I go, I find such people. And beyond the handful of activists there seem to be hundreds, thousands, more who are open to unorthodox ideas. But they tend not to know of one another's existence, and so, while they persist, they do so with the desperate patience of Sisyphus endlessly pushing that boulder up the mountain. I try to tell each group that it is not alone, and that the very people who are disheartened by the absence of a national movement are themselves proof of the potential for such a movement.

Revolutionary change does not come as one cataclysmic moment (beware of such moments!) but as an endless succession of surprises, moving zigzag toward a more decent society. We don't have to engage in grand, heroic actions to participate in the process of change. Small acts, when multiplied by millions of people, can transform the world.

Even when we don't "win," there is fun and fulfillment in the fact that we have been involved, with other good people, in something worthwhile. We need hope. An optimist isn't necessarily a blithe, slightly sappy whistler in the dark of our time. To be hopeful in bad times is not just foolishly romantic. It is based on the fact that human history is a history not only of cruelty but also of compassion, sacrifice, courage, kindness.

What we choose to emphasize in this complex history will determine our lives. If we see only the worst, it destroys our capacity to do something. If we remember those times and places—and there are so many—where people have behaved magnificently, this gives us the energy to act, and at least the possibility of sending this spinning top of a world in a different direction. And if we do act, in however small a way, we don't have to wait for some grand utopian future. The future is an infinite succession of presents, and to live now as we think human beings should live, in defiance of all that is bad around us, is itself a marvelous victory.

Howard Zinn is the author of A People's History of the United States, *among other books that nourish and sustain!*

MEDITATION
The Settled Mind

Juʟʏ 23, 2010

If the mind is always calm and still, dark and silent, not seeing anything, neither inside nor outside, free of all thoughts and mental images, this is the settled mind, which is not to be conquered. If the mind gets excited at objects, falling all over itself, looking for beginnings and ends, this is the confused mind, which ruins the virtues of the Way and undermines essence and life—it should not be indulged. Putting your nature in order is like tuning a stringed instrument. If the strings are too taut, they will snap. If they are too loose, they will be unresponsive. When tautness and relaxation are balanced, then the instrument is ready.

—Wang Chongyang

MILAGROS DE LA VIDA TURTLES

DECEMBER 4, 2008

TODAY, A FEW HOURS BEFORE SUNSET, I went with friends to place sixty-four tiny turtles back into the ocean. They had come ashore months before as embryos in their mothers' bodies. The mothers had laid the soft, leathery eggs in deep, undersand nests, covered them carefully, and left them to hatch, before returning to the ocean's depths. My sweetheart and I had walked our dog along their nesting trail in May, marveling at the igloo-like bubbles that covered the beach. Now, in early December, under large plastic buckets, dozens of baby turtles wriggled and crawled, over and over each other, and into our lucky hands.

That is what I felt, incredibly lucky to be there to help them go home. Home to a giant sea that, even as we lifted the tiny dark-gray milagros de la vida (miracles of life) from the sand, roared and crashed against the shore, sending foam and spray well above our heads.

I have been coming to this beach in Mexico, this same stretch of ocean, for twenty years, but never at the right time. Usually I have been writing in such seclusion I've missed this astonishing event. Two years ago I came to help with the turtles for the first time. It was one of my most intense spiritual experiences. Them, so dark, suede-scaled, and determined; me, speechless to find them so tiny that five of them, if they were still, might fit in one hand, yet know their way home. Scooping them out of the bucket, we barely had a moment to prevent them from falling from our hands, before they, flippers working ceaselessly, followed the smell of the sea, the spray on their bodies, and began making a dash, their kind of dash, more like a happy waddle, to the water. Going back to Mother.

Not many of them will survive their journey to adulthood. They will fall prey to many predators before they are the huge size a few of them will attain. But some will make it, and come ashore years from now as mothers themselves, ready to start the cycle all over again. I said to my sweetheart how odd it must seem to the turtles to have lived eons without needing the help of humans to keep their numbers viable, after having been hunted almost to extinction. Then I thought of how long it would take for our intervention in the cycle to become a part of what the turtles expect, a part of their DNA. We laughed, thinking of the baby turtles to come, scrambling around in the coming thousands of years, patiently waiting for us. *Where's that human hand that's supposed to appear around about now?* they would ask themselves. We laughed more, if soberly, hoping that, with still more luck, we as that human hand would always, if still needed, be there.

FACING LA MADRE

December 10, 2008

Facing La Madre, the fountain.

Meditation. Sweeping. Making and drinking tea. Speaking Spanish with Manuel*, whom I have named, to myself, Wise Heart. Because he is one of the wisest people I know.

Yesterday a beautiful black or dark brown snake came into the doorway. I called Sweet Heart[†], my partner in these adventures, who gently picked it up and placed it back into the garden.

Finally, the right spirit!

No question at all of harming it; only admiration for its sleek and fearless regalness. I felt the closing of a circle in my life, regarding snakes. From wonder and fascination (which I would have experienced as an infant), to the heavy indoctrination of my church and parents, to having fear and loathing instilled in me, then coming around again to wonder and admiration.

This little one, about two years old, Sweet Heart thought, was a gopher (or Mexican equivalent) snake.

Next day, Wise Heart encountered a huge rattler in the road. He took a photo of it and helped it on its way. In Spanish it is called *cascabel*.

---

*Manuel Vejar Castastañeda
[†]G. Kaleo Larson

Jumpy and weird yesterday because I opened my computer and found myself in the news. Emory presenting my talk as I gave my papers to the university earlier this year. It is odd, unexpectedly seeing one's self in this way. I feel far away from that sweet persona, in that role. Here, we worry about ants, *las hormigas*, eating everything we plant.

We've been studying further uses of our magical Vitamix. We can make compost with it. This excites us no end. Sweet Heart made almost a quart of liquid compost from the remains of our breakfast green smoothie. Banana peels, eggshells, apple cores, etc. I poured it over the collard and arugula starts.

Sweet Heart is practicing scales and I should be too! I can now play "Amazing Grace" and half of "Lift Every Voice and Sing!" Which I love. Generous Heart* at East Bay Church of Religious Science in Oakland is one teacher; Sweet Heart is the other. Between them and my keyboard I am coming back to the lessons I left when I was eight or nine years old.

Another circle, longing to close, closing.

*Jacqui Hairston

GIVING, AS GENEROUSLY
AS THE EARTH

December 11, 2008

As the *hormigas* appear to be winning this year, I have had to take other measures. Neither Sweet Heart nor I wish to be without our own patch of collards, no matter where we are. So, we went with friends to visit a small family farm near Villa (named for Pancho) and asked if, in exchange for a financial offering, I might create a small garden on their land: for peanuts, collards, sweet potatoes, okra, beans. They have land, a few hectares near the river, but no cash. Farmers around the world face this predicament. They live in a dwelling considerably smaller and less substantial than the shacks my family inhabited when I was a child: constructed of tin, a few slabs of wood, a dirt floor. It was like visiting my own family, in the 1950s, in fact. A mother, father, and one small, friendly daughter with, apparently, Down syndrome. *La Señora**, graying, bright-eyed, and energetic, talked a mile a minute, while Sweet Heart helped *El Señor*† to drag a huge *manguera*, hose, to drip irrigate what looked like a long row of fledgling papaya trees. Before long we were smiling, at ease with each other. In fact, being with them felt right, as if we already belonged to each other. We didn't want to leave: talking the while about broken-down tractors (his), her missing goats (I think they had to eat them), how much I would like

*Nieves Orendain
†Aureliano Naranjo

the cheese she makes if she still had goats, the medicinal plants that surround their house: for diabetes, arthritis, and liver troubles. In my excitement that they had chickens, for which I lust, I immediately thought of eggs, which, turning around, I saw she'd brought me. Eleven of them, exactly, as the hens and roosters responsible for this bounty, strutted about proudly. She also gave me several *calabasas*, pumpkin/squash–like vegetables, which my friend, Organizer Heart*, who had introduced us, told me would make delicious soup.

I was reminded of why, as a child on a "poor" sharecropper's farm, I never thought we were poor. Because we were always giving. It was giving, as generously as the Earth did, that made us feel we had plenty. In fact, my sense of this family—the husband and wife unself-consciously holding hands, while talking to us—was that they were richer than almost anyone I'd met lately.

* Yolanda Padilla

SEEKING COUNSEL FROM DIEGO AND FRIDA

December 15, 2008

MY FRIENDS DON'T WANT ME TO BE stressed out by the violence, caused by drugs, that is occurring in Mexico, and the attempts of the government to expose and bring to justice those who are harming Mexican society so grievously. When we walk along the streets in Mexico City, with its ubiquitous fountains and wonderful art—a city I like a lot, though breathing the air, after a few days, is a challenge—they snatch me away from kiosks where there are screaming headlines and lurid pictures of the latest atrocities. Brutal and grotesque messages from the drug cartels. I recognize and share the suffering I see in their eyes. It is our own suffering in the United States, as we've watched our disintegrating communities struggle against an enemy so implacably cruel that it is almost impossible to know how to respond to it. Countless lives have been broken, utterly, by this unequal and unexpected fight. And we have been abandoned by our government. In fact, our government has played for the other side. That this suffering should befall anyone is tragic, but that it should befall the people of Mexico, legendary for their warmth and hospitality, their generosity and patience, is deeply painful. So much like ourselves they are, and have been.

Going into Frida and Diego's house and studio, her side blue, his white, I am troubled for the people, and the country, they loved so much. And that I also love. They did not live in these times; what would they make of them? Inside, I saw, on a small round rug, a pair of Diego's shoes. Enormous. I placed my own bare foot beside his shoe. Tiny, by comparison. I thought of their connected lives, their deep trust that in finding each other they had discovered a way to reach what was most profound, and perhaps most challenging, in themselves. What would they say to the people of Mexico today? Would they ask Mexicans, who so bravely fought a revolution, over a hundred years ago, to free themselves from foreign and domestic oppression, to remember to look for the root of their present calamity: poverty, hopelessness, too many children, beloveds, and kin left behind in the wake of mass migrations north? Too many humiliations, brutalities, and deaths, of people trying simply to locate, on this broad earth, a better life for those crossing borders and those left behind? To think of the loneliness, the desperation, the feeling of abandonment by everything that speaks of ease and joy in life. And naked hunger, and literal emptiness, that for a moment a drug can mask. It would be horrible, I think, for them to contemplate the wall that the United States has built in its attempt to keep Mexicans—whose hard work keeps so much of our economy going— out of *Gringolandia* (Frida's word). I can imagine Frida's proud scorn, and Diego's bellow of defiance.

No one profits ultimately from the humiliation of others. Surely this is a law.

Hold dear your families and especially your children, which has always been paramount for you, I imagine Frida and Diego saying. Insist on government that responds to your suffering, and if it does not respond, change it. This is a harsh passage, but only that; there will be, there must be, an end. The drug war is not just Mexico's and not just the United States', but a global struggle. It is for the people of the planet to say "No" to every kind of enslavement. Every kind of violence. They must gather in whatever ways they can to make their stand for the sake of humanity. Above all, do not abandon your faith that you can change your environment. You are a revolutionary people, a proven model for the world. Many people stand taller for the course your ancestors pursued. It is the consciousness of the whole world that has to change, and that change is happening. Not because of human enlightenment, necessarily, either, but because Earth is sending its own messages of atrocity that are far grimmer than those sent by the drug lords, in the form of earthquakes, fires, droughts, hurricanes, and floods. Human beings will awaken to these *noticias* (news reports) from *La Madre* (The Mother), or perish.

HITTING THE MARK

December 15, 2008

MUNTADHAR AL-ZAIDI, THE IRAQI JOURNALIST who tried to hit George Bush with his shoe, has captured the world's imagination, causing each of us to wonder: if we had the opportunity, what would we use to hit Bush? I am the least violent person I know: I cannot imagine hitting anyone, though I do not deny an occasional urge to strike out when words and careful ceremony fail me. I literally pray to be nonviolent, having learned from observing over half a century of violence, how incredibly stupid it is. Thinking about this, in Mexico, during the twelve-day celebration of the *Virgen de Guadalupe*, where children in white, their parents and neighbors beside them, march in procession in every little village, I have had a thoughtful time, holding these opposites: a world that still honors the feminine face of God, the Goddess, and a world that seems, by now, almost entirely masculine, where something so wonderful as a dog is considered contemptible, and the Earth, from which everything is given to us, even more so. Whatever touches the Earth is blessed, in my view, and what is of more humble service to humankind than the shoe?

Still, I do realize cultures differ.

With what would I hit Bush? This man who has caused so much suffering, death, despair, and pain?

Remember how Bob Marley sang: One good thing about music, when it hits you feel no pain. Hit me with music, hit me with music, now? I think of this—what a genius he was, making us think in new ways, almost constantly—and I think of George Bush. About whom I have tried not to think too much, over the years. What I would hit Bush with, and what I think we all need to consider hitting him with is . . . understanding. I may be completely mistaken, but it is my sense that no one understands this person. I remember once, sitting in Chinatown with a Chinese family the night Bush was reelected (or re-selected!) as president of the country. We were all of us feeling despair, but it took the eldest person at our table, a grandmother with wispy white hair, to put into words some of what we felt. She simply couldn't believe Bush had been placed at the "top," as she put it, of the country. Shaking her head, frowning, totally incredulous, speaking partly in dialect, she refused to believe he was the people's choice. But why do you think it's impossible that Americans have chosen him? asked one of us. Because, she said, as if it were the most obvious thing on Earth: he has the eyes of a thief. That is the way people in the old days used to think, to size people up, to save the community and the family a lot of trouble. What happened to this ability?

We don't understand Bush. I don't. I remember marching, alongside millions of other people, against the war, speaking out against the war, being arrested protesting the war, all the while thinking: it is really strange that Bush ignores us. We knew perfectly well what happens during war: people are mutilated, murdered, made homeless, and things even worse. He had to know this too. And then the long years of every ominous prophecy being fulfilled: hundreds of thousands murdered, raped, butchered, burned, bombed. Children blasted away in their orphanages, young girls raped before their parents' eyes. There have been days and nights over the past eight years when I, like so many others, could not sleep. We knew what it meant when the media talked about things being more "calm." Our neighborhoods would be calm too, we muttered, if nobody still lived there but had fled to some other country where they suffered the indignity of being unwanted refugees. Very calm and peaceful too, are the dead and buried. But to our haggard faces, Bush turned a beaming countenance, year after year. And even now. He plans to leave the White House, he beams, move into a new place, start building his library, and write his memoirs. His memoirs. If I understood him better I could tell him, there's going to be a little child sprawled bleeding behind every page. What I understand so far is that the suffering of that bleeding child is not the story he's interested in telling, and this makes it all the more necessary that we ask ourselves, as a country that elected/selected him: who is this?

The world's people will demand that we get to know this man, so as not to let another like him loose on them. There will be more than talk about war crimes and crimes against humanity, fairly soon, for Bush and all those who collaborated with him in bringing such terror— shock and awe, indeed—to the Earth. We might as well get ready for it. But thoughtfully. The least Americans can do to show we recognize our complicity in the wrongful assault on a country that did us no harm is to honor our own history of a belief, finally, in justice. Justice for the "evildoers" we permitted to lead us; no more and no less. We will have to hit Bush with something. And it won't be a shoe. But it will be mean- ingless beyond words, if we hit him only with vengeance or revenge or simple hatred, in an attempt to attach all the blame for our disaster to someone so out of touch, not only with reality but with himself, as he appears to be.

As for the Iraqi journalist, I would wish to have the courage to ex- press my outrage in such a well-aimed and culturally apt way, if I were in his position.

George Bush has destroyed Muntadhar al Zaidi's country, abused his people, and disappeared countless children, colleagues, and friends. I understand him, at least I understand his behavior, completely.

THE VICTORY
BELONGS TO LOVE:
SO WHAT ABOUT
MARRIAGE?

DECEMBER 19, 2008

IT SEEMS TO ME SUCH A PRIVATE AFFAIR, to which one invites
only the public that one loves. I was married once, illegally, as has been
well documented. I was very much in love with the man I married, and
could not agree with the state that his color made him unacceptable
for matrimony. But there has been such a long history of intrusion into
matrimony in our country, in the world, I suppose, that this certainly
seems a good time to interrogate it. To look for instance at the ban
against enslaved people marrying, and how they coped with that. What
could they do, really. There they were, these brown and black and tan
and chocolate and yes, alabaster, lovers, wanting more than anything
to do the right thing by the community and church (although church
too, for them, was banned for quite a long time). No public sanction
for you, they were told. You can't marry because you're not even human beings, you're property. And sure enough Ole Miss and Big Miss
and Master Bubba could at any time sell the bride-to-be and the groom-
to-be a thousand miles downriver. In separate directions. What would
have been the use of nuptials then?

I never intended to marry. But when a handsome prince appeared,
and I faced the illegality of claiming and being claimed by him, it
seemed a no-brainer. Whose business was it who I married? In what
way was my happiness an affront to theirs, assuming they had any?
Which I doubted because, having observed people who spent more

than a few minutes digging into other people's personal love intentions, I realized they had no similar love to be fascinated by in their
own. Think of all the times you've been content with your affectional
choices and your life. How much time did you spend wondering about
what other folks, especially those two kissing and hugging over by the
elevator, did? Did antebellum (before the war) folks care about society,
and family, and civilization? Could one honestly say that slave owners
cared about any of this? Impregnating their own relatives and offspring, selling their children who, because of their mothers' condition, were now slaves, and, through sheer avarice, destroying, through
overproduction of crops, the very earth beneath them, as they did?

It was Daniel Ortega, president of Nicaragua in the 1980s and currently, who said, The victory belongs to love. It was the most astonishing of the things I heard and experienced on a trip to Nicaragua during
the Sandinista government's battle against the Contras. There he was,
with his wife, Rosario, having fathered nine children, all of them, if I
remember correctly, boys. I still remember the charm of their wooden
house that seemed to have no real walls, only partitions made of tall
houseplants. Flowers were everywhere, and rocking chairs. Over a half
dozen of them. And art. It was a wonderful house, or nonhouse. They
seemed not so much to live there as to float through it, as we did, their
guests. I did not fail to notice Ortega's trips to the refrigerator, however, and the thick rows of cold Coca-Cola cans. Even sipping a Coke,
grateful for the snowy fizz in the tropical heat, I thought: oops. Almost
free.

So what does this have to do with marriage? Something about
choices, I think: how to live, where to live, what are the whimsies and
challenges each of us deserves to make for ourselves. Nobody yet being
perfectly evolved. Five thousand years of something that makes people
unhappy is long, but given the age of the planet it's almost nothing.
Besides, we now know that Mother rule, which preceded patriarchy,
smiled then, as now, on love, whatever its orientation. The way God
sent him, is how a recent Oaxaca mother described her gay son.

Besides, the same God who restricted marriage to a woman and
man also gave man dominion over the Earth. 'Nuff said.

Almost two years ago I awakened to the realization that I felt married to my dog and my cat. This feeling arose in me: that I would willingly assume responsibility for them for the rest of our lives. That I

would love and honor and cherish them. That together we were a family. Calling in a priestess friend, we arranged a wedding ceremony, which was beautiful. Was this an affront to the marriages of men and women, so many of which end in divorce? I don't think so. I experienced it as a strengthener of spirit, a movement forward in my growing ability to connect with animals other than human. I've sometimes wondered how the event felt to them. My dog, Marley, died within months, well loved and well cared for to the end. My cat, Surprise, reigns in our household, secure in her recognized place of queen.

I sent out invitations to our ceremony that read: Marriage Happens! Because that is how it seems to me. That you go along in a relationship of whatever kind, and one day it dawns on you: this is it for life. In truth, you're already married, when this happens, but perhaps it is human nature to want to share our joy.

THE CLARITY

SETTING OUT COLLARD STARTS IN A BED where they may be eaten by ants overnight, I had some insights: one was that some old, unconscious programming is still alive and well in my head, and probably in my whole body. I was becoming tired from bending, and hot from the morning sun, which, though delightful at eight, was not so at ten. My body and I, conversing, as bodies and minds will, said: I think it's time to do some watering of the new plants, because they need it, having just been set out, but also, it will give your lower back a chance to recover. Fine. I immediately looked about for the hose. However, the old internalized voice (whose? Father, mother, grandparent, older sibling, teacher?) said: Now, now, you must always finish what you start! Never stop in the middle! But this is how I've always worked, I thought, remarking the voice, but asserting myself. And that is why I have been able to work so much. By taking breaks that change, if only slightly, the work's direction.

I'm a writer, probably because I could not abide a job that required repetition. Hardest for me was a job I had for a summer once, as a file clerk. The monotony bored me. I will always feel I left a part of my life in that office. I could have done so much more there than file, left to my freedom; if only the bosses had understood that. Anyway, I have reached the period of life where it is a joy, really, to ignore ancient programming. I not only watered the tiny plants that I may never, after today, see again, but I sat right down and ate a papaya.

The second insight was: when I am mad at another person, I make myself mad. Now this is probably Insight 101 to all Dharma bums everywhere. But it seemed really fresh, this morning. I was in a snit because my greens were not as high as my knee already, and because so many previous efforts (more anon) to grow them had failed. So when someone sweetly asked if he could help me, I, exasperated, said: I needed help three months ago. I think I'm so small I can never terrorize anyone, but I think my response was dampening, at least. And then, for the next hour, I worried over it, still being mad, while he went off to do some other wonderful thing that he's good at. And that's when it came to me: being mad at him made me mad. He had nothing really to do with it. Although in truth he could have planted the collard starts three months ago, since that is his job. Even so.

This is one reason I love mornings! And gardening meditation. The clarity! The stretched muscles! The cleansing of the pores through sweating! The reward of fresh fruit!

OVERWHELM

THE FIRST MORNING WE WENT OUT TO the farm at which my ant-free produce might grow, we found a huge field had been raked over by somebody else's tractor, since the farm's vehicle needed much more work. It was a vast field. I tried to explain once again that I had wanted an area more like a large rug, not something broad enough to play soccer. I once again pointed out the area: just between these four palm trees, *por favor. Esto es suficiente.* Fine. Leaving offerings to take care of the tractor, the diesel for the tractor, pump repair, and several other necessities, we left with the understanding that by *sábado* all would be ready. Three days! Excitement was building, not only in me, the farmer (small-time though I might be), but also in Sweet Heart, who has never farmed and knows little about it, preferring to grow music from his golden *trompeta*. Saturday morning, at dawn, we were at the farmer's gate: not only us, but other helpers who had volunteered and joined us along the way. However, first of all, there was an enormous dogfight occurring at the gate, which right away felt like an ill omen. Half a dozen dogs, snarling, growling, barking, biting. So early in the morning it seemed surreal. However, courageous. But then, behind them, we began to see *las vacas*, cows, many of them, loose in the farmer's cornfield. And to make matters worse, they were ankle-deep in water.

The farmer, perhaps I should call him Overwhelmed Heart*, came up to the car to tell us what we were seeing: his neighbors' cows had broken his fence, come into his cornfield, were eating his corn. *!Que lastima!* More than that, they had managed to break his water pipes, which we could see were made out of fragile white plastic, and the result was a flooded field. *Oy vey!* My tiny, rug-like patch of land, surrounded by the soccer field, was flooded and would not be dry enough to plant anything for at least three days! Could we come back then? *Sí.*

Wise Heart, with his typical compassion, opted to check on the situation for us, to prevent our tumbling out of our cozy beds to no purpose. Three days later we asked for a report. Nothing's moving, he said. Neither the cows, nor the water level. Besides, Overwhelmed Heart says another field is too much work. Considering the overwhelm I had received on viewing the cleared soccer field, I agreed with him.

What is the lesson? Today I am feeling regretful that my Spanish, after all these years of study and learning, is still so poor I can't sufficiently emphasize the difference between rug-size and soccer-field-size. And I wonder, as well, if my approach was somehow wrong. Longer meditation might help me here.

One lesson seems to be to recommit to my own yard and garden, and to take my stand here. Wise Heart and I immediately decided to tear out the humungous stand of red ginger and palmas that was about to eat the side yard, and to plant collards, okra, kale, and garlic there. With two other young men he went at it with a will, and made a circular bed ten feet across. The roots of the palmas are still there, however, and will be hard to remove.

I woke this morning feeling reckless: I will just put seeds there anyway. Maybe most of the plants will be devoured by *hormigas*, or strangled by palmas roots, but maybe a few will survive for us.

*El Señor Naranjo

QUEEN SNOWS

DECEMBER 30, 2008

I WAS SURPRISED BY THE DISAPPOINTMENT and sense of loss I felt because my plan to have a vegetable plot in a farmer's nearby field did not come to be. I found I missed the sweetness and mystery of the faces Sweet Heart and I loved, practically instantly. Out of that sadness came the poem "I Will Keep Broken Things."

In this way:

True to his empathetic spirit, Wise Heart said to me, as he stacked row upon row of red ginger that he'd removed from what will hopefully be our next garden in our yard, *¿Que piensas?* (What do you think?: which is how we both start many a conversation.) Maybe we should give some of these flowers to Snows, the English translation of *Nieves*, which is *La Señora*'s name. I was delighted by the thought! There had been many medicinal plants around their house, but no flowers. Yes! I said. Excellent. And so he took the plants to Snows, and in return we received, from Queen Snows, so naturally elegant in her generosity, a bushel of *pepinos* (cucumbers)!

And so I was taught, again, that the original of anything may be broken, but what is left can be usefully different and often well worth keeping. Our connection survived.

I WILL KEEP BROKEN THINGS

I will keep broken
things:
the big clay pot
with raised iguanas
chasing their
tails; two
of their wise
heads sheared off;
I will keep broken things: the old slave market basket brought to
my door by Mississippi a jagged
hole gouged
in its sturdy dark
oak side.

I will keep broken things:
The memory of
those long delicious night swims with you;
I will keep broken things:

In my house
there remains an honored shelf
on which I will keep broken things.

Their beauty is
they need not ever be "fixed."

I will keep your wild
free laughter though it is now missing its
reassuring and
graceful hinge.
I will keep broken things:

Thank you
So much!

I will keep broken things.
I will keep you:

pilgrim of sorrow.
I will keep myself.

From Hard Times Require Furious Dancing. *New World Library,*
2010.

ALL THE STARS

JANUARY 11, 2009

BACK ON THE BLOCK IN THE EAST BAY and right away went to see a screening of the new movie *La Mission*. Was I ever glad I did. It is extraordinary. A film of now, a film for us, for the emerging conscious-ness of what needs to happen in the heart and conscience for humanity to evolve beyond violence. It is also a film about love in the same way *Casablanca* is a film about love: the true Big Love that recognizes we humans are small and the problems gigantic. But notes also that hu-mans are a feisty lot and up to the challenge if given half a chance. Furthermore, it is exquisitely beautiful, displaying in almost every shot the surprising and vibrant colors of Mexico and points even further south. The soundtrack is a soul feast. The cars, high art.

And who is responsible for all this joy? The Bratt brothers, who used to be brats when they were growing up, one has heard. Peter and Benjamin Bratt. Peter as writer-director, and Benjamin, co-producer with Peter, and also starring as a bus driver named Che. (We knew something good was going to happen right there.) And it does. Benja-min Bratt as Che models all the anger, rage, hate, and homophobia that could possibly live under the placid courteousness of many people we meet. The woman he falls in love with carries all the strong bound-aries one is likely to accrue in a lifetime of dealing with faithless and brutal mankind. His son, all the passionate honesty of someone com-ing to understand the meaning of his choices, and deciding to defend his own choice of whom to love, come what may. There is of course a *tía* and *tío*, aunt and uncle, for the younger lover to run off to, as is proper. They are just the couple who, at the end of your running away, you hope will open the door.

Like *Follow Me Home*, another amazing film, also written and directed by Peter Bratt, *La Mission* will be a classic. It will be around, like *Casablanca*, and like another more recent film I also love, *Something New* (which makes me think of yet another film I think is wonderful: *The Best Man*), for a long time, if we in fact have a long time.

Lucky for us, the artist doesn't care about time; who knows how long it took the Bratt brothers to make this graceful offering? The artist cares about beauty, soul, bringing the light; the artist cares about us.

All the stars. Not five or six or ten.

THE KILLING OF TROY DAVIS: WHAT DOES IT MEAN?

MAY 12, 2009

WHAT DOES IT MEAN TO KILL a human being in cold blood? What does this say about you, the murderer? If taking a life—the crime for which Georgia wishes to execute Troy Davis, who appears to be innocent—is wrong, then it is wrong for the State of Georgia, acting for its citizens, to commit this same offense.

Have we learned nothing from our Sunday School lessons, from our parents, especially our grandparents, and from our New Testament Bible and the teachings of the wise and compassionate spirit, Jesus?

Who are we if we cannot forgive? If we cannot make our way beyond ancient programming and prejudice? Who are we, indeed, as we look into the trusting eyes of our children, and, especially, into the eyes of our grandchildren, who will inherit all that we have done? They believe that we, though fallible, as all humans are, are still just. That justice matters of us. Why wound them with our intolerance, our prejudice, our dissatisfaction with life, to the extent that we can feel alive and powerful only when we abuse, torture, or kill another? Someone who, in this instance, has been living for many years in a cage? How will they look at us, when they know what we have done?

This time on Earth for human beings is like no other time. The very Earth, tortured and maimed, imprisoned in so many ways, is receding from us. Only the most radical compassion for ourselves, for other humans, for all creatures and creation will bring Earth back to us.

Free Troy Davis. Not only Free Troy Davis: give him your blessings and your prayers, in faith that when it is your own time to be judged, you will not stand alone. That friends will see your true worth and radiance and will come to your side from all the corners of the world.

The only punishment that works is love. This truth has been proven endlessly in our public and private lives.

Free Troy Davis, and free the goodness, even now longing to be expressed, that is imprisoned within yourself.

I was born in Georgia, and I believe in its ability to change, to grow, to carry a light for the human race. I have witnessed this transformation in my own lifetime.

Free this man, and let us Georgians, with the rest of conscious humanity, seek other ways than murder to further the cause of human enlightenment.

Troy Davis was executed on September 21, 2011.

THE G IN "ODE TO JOY": JOURNAL

June 7, 2009

THREE DAYS AGO, ONE OF THE HAPPIEST MOMENTS of my life. My teacher showed me the missing left-hand G in "Ode to Joy." This music is the first I've been able to read completely by myself; it is simple once you play it, but I didn't know where or what the missing note was. Had Beethoven left it out? Etc. I love "Ode to Joy," and so does my teacher. We talked about Beethoven's African heritage; all black people seem to know about this, which is amusing.

I told her about one of my favorite films which I'd just seen for the fifth time, last week: *Immortal Beloved*, the story of Beethoven's life. I told her about how his father's beating of him when he was a child caused his deafness. She said: And did the film talk about his African heritage? I said: Of course not. We are used to this, so we laughed. But then I wondered: was it partly that he was darker, in white Germany, in those days, that caused his father to abuse him so? To even, perhaps, as implied by the film, assault him sexually? In the film the father's rage is because Beethoven as a child prodigy did not compare to Mozart, also a child prodigy, whom his father wanted Beethoven to imitate. To become the trained monkey many assumed young Mozart to be. I adore Mozart, too. (A character in *The Temple of My Familiar* shares this adoration.) Also just reviewed for maybe the sixth time the amazing film about him, *Amadeus*. Though I had to stop in the middle because it hurts too much to see him being destroyed by someone he so naïvely trusts. I love this film because it really helps you see how self-torturing envy is, and how it can completely corrupt and destroy the soul. Also, that genius of any sort is a divine gift and just occurs. At the same time, the soul through which it pours obviously has to be made large enough to accommodate it. This was the puzzle for Salieri, who so coveted Mozart's gift. How could God send such a profound musical gift through such a smutty-mouthed, vain, silly boy as Mozart?

But the Divine doesn't care, as far as I can tell. It's got a gift it wants delivered and doesn't pause one moment to wonder who's driving the delivery truck. On the other hand, the delivery truck always seems to have survived quite a few wrecks.

FROZEN RIVER IS A MOVING SURPRISE

June 9, 2009

THE FILM *FROZEN RIVER* IS A MOVING SURPRISE. I'd never heard of it, but once we got our Netflix going, there it was to be considered. It is such a relief to see a film that shows the true anguish of poor Americans, to acknowledge the anxiety and poverty in which so many Americans live. I especially appreciate the relationship that develops between the white woman, working at a crummy, low-paying job to feed her boys, and longing with all her heart for a "double-wide" trailer home, the down payment of which has been gambled away by a husband who has disappeared, and the Mohawk woman who has lost her child to her husband's family after his death by drowning. That they team up, reluctantly, to make some money by becoming smugglers opens a window on a world I had not thought much about. How do the millions of "aliens" get into the country after all? Who helps them, and why? Even more pressing: how are they received, how are they treated once they get here? This film is a stark memo to the oblivious that slavery has perhaps never been over, only newer slaves imported. The acting is so excellent the "characters" feel real. There is also the wonderful "aha" that happens when realization dawns on the white woman: that the quickest way to be treated like a person of color, a Native American in this case, is to be poor, but that the solution is not to flee from this belated understanding, and suck up to the common oppressor, but to embrace and strengthen the solidarity. A radical film by serious filmmakers.

MAY I BE FRANK

THERE'S A LOT ON OUR PLATE in this life, as the world awakens to the crisis we're in. What is the most revolutionary thing one can do? Especially if there are a million choices of things that need doing, not just last year, but a couple of centuries ago? I think the most revolutionary thing each of us can do is reclaim our health. Or, preserve it, if—oh happiness and no Big Whoppers—we never lost it. The second most revolutionary thing is to help others reclaim or protect theirs.

There is a new film, *May I Be Frank*, that shows what this can look like. A big-bellied, overweight, guilt-ridden, drug-dependent but still quite loveable Italian American named Frank Ferrante is taken on as a project by three young men who manage a Café Gratitude restaurant in San Francisco. This is a place that serves only raw, vegan, organic food. They sign him up, to eat only this food, for forty-odd days. They coach him through colonics, spats with his family, crying jags, and rare moments of breakthrough and bliss. As the body becomes clean and light and the attitude shifts, as the guilt is disposed of by letting it surface and by seeking forgiveness, and as the foreskin is glimpsed for the first time in, maybe, a decade, we see the spirit, the Frank, that might have been had not drugs, alcohol, anger, and self-centeredness so overwhelmed it. It is a beautiful sight. The caring behavior of the three young coaches is the essence of the revolutionary spirit that Che Guevara meant when he said, "True revolution is about tenderness." This is true! They are a model for any young man, or woman, seeking one-on-one ways to be with the causes of misery in the world.

There are armies marching still, bullets flying, bombs being dropped, people being tortured and their homes demolished while they sit beside them, those left alive, wailing. But this is never going to change the world to a planet of peace. In fact, it is old news. Dead, just unburied, as acceptable human behavior. It is so obsolete as to be embarrassing. That is one reason it is difficult for us to look at our television screens. We are thinking: Are we, humans, as degraded as all that? All of us? Everywhere? Well, no. We're not. Some of us have taken our unruly selves in hand, the prerequisite step for liberation and peace, and some of us have dedicated ourselves to helping our sisters and brothers along. Not for the "doing good" aspect, which is fine, but simply for the fun of it. It is, finally, fun for these three young men to help Frank find his true and radiant self. Or joy, that word for which I am convinced our planet was meant.

¡NADIE TE QUITA
LO BAILADO!

*No one can take away that
which has been danced!*

DECEMBER 4, 2009

MY FRIEND ANDRÉS C.* HAS BEEN in the Brazilian embassy in
Honduras with the president of Honduras, Manuel Zelaya, for two
months. We last saw Andrés and his sweetheart Paulina C.† when they
came to stay overnight with us in the country. Andrés is a wonderful man,
filled with love and light, a believer in justice and human rights. An en-
joyer of beauty and freedom. He left me with many wonderful thoughts,
one of which I wish to share for no other reason than that it is good to
know deeply in one's heart in these times of fruitless war and endless
waste. It is apparently a folk saying of the people of Honduras: *¡Nadie
te quita lo bailado!* No one can take away that which has been danced!

This is worth remembering.

Thank you, Andrés. May you and the president and his family, and the
people of Honduras, be safe. The world sees what has happened and is
happening. We are awake. And, perhaps now, after the elections, you and
your friends are free to leave the embassy and you are on your way home
to your friends here. I have been unplugged from all media, including our
beloved *Democracy Now!*, to do other work; so I am not current with the
situation. I hope for a peaceful resolution to a crisis poorly handled by
those who might have been more honest, forthright, and helpful.

Your bravery and caring are inspiring. We are glad to share the planet
with you.

*Andrés Thomas Conteris
†Paulina Contreras

LOVING AUDIOBOOKS
BUT NOT THE
SEGREGATION OF
BOOKS AND LITERATURE

AUGUST 9, 2010

I WOKE THIS MORNING THINKING of two recent audiobooks that I admire: *The Inheritance of Loss* by Kiran Desai and *The Blood of Flowers* by Anita Amirrezvani. I listened to both these books over the summer and they have haunted me ever since. They are quite strong medicine and unquestionably powerful, if not for everyone.

The one set mostly in India tells more than I sometimes could absorb about the challenges of immigrating to this country from India, if you are poor; the other, set in ancient Iran, follows the life of a peasant village woman who develops into a designer and maker of fine carpets in a society that demands that, outside her house, she be completely subservient to men and also wear the chador.

It is a wonderful thing to be read to, and the narrators chosen for these novels, set in modern-day India (and Manhattan) and seventeenth-century Persia (Iran), are superb. It is easy enough to Google reviews, so I won't attempt one here, and for all I know these books met with great notice and acclaim when they first appeared. I hope so.

I recently committed my own novel of twenty-eight years ago, *The Color Purple*, to audio: it is now available from Recorded Books. The novel has had a long life as a book, then as a movie and then as a Broadway musical (and still touring); the circle completes itself with the book read/told by me, as messenger from ancestors and kin I knew little of at the time of the story's unfolding (before my birth), but loved nonetheless.

In my passion to locate more books by writers from other cultures I took a turn around the Kindle and Amazon sites, to discover something that seems truly amazing: books by black authors are segregated by race! This would be hilarious if it were not so troubling. If, after all of our struggle to integrate into this questionable system, we may enter a bookstore and stand anywhere, but our books must reside in a corner, the world has not changed nearly as much as I, for one, assumed it had.

There are writers from Iran, Japan, Ireland, England, India, China, Israel, Korea, Tibet etc., all listed and shown to be writers of Literature. But when looking for my own novel (which worldwide has sold perhaps fifteen million copies) I found it tucked away with twelve or so books by other African Americans under African American Literature. To make matters worse, no one had bothered to read the book to verify the narrative. A synopsis has the main character raped by her father rather than by her stepfather (her father was lynched when she was an infant), a point that is crucial to comprehending the dynamics of the heroine's rise from disaster.

I had noticed this segregation before, disturbingly in a Borders bookstore in Berkeley/Emeryville. There, books by African Americans, all twenty-five or so of them, were stuffed into a dingy circular kiosk that looked as if it had not been straightened out or freshened in months.

Recalling the child I was who was not allowed into the public library of Eatonton, Georgia, I think of children, especially, who will receive a subliminal message that somehow literature by African Americans isn't really Literature. That it is a separate and smaller, i.e., lesser, creation.

What could be the rationale for such segregation, today, 2010, when our president and First Lady and their children are African American? When Oprah Winfrey sells more books by writers of all colors than is even imaginable? Maybe booksellers assume black people only read books by other black people and want to find them quickly without having to consider what other writing might be going on in the rest of the world. There is also the amusing notion, held by some, that when black writers write about Life it isn't about Life but about being black. That this is ridiculous can be determined by thinking—for a moment, no more—that when white writers write about Life they are simply writing about being white. Imagine how bored Charles Dickens would have been.

It is too late for segregated thinking; it harms by blinding us to what is most useful for us to know: how to survive as feelingly human, how to thrive, worship, and dance in this life. As selves unique.

The Color Purple, for instance, whose first words are "Dear God" is about God. About the need to abandon a God who is incapable of hearing us, and to find a God in Nature who not only listens to us but unfailingly responds.

We are beyond a rigid category of color, sex, or spirituality if we are truly alive. Not to be alert to the challenges and wonders confronting humans today is to miss what could be the last chance to understand and celebrate the wonderful multi-everything mystery that we are.

The responsibility for changing literary segregation rests with readers. Would you drink from a segregated water source? Eat in a segregated restaurant? Buy a dress where I could not try one on? Buy a book where black writers are discriminated against?

Changing our society and the world is up to us, even in what might appear to be small choices. Any hope of our communal happiness depends on our private honoring, to the best of our knowledge, of the dignity of all, and of what is right.

AT SEA ON THE
AUDACITY OF HOPE

JULY 1, 2011

TODAY IS, I THINK, the 31st of June (Friday?) or is it the 1st of July?

We have been in Athens since the 21st—trying to get to Gaza. Many impediments orchestrated by the Israeli government. But what a wonderful group of humans.

Therefore: we've won. We're in Gaza. To be in Gaza is to feel this love. To know there is always a part of humanity that is awake even though the overburdened or the bewitched remain sleeping.

My throat is sore from breathing the tear gas that drifted into our hotel windows, as Greeks, mostly young, battle police, their brothers and sisters who are paid to keep them in line. This is the tragedy. I feel so much compassion for both sides my eyes tear and not only from the gas.

It was hard to breathe. My lungs were fighting hard to protect me. How I adore them, my lungs. And so many of our group tried to protect us, my lungs and me, too. A lovely young man named Steve gave me his own gas mask and someone else, a beautiful young woman with straw-colored hair and blue-gray eyes, gave me the benefit of her knowledge of how to wear it.

I do not like calling such angels "blonde" as I feel the word is so loaded now and it sets them outside of Nature and somehow diminishes them.

I spent a blissful hour yesterday massaging Hedy's feet. She has the most wonderful gray, or are they hazel, eyes—full of humor and light. She'd never had a foot massage before, she said. And she is eighty-seven! Hard to imagine.

Hedy, I said—when she told everyone who passed by us: "I'm being spoiled"—I have a full body massage at least once a week!

This was a high point for me, as it is well established by now in myself and among my friends that I like to massage the feet of anyone who stands up for us. Humanity, I mean.

Or the other animals.

Hedy, holocaust survivor, inhaling the gas in Greece, but even more poignant, anticipating being teargassed by the Israelis, who are doing everything they can to threaten our boat.

I have no computer—they said not to bring one on the boat because it would likely be destroyed or confiscated—only this small notebook in which I have been avoiding writing the poem that starts and stops in my head.

STUBBORN FLOWERS CLIMBING

MAY 11, 2011

Writing is like taking a scalpel to one's thoughts every day. Or a rose petal.

I'VE BEEN SOBERED BY HOW SHOCKING my experience of Zion was. Few could imagine what's transpiring there. The insanity of the occupation, the brutality of it. That our government supports this is tragic. I will pray for guidance how to proceed for the highest good of all—nothing else makes sense to me.

We've decided to go on the boat to Gaza. I will make this journey in honor of the black Southern movement for human rights. Especially for my parents—such good and honest, generous and brave, people. My feeling of indebtedness to them grows as I see their lives reflected in the poor I encounter around the world, who try so hard to live by rules they've had imposed upon them.

It helps so much to look up from the page and to see a flame-red bougainvillea climbing over the ledge and onto the deck.

They can destroy the Earth and take everything it has, but there will always be stubborn flowers climbing whatever walls are left.

How anyone cannot see that Nature is God is amazing to me: that they'd rather worship something that can only exist, really, in their own minds.

Mother, Father, Grandparents, Ancestors, this time is no different than all the other times: I ask for your guidance, your wisdom, your love. Help me find the path that leads to what is best for all. Thank you for leading me back to the chickens—this is a wonderful gift. Thank you for allowing me to see Kaleo as he worked on my sink.

For letting me hear the cries of Surprise sitting in the shrubbery. In all cases Love calling out to me.

I begin to live in the time of last looks. To drink in the loveliness of what may never be enjoyed again. I am so grateful for every leaf, every petal of the billions of flowers. And Creation might have stopped right there! But didn't.

And so, wonders upon wonders!

Heaven is consciousness of this.

Listening to The Life of Helen Keller *(both blind and deaf)—there it is! Perhaps it is the obliteration of this consciousness by enforced religion that has driven men to madness. Women retain a tenuous hold through giving birth, miraculously, to children.*

The birth of my beautiful big baby! What a miracle and what a surprise. Nature at its most strict, most painful, and most playful! Look at this! it cried. I bet you never thought we could do that!

I didn't.

WINDOWS:
DISCOVERING URI AVNERY

AUGUST 4, 2011

MY OWN WORK HAS BEEN BANNED A LOT. In fact, there is a book about that called *Alice Walker Banned* that fascinates me to this day. In one instance my work is banned because I am accused of being "anti–meat eating" and in another I am said to be "anti-religious." That I permit young women to speak about sex in the crude euphemisms of their culture is considered abominable. I have also been censored for "political" views that to me constitute merely average humanitarian concerns.

With time, and the gorgeousness of Life to distract one from the arrows of pettiness and slander, one can forget how sad it is that one's best medicine, offered with devotion, is routinely denied its usefulness and is instead thrown out of the proverbial window.

All of which is to say I only recently discovered the work of the Israeli writer Uri Avnery, who is not young. He is wonderful and courageous and all those things we want in writers. But I never heard of him until two weeks ago. Why? Because obviously he's been kept away from most of the uncurtained windows of Israel into which curious outsiders might look.

In fact, looking him up on the Internet (where he has a regular column! so perhaps I am solitary in my late rejoicing) I could barely stand knowing some of what has been done to him, as he followed his inner guide. Including the breaking of his hands.

In any case, not to rouse my calm heart to weariness and rage, I offer these recent pieces that came to me via members of the fabulous contingent of humans who made up the Freedom Flotilla II en route to Gaza, Henry Norr of KPFA, and Jane Hirschmann of All Over What's Going On.

I am so thankful to encounter this voice. I wrote to Uri Avnery at once and thanked him for helping me, and others, take in a full, deep breath, aware that another human being has been off his knees and standing all this time.

His life is a medicine for our time, to be absorbed with gratitude, not to be thrown away.

In a style reminiscent of the great and daring Howard Zinn, Uri Avnery just goes on speaking his word. See articles below. How refreshing!

- "Instilled Memory": http://zope.gush-shalom.org/home/en/channels/avnery/1310296614/.

- "It Can Happen Here": http://zope.gush-shalom.org/home/en/channels/avnery/1310733120/.

- "Bibi and the Yo-Yos": http://zope.gush-shalom.org/home/en/channels/avnery/1306359471. This is another great piece about Netanyahu's recent visit to the U.S. Congress that appears on Avnery's website, where I discover he is also a founder of Gush Shalom, an Israeli peace group. Which explains a lot.

RECLAIMING THE CROSS

An old friend was upset because she saw a photograph of me wearing a cross. That's a cross! she said with fear. As if she thought I had regressed into something dangerous. And your earrings, she said, are little crosses! She was alarmed. The cross has always preceded torture and attempts to eradicate her people.

I started with the earrings: No, I said, the earrings are small dragonflies.

They had never for a moment looked like little crosses to me.

Oh, she said, really? I guess I've never really looked at dragonflies before.

I love dragonflies, I said, finding the tiny earrings and handing them to her. They are some of my favorite beings.

Why is that? she wanted to know.

They're so optimistic, I said; you feel this because their wings are shiny. They also like to dart.

She looked doubtful.

And when you're near a pond they will simply appear, like tiny lights, cruising for a snack among smaller insects. Being absolutely stunning to humans, and not caring that we're stunned.

Yes? she said.

Yes. And they come in so many colors! When you swim in water that draws lots of dragonflies you find yourself counting: black ones, red ones, green ones, blue.

No, she said.

Now the cross you saw around my neck isn't a cross, either. This necklace, I said, handing it to her, noting again its tiny symbols that include mountains and arrows, was made by a Native American artist; it represents the four directions. There have always been four directions, you know, long before there was a cross.

Oh? she said, taking it, and looking closely.

Yes. And in fact like most symbols, the cross as we know it is based on the strong symbolism that came before it. There was the ancient Egyptian ankh, for instance, that becomes a cross if you remove the feminine loop at the top.

MONTHS LATER an African American artist, a thealogian (the feminine of theologian), presented me with another beautiful necklace whose pendant looked like a cross.

Is this a cross? I asked. And if it is, how do you relate to it? I was not sure I would wear it if she had made it as a symbol of suffering and death.

I think for most folks the cross is something people die on, she said. But to me, when I was making the necklace and pondering its four directions, it seemed to represent choices.

Looking closely at the necklace, I saw it was covered with flowers and leaves. An inviting crossroads, it offered many paths from which to choose. I liked it very much.

That reminds me, I said, of my favorite definition of the cross: that the cross represents the place where spirit crosses matter.

Hummm, she said, appreciatively. I like that.

Yes, I said. To me too, it just fits. After all, that is where we are really, all of us in existence, in these bodies, that place where for a short time spirit crosses matter. After spirit completes the crossing, I said, we return to matter. But what a divine experience we have had!

These conversations started me thinking how true some symbols are to ancient emotions and beliefs humans have always had. Jung would say that's because they already exist within the psyche; we are never free of them. Their external manifestation—which we appear to achieve any way we can—is our attempt to speak and share an inner mystery

whose ultimate meaning might well be unknowable, except for what each of us makes of it.

It delights me that artists are reclaiming a symbol that has been used for millennia to intimidate and frighten us. Doing this without fanfare, and with fidelity to our own psychic memory.

MEDITATION
"This Is What You Shall Do"

A RECIPE FOR
DIFFICULT TIMES:
ANXIETY SOUP

OCTOBER 31, 2008

YOU KNOW AS WELL AS I DO that in the coming elections we will choose world leaders who will be required to stand with us through perhaps the most difficult period, for humans, on planet Earth. Our anxiety about this situation is understandable. Looking at some of the candidates we see there has already been a great deal of shrieking and groaning; the dismay we feel is equaled only by our alarm. There are many ways, however, to encounter this lack of confidence, this unsteadiness of emotion, this terror, and we will no doubt use all of them, as the final day, November 4, approaches. Some of us will drink more than usual, some of us will do drugs, many of us will pick fights with friends and family, as well as feel hostile and aggressive toward others we don't know. Millions of us will feel hopeless and depressed, believing that no matter what we do we cannot avoid the karma that is coming—especially the karma that is coming to the United States. Even a cursory meandering through our history and a glance at how our government has treated others, for centuries, would make us throw in the towel, climb into our beds, pull the covers over our heads, and wail.

I would be remiss, as an elder of the planet, to remain silent at this point about some of the ways to deal with this period of emotional, psychological, ideological, and financial instability. For I have by now lived relatively long, compared to some of you who are mere children, though you might be in your twenties and thirties. I am definitely at a

July 30, 2010

This is what you shall do: love the earth and the sun and the ani-mals, despise riches, give alms to everyone that asks, stand up for the stupid and crazy, devote your income and labor to others, hate tyrants, argue not concerning God, have patience and indul-gence toward the people, take off your hat to nothing known or unknown or to any man or number of men, go freely with pow-erful uneducated persons and with the young and with the moth-ers of families, read these leaves in the open air every season of every year of your life, reexamine all you have been told at school or church or in any book, dismiss whatever insults your own soul, and your very flesh shall be a great poem. . . .

—Walt Whitman

plateau that makes the teenage years seem doable, and the adolescent years nonmysterious. The late twenties and all of one's thirties are hellish for everyone, as far as I can tell, but at least you've been warned. And so I wish to offer something that I take myself, which is the only kind of medicine I offer—the same as I take myself: Anxiety Soup.

First of all, Anxiety Soup keeps growing and expanding; it is eclectic, it is self-choosing, and it is already within your reach. The main thing it assumes is that you are coming to it in your right mind: that you've put the liquor bottle back on the shelf, said no to drugs of all kinds, and made the manly or womanly decision not to pick fights. In fact, it assumes you consider yourself free. That being so, you are ready for ingredient number one. Ingredient number one is dance. Actually there is a toss-up between dance and meditation, but for me, during this period, I find dance trumps meditation, at least sitting meditation, because while listening to the rhetoric of our politicians I find it increasingly difficult to sit still. That is when I put on one of the most instructive, intelligent, historical, and danceable CDs ever made, *Back on the Block*, by Quincy Jones and a host of fabulous musicians who tell us the wonderful history of our most soulful American music while rocking us into a drenching sweat. I also use this medicine CD, along with Tina Turner's astonishingly mature, dark-souled, and survival-oriented *Twenty Four Seven* to pump me through five or six miles on my exercise bike. There is also *Deep Forest*, the reassuring CD that features the voices of our rainforest ancestors, and almost anything by Oliver Mtukudzi. But you will make your own list, and many of you, feeling the need for this medicine, have already done so. Having made the list, use it. The best time for dancing and biking, I find, is the morning. If I can get up early enough to spend at least an hour enjoying this medicine, I can listen to most political craziness with a relatively detached mind.

Ingredient number two, in other times, would be ingredient number one: sitting meditation. In my experience, nothing beats meditation, for everything. No matter what the problem, my opinion is: meditation is the solution. I share this belief with a lot of people, most of them more disciplined than I am. I began meditating as a child—and it still seems to me the most natural human state—and learned formal meditation in my thirties. It has saved my life. For this, any private corner of your house or car will do. When I lived in Mississippi, and the Klan occasionally left its card in our mailbox, I used to meditate in motel rooms. Sit with a tilted pelvis, breathe so that you notice your breath more than anything else that is happening, keep a watch nearby, if you have to be careful of the time, and for twenty minutes or an hour, sink into the bliss of mental flossing. Political idiocy, no matter how irritating, can be cleansed from your mind, the same way cheese is removed when you floss your teeth. It will be gone, as the profound irritant it was, forever. Though you may recall it, later, in tranquility. What I like best about meditation is an experience that we can also achieve while sitting on the ground and allowing ourselves to drift into the trees: the taste of eternity. It is this taste that reminds us we will be around longer than four years of confusion and disaster; longer than even eight years of complete ruin. In fact, once we slip out of mere time and into eternity, fear leaves us entirely. We become aware we've always been, in some form; that we're not likely to be going anywhere, since the universe, though vast, is probably a closed system, so we might as well relax. There may well be nuclear bombings and a deep global freeze in our future, but who dies, ultimately? No one. Of course you and I might, and that would be regrettable, but after a million years of ice, even plutonium will be turned into fertilizer and I'll probably see you out of the eye of an amoeba. Whatever that eye looks like by then.

Ingredient number three: I just read a statement from my financial planner, who happens to be a good writer, lucky for me. While dealing out the horrid news of financial loss for almost everyone these past weeks of Wall Street meltdown, he mentioned the one stock that has not gone down, but has, in fact, gone up.

Campbell Soup. And that brings me to ingredient number three of Anxiety Soup, which is actual soup. But it is soup you make yourself, from scratch. Soup is an amazing food because, like salads (using only fresh ingredients for those) you can make it out of anything: old, dead, or dying celery stalks, shriveled-up tomatoes and potatoes, crinkled-up mushrooms, sourpussed rutabagas and turnips, dried-out beans. Whatever you have on hand will do. And soup, no matter what's in it, always tastes good. No old shoes! But this is a part of soup's magic: you can only go wrong if you have no sense of taste whatsoever and put in a cup of cumin when you should add a pinch. Choose your biggest pot, concentrate on cleaning out your entire refrigerator. If you don't have anything in there, go out and shop. Buy lots of different vegetables, even some you've never seen before. Spend an hour chopping off heads and splitting things down the middle; this will relieve tension you weren't aware you had. Put in lots of onion and garlic, you want to have strong breath; let your tears fall into the pot, you're crying for your country. Put on music as you chop and stir, or use the time to do silent meditation, thanking the vegetables for appearing in your kitchen, ready to sacrifice themselves for you. Invite someone to share the soup with you; ladle it out in big earthy bowls. Add brown rice or quinoa if you have it, nutritional yeast (for your nerves), and, if you can, eat it in front of a nice homemade fire.

And now, for the last ingredient: snuggling. I have friends who sleep with their dogs and who laughed at me because I didn't understand why the band Three Dog Night called itself that. My dog was always too heavy and hot for me to feel comfortable sleeping with her, but I have enjoyed sleeping with my cat, which is perfect except I become so conscious of her comfort I cease to move, leaving me with various cricks in the joints. The best snuggling is often with a human; this I have found through much trial and error. So if there are animals around, or a human, you are in good shape. And if your person or animal isn't a snuggler and you are, this is serious business. You want someone who adores a big fluffy bed, someone who likes the look of lamp or candle glow, someone who enjoys the sound of rain and turns over and smiles when you say I think it will snow. Snuggling is the best ingredient of all for Anxiety Soup because it is free, it is fun, it goes well with old movies, it goes well with pizza, and it goes well with two people reading great novels or listening to great tapes. It goes really well with drowsing and snoozing and hugging and cuddling and the flinging over of arms and legs and the intermingling of delicious breaths and the deep peace of happy snoring!

And so, here is a recipe for Anxiety Soup! May we continue to be a hardy race that outlives our tormentors—as one of my grandmothers outlived a century of people who thought they owned her. She did this simply by living to be a hundred and twenty-five. As we might, for all the talk of our country's wrongheadedness and multitentacled demise. Part of her Anxiety Soup was the belief that we must never cover up the pulse at our throat, and, even in deepest winter, she left her own throat bare. Proving, during one of the darkest periods of our Republic—when people were owned by regular folks they saw everyday (and were often related to), and not by faceless corporations that hide behind their advertising—that a good Anxiety Soup can be made out of anything.

EVERYONE'S
A VICTIM

November 18, 2008

WHAT I REMEMBER MOST about being shot is how quick it was. Like a streak of lightning, searing my right eye. One second I was an intense, whole, and scrappy eight-year-old, the next I was down on the tin roof of our makeshift garage writhing in unfathomable pain, a victim of my brother's pellet gun, needing to be led off the roof by another brother, never to be the same again. It is this moment that I relive when I think of the children in the world who are harmed by war; some are bombed or shot or napalmed outright, killed instantly, others are maimed. I lost the vision in the affected eye and it would be years before I received proper medical care. It is of this I also think as the countries to which children belong are obliterated and they are left to fend for themselves.

I think of my brother, given a "toy" gun by our parents before he was wise enough to use it, who was never able to say he was sorry for what he had done, and whose guilt turned into bitterness against all females and lack of honor toward himself. Later in life, violence and cocaine were his crutches of choice, until he died an untimely death, quite recently.

After 9/11, when the U.S. government chose to bomb Afghanistan—as if no children lived there (this is what small children believe: that of course if grown-ups who bomb countries knew that children lived there they would not bomb)—I was distraught to discover there were 700,000 disabled Afghani orphans. Many of these children were blinded; many had lost hearing and limbs. Who would they turn to, where would they go? I wondered. Who would feed them, take them to safety, put them to bed? Now we know their orphanages were not spared. We, who paid for this destruction, must live with this.

My sweetheart, a Vietnam veteran of Korean-Norwegian descent, tells me harrowing tales of his tenure there. Drafted at eighteen, he was ordered to come to the induction center to arrange for reclassification of a student deferment. Once there, he was steered onto a bus and sent off to boot camp, without even, he says, a toothbrush. There, he was confronted with the rigors and horrors of training, hardened men giving crude and shocking orders to teenagers who had no recourse but to obey. Within a short period of time he was sent halfway across the world to fight people he barely (except for the news) believed existed. What is more, because they were Asian, they looked like him. He tells me something I have never heard before: that though in boot camp the army issued each recruit a gun with a heavy wooden stock, a necessity for hand-to-hand combat, in Vietnam the soldiers were issued guns with lightweight plastic stocks, made by Colt but designed by the toy manufacturer Mattel. Against the heavy, wooden-stocked AK-47s of the Vietnamese combatants (supplied by the Chinese communists) these guns that jammed, misfired, and often shattered on contact, were almost useless. Frightened and frustrated soldiers appealed to their superiors for Thompson .45 caliber machine guns, antique relics of previous wars, and wrote home for their fathers' and grandfathers' sawed-off shotguns, and went out to fight "the enemy" with those.

He tells me of the immense suffering of soldiers. Of the rivers of heroin, supplied by the Chinese communists—who were helping their Vietnamese communist comrades on this front too—that flowed into camp, and how this "medicine" that soldiers turned to in order to blot out the terrible things they had seen and done became a poison that turned everyone involved in its sale and use into demons of instability and pain. He tells me of the young man he was at nineteen, alone, far from home, at the mercy of a war he didn't understand, forced to live by his wits, even as he deliberately scrambled them with what he thought was cocaine but was, in fact, 94–97 percent pure "China White" heroin, one of the deadliest drugs known. He tells of being put in a metal box for 21 days and "cooked" at 114 degrees, to cure him of addiction. A torture many of his mates did not survive. He tells me of the suicides.

I weep with him, and hold him, as he tells me these tales. This was nearly forty years ago, and he is still suffering, deeply. *Why haven't I heard these stories before?* I ask. Because nobody has wanted to hear them, he replies. Some people have. In remembrance of some of those people we watch *Born on the Fourth of July* (one of my favorite films), *The Thin Red Line* (the most lyrical of war films), and *Platoon*. We watch the compassionate masterpiece *Coming Home*. There have always been people who understood everyone's a victim in war. May our numbers increase.

I wrote this as an op-ed piece while promoting my book for children, Why War Is Never a Good Idea, *illustrated by Stefano Vitale. It was never published.*

SISTERLOSS

JANUARY 15, 2009

MY SISTER ANNIE RUTH WALKER HOOD died the morning of
December 27, 2008: throughout the four days leading up to her death
in hospice, friends and I sat in ceremony, thousands of miles away,
chanting, praying, meditating and speaking at times to her spirit and
soul. It was a difficult transition for her; at the end, for us at least,
there was a palpable feeling of release, of peace. We were close as children, but grew apart as the years turned into decades since we lived
near each other, and our ways in the world proved very different. She
didn't believe in voting, for instance, which I found an affront to those
who, voting even when their lives were endangered, made attempts
year after year to change a system that kept her and others like her
relatively poor, without health care, undereducated, and largely ignorant of anything not seen in a flash on television. Just last year she discovered, and believed, the Earth was in trouble, running out of resources,
and immediately decided to recycle her paper napkins and garbage
bags. But voting, no. Seeing Earth as divine, rather than a fundamental-
ist religion that encourages passivity and "heaven" for a few thousand
souls, no. So we disagreed.

The morning of her death my friends and I moved our circle from
outside the house to the dining room table. Holding hands we urged
her to let go. I had written a poem for her, and letting go was its theme.
During her cremation, we again sat in a circle, just my partner and I this

time, a two-person circle, and waited until my niece called from Atlanta, to tell us the machine had stopped and the cremation was done.
No pun intended. But my sister would have enjoyed this, even if one
were intended. Anything to do with cooking, eating, ovens, and refrig-
erators aroused her interest; she loved to eat. This had, unfortunately,
contributed to her ill health.

So this was our Christmas. The day after my sister's death I felt
lighter than I had in months. She had been very sick for years, fighting
it all the way. The day after her cremation, however, Sisterloss set in. It
felt exactly as if I had lost a limb, or some other part of my own body.
My body felt too heavy and wobbly to carry; I had to lay myself down,
as if I were wood, the remains of a tree from which a huge branch had
been removed. I found a hammock way at the back of my house, hidden behind cactus plants, and swung in limbo. Earlier I had had a
dream that I thought of now: I was being informed by an old friend
that he was leaving. He showed me the symbol of his new life: a green
apple encased in a moist, spongy kind of cake. I seemed resigned to his
moving on, but at the same time I experienced a piercing pain in my
heart, so agonizing it threatened to wake me; but I went up to the table
(that suddenly appeared) in the dream, a table spread with all that remained of enjoyment in life, and I tried to find a new place. A place
not for two, as had been the case until now, but for the solitary one I
had become. The dream had done the thing that dreams do so well:
given all the symbols my psyche needed to prepare for the devastation
I was feeling in the hammock as I swung.

Going from this state to encounter the news of the outside world
was probably a mistake. I don't know why I did so. Curiosity, love of the
world, concern over our collective well-being. More curiosity. In any
case, the first thing I encountered was Israel's attack on Gaza, illustrated
by a row of little girls, looking sound asleep but obviously dead, their
grandmother wailing over their heads. And then, in the same frame, or
close, Nancy Pelosi, Democrat Speaker of the House, saying that Hamas,
the elected representatives of the Palestinian people, are "thugs." Had
she seen these children's bodies? And then, a fragment of news that has
kept me awake every night: in one house, bombed by Israel with money
their state (more important by the attention it gets than any of our le-
gitimate states) received from American tax dollars, five sisters had been
killed. Five sisters. Their mother was critically injured.

We know that Gaza is comprised largely of refugees. That refugee settlements are generally 80 percent women and children. What are we to do with this assault on a people who have been forced into a space too small for them, deprived of water, food, medicine, and mobility? Of fathers, brothers, and husbands? Five sisters, on whom a thousand-pound bomb was dropped. And on their mother. How are we to live with this?

This tragedy to the human race is unbearable. How are we to raise children in this atmosphere of savagery? Every child on the planet real-izes he or she is in danger from grown-ups gone mad. When I think of children left alone with images of bloodied corpses of children just like themselves I can hardly sit still, let alone sleep. When I visualize the five sisters, they are wearing green. Green dresses with billowing skirts. The mother alone is dressed in black, and at her throat she wears a white embroidered collar that can be detached. Is she still alive? And if she is alive, and if they have told her about her daughters, how does she feel? As if all her branches are gone? Her root? Were there still more sisters left? One sister? There are now hundreds of people dead, thousands wounded. Even before this attack medical supplies, as well as food and water, were miniscule. I had a glimpse of the horrendous wall the Israelis have built around Palestinian settlements and noticed they have a ledge on the Israeli side for soldiers to stand on in order to shoot down into the imprisoned population. Doesn't this remind the world of images we've all said Never Again to, and tried to grow beyond?

I am convinced that, unless the world takes the time to unravel the skein of hatred that binds the people of the Middle East, our end—the end of the world citizens have made—will come from there. That though all focus appears to be on which Arab nation is likely to strike the United States, in my awareness of the unpredictability of evil, I imag-ine Israel just as capable of doing us nuclear harm. This is because the United States and Israel, working together (and with Britain) have done terrible things to others in their greed to take resources away from them: and it is the nature of thieves to eventually have a grand falling out. More, Israel, with our help, has the weapons of mass de-struction for which Bush looked in vain in Iraq. One senses, in Israeli rage, unhealed wounds that may well be unhealable. As a world we continue to feel grief for this, as we feel grief, unspeakable grief, know-

ing four and five hundred years of enslavement and unimaginable brutality inevitably damaged our people. Human people. All people. Not
just the blacks, browns, yellows, reds, and whites that were enslaved.

But what is the remedy? Is it to claim the people who fight the madness are "thugs"? While the people who drop bombs on women and
children are justified?

Three years ago I called a Peace Camp to which I invited African
American and Jewish women, feeling completely sure that peace is not
to be entrusted solely to men. About twenty women came, and we had
a couple of days of talking together, no holds barred. I called the circle
because what frightens me more than anything is the silencing of people who object to Israel's behavior, which I have experienced personally,
as have many other African Americans. My position was, and is, that
in every single movement for change and betterment of lives on the
planet in which I've found myself, I've been flanked by at least one Jew.
Sometimes this has been a male, sometimes, often, it has been a female. Only in the last three decades have I felt a chill as we tried to talk
to each other about the Middle East. This precious and unlikely alli-
ance, two beleaguered peoples, determined to witness and affirm each
other's struggle, seemed too essential to relinquish without a word. Or
many. At our Peace Camp we talked through the day and into the night.
What was accomplished? For me, the certainty that this circling around
this issue, globally, might just lead to the kind of change that real conversation, real telling and real listening, can lead to. I was able to express how being called anti-Semitic hurt, when I dared, in the seventies
and eighties, to express the fear that what is happening in Gaza would
one day occur. To say to a beloved Jewish friend who dreamed, she
said one day, that she was kissing Ariel Sharon, that in the absence of a
nondream sharing of what this symbol might mean, I had felt the need
to withdraw from her. (Being true friends, we of course talked our way
back to our senses on this.)

I remember one of the women from Israel who explained to us that
she worked in Israel with Arab women in the cause of peace, but
that she never thought of the Arab women as friends. This was sad to
hear. And the other African American women, silenced for decades,
struggling now to pull back into focus a cause that—with all the calamities befalling our own communities—they had mostly lost. What
happens when one's words of concern are thrown back at one as if one

has no authority to speak is that people learn not to pay attention, not to care. But of course this is impossible. This is a very small planet and by now most of the humans on it are endangered, one way or another, and very scared. It is in no one's interest to let any nation, no matter its history or claim to sympathy, further terrorize us.

And that, I feel, is ultimately what I am objecting to: the terrorization of the planet by the United States and Israel. And yes, I know African armies and Indian armies and all the other smaller armies are imitating the big guys as best they can. I happen however to be attached to the United States and Israel through the strongest possible bonds: birth and taxes. These overly armed countries are attacking people who cannot possibly put up an equal fight, which makes attacking them sadistic. Where is the glory, the freedom and bravery, the wisdom, the profit in this? All the oil in the world will not wipe away the bomb scar now seared on the hearts of billions of Earthlings, cowering in their beds or losing themselves in licentiousness and drugs.

In the film *The Thin Red Line*, the main character, a conscientious objector to the war in which he finds himself, asks, contemplating the slaughter on both sides: Who is killing us? That is the only question to ask, really. Who is killing us? Who is torturing us? Who is making us dance around the world going Yes, yes, yes, you are so right, when all the time we're appalled to our very core.

We have not, as a planet, been seeking to change the world so that this insanity can continue. And we must not feel limited by our insistence on nonviolence, when all around us is guts and blood. Wars of the sort that cause guts and blood cannot be won. Let us take courage from that fact. The anger, hatred, fear, devastation let loose on the planet just during the reign of George the Second will mean millions of people, people we might see every day, will carry war in their hearts. A war carried in the heart will one day mean a bomb under the table.

I place my own trust in human conscience, as exemplified by Israeli students who are presently demonstrating against their government's massacre of largely defenseless people. I call on all Earthlings to let their conscience speak, no matter what you are called, or by whom you are called it. You have a right to live in joy on this planet. You cannot do that, we cannot do that, if we are harassed and tormented by those who do not care about us, or about law and justice; those who readily insult our integrity whenever we ask simply to be heard; those who trample our dreams of peace and would deny us tomorrow because we, having been made to feel guilty and intimated by a history of which we had no part, have not found the courage to say No to them today.

Casa Madre, Mexico

WE ARE REMEMBERED
FOR WHAT WE TEACH

JUNE 28, 2009

IT CAN BE A SMALL THING: for instance, last week my friend and naturopath Dr. Cecelia Hart made a very unexpected transition. None of her friends knew she was sick, and in fact, I had not seen her in over a year. Though we occasionally saw each other at East Bay Church of Religious Science, which attracted us by its deep spirituality and vibrant soul, we had lost touch after she ministered to me during a medical situation that caused me concern. She was funny, slow (I used to read while she went to her storeroom and mixed herbs) with a handwriting that was inscrutable without a magnifying glass. I loved her dreadlocks, her short skirts, her languid way of making a diagnosis. Hummm . . . maybe it's this. Maybe it's that. Could be both. Oh no! And we would laugh. One time she gave me a remedy made from pigs' eyes, but that was as extreme as it got, and she had misgivings, being, I think, vegetarian. I took the pills for a while, in desperation, but couldn't keep it up because of a mental image of a pig whose eyes twinkled at me. When I told her what had happened, she chuckled and said, Well, drink lots of water.

The thing she taught me that comes to mind each morning is how to drink green tea, which I like a lot, and not get wired on the caffeine. I had invited her to come for a rest in the country, exactly two years ago, and each morning she watched me make my cup of tea, a weak cup, and drink half of it. At last she told me what she'd learned in China, where she'd studied for a year. You can drink green tea all day long as the folks in China do and not worry about the caffeine, she said. What you do, she said, taking my tea bowl and demonstrating as she talked, is put in the tea, put in the water, hot but not boiling, and let it steep for a few minutes. Then you pour the water from that tea, the first bowl of tea, down the drain, keeping the tea leaves. That first bowl holds the caffeine. For the rest of the day you pour hot water over the tea leaves left in the bowl. It will taste fine. That's how they drink tea in China.

I last saw Dr. Cecilia on June 3. She was a devotee of Amma (the spiritual leader who has hugged by now upwards of 26 million people) and she invited me and my partner to darshan. He was unable to come, but a friend, a devotee of Anandi Ma (another Indian spiritual leader) and admirer of Amma, was able to come instead. I had gone to see, and be hugged by Amma, twice. The first time was amazing. I fell into those warm, cushiony arms like a little bird finding its nest, while Amma chanted a mantra that seemed tailor-made for my current quest. The second time I went I left without darshan because Amma seemed tired (I was certainly tired, and so no doubt projected) and I couldn't bear to add to the number of people—thousands, it seemed—there to be hugged that day. This time, I went only because Dr. Cecilia invited me, and because, over the phone, she promised more stories about her and Amma's recent visit to Kenya, where Amma had opened a school for Masai youth.

My friend Rafiki Rama and I waited nearly an hour at the entrance to Amma's temple, where Dr. Cecilia had said she'd be. At last this extremely thin, slow-moving woman came up behind us. I didn't recognize her at first. She said she'd been holding seats near Amma's chair, and that she'd been afraid to leave them for fear they'd be taken. The place was, as always, packed. We moved along beside her, sat in the chairs she'd saved, and waited for the service to begin. While we waited I asked about her weight loss. Dear One, I said, you're really thin. What's up? She smiled slowly and whispered: parasites. She explained she'd been in India, as well as Africa, and had gotten them there. Well, I joked, there goes my trip to India and the visit to Amma's ashram! It wasn't at the ashram, she said; the food there is wonderful. But I went off on my own, exploring.

She made sure Amma knew we were there, and took us herself to the front of the line for darshan. Once again I knelt in front of this living saint, who looked less tired than before and who beamed at us as I leaned my head onto her shoulder. I love her darkness, her roundness, her deep Oneness with the Feminine and devotion to the Mother. Her clear and well-expressed intelligence on any and all matters of urgency afflicting our planet. Once again she whispered a mantra that seemed perfect for that moment of my life. We sat near her for a little while, Dr. Cecilia using her limited strength to get our three precious chairs to follow us, and then we left the temple. As we walked Dr. Cecilia uphill toward her car, it was easy to see her strength was failing. We walked along beside her, very slowly, up the hill. At her car, Rafiki helped her inside. I sat beside her as she found and inserted her key. She had the look of someone who wasn't quite sure what a car is for. Come with us, we said, we will drive you home. No, she said. Well, let us tail you, we said. No, she said, that's all right. I can do this. She started the car. I joked about the intelligence of cars, and how sometimes, lucky for humans, they seem to know the way home. I have experienced this in my own life. We still worried.

A little over two weeks later, she was gone. A friend alerted me to the fact that she was in the hospital and that it looked serious. I sent flowers to her and alerted our friends who might not have known she'd been taken there. Several of them went to visit her. Rafiki was able to be there to watch over her while she slept and then sing for her. Henri Norris and Angel Kyodo Williams were there. Our wonderful Reverend Elouise from East Bay Church of Religious Science was with her when she made her move, as was Reverend Andriette. That these two precious women were there, at that moment, brought tears of joy to my eyes. I had called every day, once I knew she had a phone, and at last was able to get through to her. I had learned she was an only child, that her parents were dead. A male cousin answered the phone, a person with a gentle, angelic voice, and placed the phone near her ear. She could make only sounds, not words, as I talked to her. My Darling! I greeted her. I thanked her for taking such good care of so many of us in our community, leery as we are of what passes for medicine in the modern world. I thanked her for her humor, her slowness in filling out prescriptions, and her inscrutable writing, which we all complained about and all adored. (I believe she chuckled.) I thanked her for her thick head of copper-colored locks, and for her love of Ethiopian food, which she shared with quite a number of us. I thanked her for being our teacher, and for loving us enough to go to distant lands to study new and ancient ways to keep us healthy. I thanked her for her mysterious Being.

Because, finally, she was such a mystery. How could she have become so ill and none of us know it? And what does this say about our vaunted belief in community?

While she was in the hospital, I read for the first time a note she had left on her visit two years ago. It was in a blank journal that is kept beside the bed where she slept. She said she'd come without expectations and received a healing she was unaware she needed. That is how I feel about my visits to her office on Ashby Avenue. Expecting nothing as I ambled up her walk one troubled day, I had found not only a funny and loveable healer, but a teacher and a friend.

EDWIDGE DANTICAT,
THE QUIET STREAM

JANUARY 23, 2010

ALL THIS TIME, SILENCED, SPEECHLESS, grateful for my meditation cushion, I have been thinking about the writer Edwidge Danticat,
whose writing for me, so pure and grounded and wise, is the quiet
stream flowing in the background of the present chaos and noise in
Haiti. Danticat explores with acute attention and tenderness the complex reality of Haiti and its people, and like Arundhati Roy of India, it
is impossible to think of her native country without her.

I remember reading not so long ago the exquisite, word-perfect
memoir of Danticat's childhood in Haiti, living in the home of her
uncle, her father's brother, before being sent eventually to America to
live with her parents, who, desperate to find a better place and life for
their children, had gone there years before. The love and respect between the brothers moved me profoundly, for such fidelity and trust as
existed between them aroused my longing for a more prevalent example of honor in our day-to-day lives, an honor exemplified in the relationship, lasting decades, of these two men.*

A writer's heart, a poet's heart, an artist's heart, a musician's heart
is always breaking. It is through that broken window that we see the
world; more mysterious, beloved, insane, and precious for the sparkling
and jagged edges of the smaller enclosure we have escaped.

*Danticat, *Brother, I'm Dying* (Knopf, 2007).

Edwidge, my younger sister, *couraj, ma chérie.*

There are millions of us thinking of you, with you, of Haiti. Learning what we must. Doing what we can. Understanding that someone labeled "criminal" for "looting" a box of candles may have a loved one crushed and bleeding to death in the dark. Who among us—so plump next to almost any Haitian—is put to this test?

Know the sturdy structure of words you have constructed about and for Haitians no earthquake can destroy. Your words will be part of the mortar that rejoins the soul and self-confidence of your people, so beloved by you: as they rise, once more; which, being Haitian, they will.

Wherever you are.

Sharing strength,
Alice

MORE MEDITATION
REQUIRED!

MAY 25, 2010

A SHORT WHILE AGO I published a small book called *Overcoming Speechlessness: A Poet Encounters The Horror in Rwanda, Eastern Congo, and Palestine/Israel.* In it I write that the horrors of the world are so great, and have been for such a long time, that most humans have no words for them. That we become speechless before atrocities done to other humans, to animals, and to the Earth itself because it is almost impossible to believe what we are witnessing. I have spent a lifetime finding and using my voice, so easily silenced as a young person by the overwhelm of grief. Looking back, I see that claiming my voice, asserting it in writing, became a practice that in many ways saved me. Saved me from despair, from hopelessness, from total and complete withdrawal, emotionally, from other human beings. Those human beings I knew, and those I did not know.

Turning to the news recently I discovered major spiritual assaults against the integrity and pride of black and brown people, atrocities in their own way: a Republican senator from Kentucky saying, after winning a seat in the Senate, that the Civil Rights Act of 1964 should perhaps have provided for the right of a private owner of a public establishment to determine whether or not to admit or serve people of color; and the governor of Arizona signing into law two outrageous bills against people from Mexico and other Latino cultures. She signed into law a document that would permit policepersons to stop anyone who looks—to them—like an undocumented worker and to demand proof of proper residency in the United States. She also signed a bill that would erase Latino studies. For those of us who remember the sixties, especially the losses to our ranks of people we so devoutly loved, as we struggled to change political, economic, and social apartheid in this country, and to teach ourselves and each other who, in fact, we are, the very idea that anyone would think this way, and feel comfortable saying or doing such things in public, is so shocking as to be initially disbelieved.

However, articulate voices have been immediately raised in both these instances. Both African Americans and Latinos are clearly not going to take the disrespect to their people and cultures represented by the senator from Kentucky and the governor of Arizona lying down. Watching the face of a young black woman on *Democracy Now!* dismantle the senator's argument for a return, basically, to states' rights when it comes to black people, I adored her. There she was black and queenly, never for a second losing her cool, alerting the world to the fact that yes, fifty years later we know who we are, how we got that way, and how firmly we stand on the ground we have secured. It is amazing how sweet it feels, as her elder, to see her calm self-assurance, and to have lived long enough to witness her understanding that for our collective freedom we stand in a not-so-shallow river of blood. Blood eternally precious to us. We will never consider going back to a time when any one of us could be told to use the back door; could be told to use the bushes instead of the restroom; could be denied a drink of water while white people sneeringly drank whatever water there was before our thirsty eyes. No amount of drugging us, no amount of sending our children to the army to fight people they never heard of, no amount of stuffing us with bad food will weaken us to that point. If this is what Senator Rand Paul and the Tea Party are about, they need to reconsider. I admit I haven't kept up with the doings of Sarah Palin and the Tea Party, but I would advise some distancing here.

The first thing that came to mind when I watched Latino students in Arizona defend their right to learn about their own cultures was how much I wanted to be beside them. It seemed ironic that they were demonstrating outside a college in Arizona, in the United States, while I was cheering them on from a small village in Mexico. It is lamentable that most Americans know nothing of the beautiful culture of Mexico;

that when they think of Mexico they think mainly of drugs and crime and illegal immigration. It is heartbreaking to have enjoyed the hospitality and grace of so many areas of Mexico, over roughly three decades, that have now been horribly hit by the flooding of Mexico with cheap American corn that sends farmers from, for example, Oaxaca, into El Norte, looking desperately for work. The abuse of Mexicans seeking employment, like that of other illegal immigrants that travel north through Mexico, is almost unbearable to contemplate. To my credit, I never see a poor farmer anywhere in the world without thinking of my father.

I love Mexico for the same reason I love many other Latino countries. It is the people, first and foremost. People who are well known for their kindness, patience, and humor. For their art and their artists. For their music and their dance. For their healing technologies shared graciously and, for an American, at little cost. For their food! Even for their tempers. I of course also admire them for their revolutions.

That there are Americans who want a return to White Culture, White Politics, White History, and White Literature is really stunning. Why would we want to do this? Once free of the notion that we could somehow become white by studying and worshipping all things white, why would any American be interested in being reenslaved? Besides, multiculturalism is light-years more fun.

More meditation required! is my recommendation to the senator and the governor and to the Tea Party, which I will now research. "Try to think like you got some sense" is what one of my characters tells another in my novel *The Color Purple*. Meditation is good for this. It is a medicine that plays no favorites: it can be used to cool out and calm, deepen and bolster in compassion, any of us: senator, governor, student, farmer, teacher, and police; any of us at all.

"WE BELIEVE"
BY STAUGHTON
AND ALICE LYND

June 4, 2010

TODAY I TOOK DOWN the wonderful photos and poems that surround me in my kitchen; they have been there, taped to my cabinets, for a number of years, giving me encouragement and strength. However, I found it impossible to take down a Walt Whitman statement about what we shall do, and a teaching about the settled mind by Wang Chongyang. I also could not bear to remove a poem and comment by my former college teacher (of history) Staughton Lynd (a new book about him called *The Admirable Radical* was just released) and his wife, Alice Lynd. Staughton Lynd was a major opponent of war in general when I was his student in Atlanta in the sixties, and of the war in Vietnam in particular. Since that time Alice and Staughton have become lawyers representing workers in the steel mills of Ohio. They have also befriended Mumia Abu-Jamal.

Each year around winter solstice they send out typed life/soul rafts made of words. These two pieces showed up in my mailbox some years ago. Though I have not seen the Lynds in decades, the purity of their lives and the integrity of purpose they have exhibited over the long haul teach and encourage me still.

Both the poem and the brief comment that follows it seem prophetic in the most thoughtful of ways. I remember the night Barack Obama (for instance) was elected president. I stood in my kitchen beneath this poem and was grateful to have this belief as part of my world. That election was only the beginning; it was to show us what we can do, not by any means what we have ultimately achieved, directing us beyond any of our current disappointments and fears.

WE BELIEVE
© 1990s by Staughton and Alice Lynd

We believe
Not only in the lengthening of days
And the return of springtime,
But in sudden reversals,

Unexpected triumphs.

We believe in the restoration
Of trust between friends,
And in the ability of ordinary folk

To puncture public lies.

We believe that the way to be safe
Is not to enclose ourselves in walls
Of cash and property,

But to live in solidarity
With those who need us.

How can we give the Good
More chance to prevail?

What can we add
To the chemistry of change?

Surely, first, persistence.
Prisoners are obliged to learn it.

How many times did Nelson Mandela
Reach for his shovel in the limestone quarry?

Soon Mumia will have been behind bars
More than Mandela's 27 years.

"Keep smiling," we told

The man serving two life sentences
For crimes of which he may be
Completely innocent.

He replied "I have to.
But inside my heart is broken."

So
While we seek to persist,

To be dogged, to stay strong,

We must also be open every moment
To that which only yesterday
Seemed impossible,
To transformations
Of quantity into quality,

To the instantaneous advent
Of the unimaginably new.

*   *   *

ALSO:

The good we secure for ourselves
Is precarious and uncertain
Until it is secured for all of us

And incorporated into our common life.

—*Staughton and Alice Lynd*

THE INNER LISTENER

December 5, 2009

Sounds True, which offers so many amazing and helpful works, has recently produced an audio set of Howard Thurman's talks. Thurman was a mystic and theologian who influenced many of today's most thoughtful leaders. I was asked to introduce a segment of this collection.

HOWARD THURMAN USED TO COME SPEAK to us at Spelman College during morning chapel and perhaps vespers. I cannot claim to remember these visits precisely, but, listening to his voice on tapes made roughly half a century ago, I seem to be once again in that atmosphere. There we were, young girls of seventeen to twenty, required to be in our assigned seats at Sisters Chapel each morning, five days a week, to hear words of inspiration that would propel us through our studies, and through our days. Services started promptly at eight o'clock. Or was it, more likely, seven? I remember sliding into my seat just as the clock struck, pajamas tucked discreetly into my socks, yawning, and thinking of the French poetry I'd ventured to translate until late the night before.

After singing, after a prayer, after wondering whether there would even be time for breakfast, there would be, if we were very lucky, Howard Thurman, and not some other speaker whose concern would be more about our behavior with boys, or with a God who was always male and needing to be feared and obeyed, than with the growth of our spirit and the awakening of a political and social and activist conscience.

In fact, what struck me about Howard Thurman then, as I seem to recall those times listening to him now, is that he was one of the first spiritual guides I encountered who could pray to a "heavenly father" with every awareness, transmitted to his listeners, that the "heavenly father" of whom he spoke did not live by himself in heaven. Thurman was capable of knowing and of teaching us also that "heaven" is inhabited by all things: ancestors, heroes of our interminable struggles for justice in the form of racial and economic equality, as well as the water in the ocean lapping at the shore, and the sunshine blessing us with its radiance. The flowers were a part of heaven, as were our own kindness and thoughtfulness. This might not seem much now when we are surrounded by spiritual guides who acknowledge mystical and pagan and animist roots, but for most of the girls in Sisters Chapel, coming as we did from strict Christian families for whom the Bible was total law, and everything dominated by one God, himself jealous and alone, it was a revelation to be told, in quite clear terms, that no, heaven was not a closed room. It was not small either, it was vast. And, even in its vastness, it also existed inside of you.

He was subversive of the very system of the school he was speaking in. I wonder how much he considered this, as he spoke to us. For we were actively engaged in the struggle to free our people from American apartheid. Sometimes leaving the chapel to march in the streets of Atlanta, some of us going to jail, reading our textbooks as we went.

The administration of the school frowned on such behavior; it rocked a boat they were comfortable rowing in. For our daring we could be expelled or lose our scholarships, those of us lucky enough, as I was, to have one. The tension surrounding any overt resistance was intense. Which is one reason I could not remain at Spelman, though I loved it very much. I especially loved the other young women, my beautiful sisters, who were so brave and determined to change the racist world that had so degraded the lives of our people. There were also others who had fought the good fight at Spelman and moved on to graduate— for instance, Marian Wright (now Edelman), who was legendary and whom I would one day, to my great if not always graceful good fortune, meet.

Listening to Howard Thurman now, I am so grateful for his life. For his presence among us: young girls who had never had anyone to tell us about the inner listener. The one Carl Jung calls the two-million-year-old man/being, who is the witness to our every thought, every move. The one who knows, even when we think we know nothing and are without guidance, and friendless. The teaching about "the inner and the outer" that is explored in one of these selections is one I wish all people, young people especially, could absorb.

For it is true, an inner discipline of the spirit develops the character that is then visible to others in our behavior, but it is also true that "acting as if" also works; which is to say, conscious development of our outer, discernable behavior, in a direction that we desire, also has the power to move us along. This truth may well be discovered as one goes along in life, but how much more useful to have someone teaching it when one is young.

I avoided being arrested while at Spelman College and have always felt I missed something special. My three arrests later in life were always, among other things, a nod to my Spelman sisters, who (a couple of years before I arrived on campus) had exhibited a style and grace as they were carried away that should have put their jailers to shame.

It is easy to see why Howard Thurman was mentor to Martin Luther King Jr. And it is moving to hear his statement made the night after King was assassinated. There is in all of Thurman's work support for the one who contemplates and also acts. In Martin there was a stunning balance that Thurman must have applauded. And then to lose him! I can only imagine his pain, a pain shared by so many of us. And can only marvel at what he saw as the value of such a death: that the day after King's death, the people of America moved one step closer to being human. That humanity is sometimes only moved forward by the sacrifices that make us weep.

FROM GRANDMOTHER'S HORSE

Tale One: Horse History

Listening to Bloodhound Bob the other day on the news talking about killing Julian Assange, Grandmother decided she needed to make her thoughts known about Julian, the Dark Knight (as someone commenting on a poem Grandmother posted on her blog calls him). Grandmother likes Julian Assange and hopes he never again dyes his gray hair. It is the sign of the fairy spirit that inhabits him, in case he didn't know. Grandmother has gray hair too, but hers came on time, when she was already much older than Julian Assange. She likes it because it connects her to fabulous old people from childhood, her grandfather, for instance, who was so adoring and so silent, like a tree that could sit on a porch without moving, or like a mysterious wind that could plant beans. Unless something truly horrible is discovered about Julian Assange, Grandmother thinks he's fascinating. (She is unconvinced he is a rapist but is willing to wait and see how the investigation of this goes.)

Bloodhound Bob comes from a long line of assassins and murderers that kept the black Southern population (and some of the white) terrorized for centuries; not a few of Grandmother's kin ended up lynched, burned, cut up, and tossed into the muddy swamps. This is what Grandmother *feels* when she looks at Bloodhound Bob's face and listens to his tone. He wants to do something like this to Julian. Is *obscenity* too big a word for you? It's like: so stinky it makes you sick to

your stomach even to look. But by now Grandmother can look at anything. Life, she finds, is a revolving door, and there's always something
you thought you'd never have to see again staring you in the face.

But she wants to talk to you a bit about something that might be a
big help to you, later on. Truth. You may have noticed that while Bloodhound Bob and others are blaming Julian Assange and (somewhat less
urgently) Bradley Manning for leaking diplomatic and other cables
between the United States and many countries, they have not blamed
the cables themselves, for existing, even once! And this is what Grandmother wants to make sure you understand: the only blame that can
legitimately be laid must lead to the doorway of Truth itself. Truth is
the culprit. Truth is to be blamed. Not to do this is to fatally misunderstand the nature of Truth. Which is, *Truth wants to be known*; that is
why Truth always leaves a record. It leaves a footprint. It leaves a mark.
Always. That is why, for instance, though every trick in the book was
used to cover up the soul marriage of white president Thomas Jefferson and his black enslaved partner Sally Hemings, every one of their
later-to-be-claimed-nonexistent children had Jefferson's flaming red
hair.

Isn't that funny? Doesn't it make you laugh? That is the other char-
acteristic of Truth. It can be as horrible as you can imagine, but because
it is the truth, it offers relief. Relief makes us feel better. Feeling better
relaxes our faces. Smiles may occur. Guffaws.

So don't let Bloodhound Bob and his ilk scare you. When you grow
up you may decide to try to save your world. You may have to do some
pretty amazing things, like find out where the Truth is kept hidden and
to set it free. Grandmother will, at that point, hopefully be around to
give you a horse. Not necessarily a four-legged one, but an imaginary
one to ride into the fray. Julian Assange is on his horse; I think the person who called him the Dark Knight is right. He comes to us trailing
odors of indiscretion, imperfection, and highly uncircumspect behavior. Still he rides to his post as guardian and protector, come whatever
the heck may. He's one of us, the motley humans, for sure.

Grandmother too, is on her horse. She's been on her horse for a while,
so long that sometimes she's not even sure her horse is still under her.
But no matter. You'll see. When you are a bit older and a passion to exhibit your love for the world comes over you, your horse will suddenly
appear beneath you.

And here's something else about the horse: During the centuries when Bloodhound Bob's ancestors could kill black people and the occasional white person with impunity, black people could not even talk to each other about it. And that is why when they met on the back roads of the South, with Bloodhound Bob's people cracking whips all over them, they would say, as their mules and horses waited patiently beside or under them: *Tell my horse.* And the horse (or mule) is the one who received direct information about our people's tragedies, never our people themselves.

That is what we're here to change.

And so, my dears, Grandmother and you now share a history that connects us to our common horse. Get on. Don't be afraid. I know it's dark. But darkness, like truth, exists to be made visible. An old white-haired man named Jung that Grandmother likes a lot has written about this. And yes, it's going to be a long and bumpy ride.

FREE DOGS AND
THE ALBANY BULB
WATERFRONT PARK

FEBRUARY 13, 2011

A DOG'S PURPOSE: A NOVEL FOR HUMANS by W. Bruce Cameron is an amazing book. I just listened to it on audio and laughed and smiled and cried right through it. The narrator, George K. Wilson, is so good that by the end of the story you think of him as a dog, and a marvelous one at that. In fact, you love him as Bailey the dog so much, and feel so intimate with Bailey's sometimes painful journey, that the sobbing is wonderful. It's wise, this book, and is sure to open the hearts of all who read or listen to it. I recommend *A Dog's Purpose* to those who wish to make the Albany Bulb Waterfront Park in Albany, California, a place where dogs must be on a leash. Bailey, the dog of the story, who is reincarnated four or five times, has much to teach us about a dog's love of liberty.

The Albany Bulb, as the park is also called, used to be in danger of becoming a shopping mall. Maybe this was just rumor, since this has not, in fact, happened. Perhaps the idea of not letting dogs run free there is also a rumor. I hope so.

For all thirteen years of her life, my black lab, Marley Mu, and I headed for the waterfront whenever we needed to walk. She trotted alongside me for endless miles over the years, free of attachment to me, except by her affection. This was a glorious time for us both: for her, meeting other free dogs, circling and sniffing, or dashing up and down the banks of grass and flower-covered rubble; for me, relishing the peace that comes from being in a community that cares, and thinks seriously, about the happiness of dogs.

I love the park just as it is: the rubble being overtaken by vegetation, the uneven walking surfaces, the sense that we can create beauty out of destruction and waste, and the arresting art, done anonymously, that makes this park unique in a world where few artists can bear to remain unknown. And I love the beauty of free dogs, running and playing, jumping in the ocean: exploring, free for a time, their extended and beautiful Universe.

ENDING THE
AGE OF WASTE

FEBRUARY 20, 2011

*The most important thing humanity can do is believe in itself.
That we can grow, that we can change, and that we can rouse
ourselves to exhibit gratitude—by respecting her limits—to the
only planet Mother we have ever known.*

UNTIL I WAS A TEENAGER I had no experience of waste. Growing
up on a farm in middle Georgia, everything we grew, built, raised, or
sewed was used until it was used up. There was no "extra." And no
such thing as litter. My parents were puzzled when they perceived the
beginning, in their community, among their relatives and friends,
among their children, of "the Age of Waste." Neither of them knew
what to do, for example, with Styrofoam containers or plastic cups.
They thought items so wondrously made, so lightweight and sturdy,
should certainly be prized. They carefully washed and reused them,
until their replacements began to appear at an alarming rate. For a
long time they collected and carefully stashed these new inventions in
the kitchen pantry, believing, I suppose, that at some point they would
come in handy. Perhaps they could be used to carry food to picnics.
Maybe they'd be useful to share food if someone came to dinner and
wanted to take food home. How could they know this plastic, like
almost all plastic from that time to this, would end up in the oceans,
killing turtles, dolphins, whales, and fish? And presenting major

health challenges to humans. All because it was used once, and thrown away.

My parents heated their homes, never more than three small rooms and a kitchen, with wood they cut and carried inside themselves, until they moved to town, where everyone used electric heaters and, in the chilly concrete rooms of the projects, ran them, in winter, almost all the time. Rarely feeling warm, even so.

My grandparents were even more frugal than my parents and lacked, for a longer time than my parents, both electricity and refrigeration. (All food was eaten fresh, canned in jars for winter or smoke and/or salt cured. In summer the favorite fruit, watermelon, was kept cool by placing melons under the bed, a magical hiding place, to me as a child, for the round, dark green treasure!) They had kerosene lamps which they lit just as darkness fell until, in their late sixties, they also moved to town. They, like my parents, grew everything they ate, except for citrus fruit, sugar, salt, and coffee, which they bought in town a few times a year. Like my parents also, they raised pigs and chickens, goats and ducks, and grew gardens of healthy produce that made them some of the best-fed people on Earth. They knew nothing of artificial fertilizer, nothing of pesticide. There was, as I recall, one major infestation of their garden, among the tomatoes, giant "tomato worms" that were carefully picked off the plants by hand. As children we chased each other around the yard with these worms, truly huge and scary to see, like miniature green dragons. The largest of them even had horns.

What I have learned, from these country folk and from my own life, is that it is not necessary to be rich, or even "well-off," to be happy. What is essential, though, is to have enough. Much energy might go into educating human beings about just what "enough" is. As a culture we, in America, have rarely seemed to know. Part of this ignorance is because we inherited the consumer-driven capitalist system, and paid no attention to the people of indigenous cultures already here who were more like my parents and grandparents, extremely careful not to waste anything. If my parents and grandparents had had health care that included even a yearly visit to the dentist, and if schools had been well equipped with teachers and with materials, and if work had provided a decent wage, our family would have been content, with a happiness that went beyond the mainly peaceful existence we managed to make out of what we did have.

Will we need to endure another war on American soil (of the many wars that have been fought here, it is the Civil War that most think of as war: the "Indian" wars—genocidal wars against the indigenous population—are largely forgotten) before we learn what is precious in life? Goddess forbid! And yet I think of a story a friend told about being in Nicaragua during the Contra war against the Sandinistas (the United States backed the Contras, alas); she said one day she watched a member of the embattled Sandinista government stoop down to pick up a paper clip that had dropped onto the floor. Nicaragua had been so impoverished by the war that there seemed nothing one could actually consider office supplies. She could tell by the look in his eyes that the paper clip was cherished. This was the most moving moment in her time of witnessing there.

This may well be how it is for us, so wasteful of so much, for so long! But maybe not, Nostradamus's prophecy of all-out nuclear war during this very period notwithstanding. Perhaps we can learn how to change our course in a way that means we, and all of Earth's resources, will not be consumed in war. War, which is perhaps the most blatantly unintelligent and unproductive activity that humans are engaged in. Of course there are others: a general waste of Earth's resources constituting a major, and unwinnable war, not only against our common Mother, but against ourselves.

The planet is fed up. The planet is tired. Of us.

My friend Bill Wahpepah, of Lakota and Kickapoo ancestry, used to come to my house exhausted from speaking up for Mother Earth, and would collapse on a bed in my guest studio, always sprinkling tobacco in honor of Her and saying to us: *Mother Earth is so tired. So weary. So disrespected and ravaged, I can hardly bear Her suffering.* Sometimes, in his sorrow, he would weep. It always felt as if he were talking about his very best friend as well as of his mother. He was. He died talking and singing and drumming to Her. Praying on top of mesas where corporations were strip-mining coal, or chanting beside pristine rivers soon to be polluted from every conceivable contamination caused by drilling, mining, "fracking," and other grotesque forms of ecological rape. He was always thinking of Her. Always in prayerful alignment. He was Her son; he did not forget this for a moment.

We must all learn to know Her as Bill Wahpepah did. To feel with her. To know She is alive. That she is alive and needing affection, caring, love. That She gives us everything. Who are we to give her nothing, but, basically, grief? Massive amounts of faith will be required: that we can change enough to be worthy of Her caring for us all these millions of years.

There is a bit of comfort in knowing that, having done all that we can, if we must go down, we will go down together, in heartfelt alignment, Earth mother and Her earthling children, hand in hand, doing our best to save each other from a fate that, unfortunately for us humans, is all too easily, without a drastic change of course, foreseen. And is already, in so many parts of the world, apparent.

I wrote the foregoing for a forthcoming book, Dream of a Nation, *edited by Tyson Miller, a wonderful book that offers innumerable examples of ways to help us evolve. It will not be used there, because another piece, containing poetry, was chosen.*

As I post this on February 24, 2011, Moammar Gadhafi is teaching the planet one of the lessons he was perhaps born to teach us: that war is the ultimate tool of those who have no faith in, or capacity for, reason, no belief that humans can settle differences nonviolently, as equals. It is an ancient and regrettable behavior that will, if persisted in, put the stability of our fragile planet in ever more desperate peril. War is as obsolete and nonsensical as the belief that by controlling a huge fortune, no doubt amassed on the backs of the poor, one can, in these days of catastrophic climate change, automatically be saved from fire, freezing, drought, earthquake, or flood.

Our outrage that a dictator turns his military forces against "his own people" must remind us that all people are our own. There is no one on Earth who is not us. We must hold this thought very dear, even if we find it hard most days to believe or even comprehend; or we will continue to oppress, degrade, mutilate, and murder our own selves, both physically and, perhaps most profoundly and destructively, psychically. And for generations to come. We now see in the lives of those harmed by war that war is indeed endless. It will take humanity the rest of its collective life to put a stop to it. But without engaging this work, if in no other place than the self, our species will continue to suffer a hideous distortion that is as unnecessary as it is unbeautiful and unwise.

The pain one feels for the martyrdom of the peaceful is great. What right has anyone to harm such precious courage? Courage demonstrated by brave humans who long simply to live their days in freedom and to draw breath in ease. We know these souls, these spirits, these hopeful, rising people. We see them, if we're lucky, in the mirror of our own lives.

Long live the revolution of wakefulness! No one need remain asleep.

THE CASE OF
BRADLEY MANNING:
WHAT ARE WE
CALLED TO DO?

MARCH 15, 2011

As an elder of color born and raised in the United States, I have dreamed of a day when young white men, en masse, might rise to take up the cause of freedom and justice in defense of those manipulated, oppressed, and stolen from around the world by our government. That time seems to be beginning. I am thinking of Bradley Manning, Julian Assange, and Tim DeChristopher, in particular. (Their names may be Googled and ten minutes spent considering their different cases.) Manning, a soldier in the U.S. military, imprisoned for leaking classified documents to Julian Assange of WikiLeaks; Julian Assange jailed for publishing documents that "endanger government lives and secrets"; Tim DeChristopher sentenced to ten years in prison for fraudulently bidding on pristine land in southern Utah in an attempt to save it from destruction by oil and gas interests.

Something transformative is happening here. We must rouse ourselves not to miss it.

Of special interest is the case of Pfc. Bradley Manning. Manning, a young man of twenty-three at the time, supposedly downloaded files that expose and elucidate the behaviors of leaders, dictators, and actors all across the globe; these files he, again supposedly (since nothing has been proven), sent on to Julian Assange of WikiLeaks who is charged with having published them. For this act, it should be noted, Assange has been nominated for the Nobel Peace Prize. I agree he deserves it.

For without someone having the courage to let us in on what is going on as people of power, prestige, and money play with our world, how are we to know if we have a chance of saving ourselves, and this fragile planet home that is becoming so obviously weary of sustaining us?

At this point in my life, any person in his or her early twenties is very young. And so, it is doubly hard to think of the following: that this young person, Bradley Manning, who has not been formally charged with anything, is forced, since last July, to live in a cell six by twelve feet, without natural light, for twenty-three of twenty-four hours a day. That he is manacled and shackled whenever he leaves his cell. That he is not allowed to exercise. That he is intruded upon every five minutes by someone asking if he is all right, and he must answer. (This is not the same as having someone to talk to.) That he is on suicide watch though resident psychiatrists have gone on record that he is not suicidal. That he is permitted to leave his cell for only an hour each day to go to a small room where he may walk but not run. He has no one to talk to. His clothes are taken from him each night and he must stand naked, outside his cell, each morning for inspection. There is more, but this is enough for adults and elders and awakened youth to wonder deeply about who we are as a culture, and as a country.

Is there anyone who deserves this treatment? Let us ponder together. Perhaps the people who bomb cities, poison water supplies, murder civilizations? Those who send drones and white phosphorus–laden missiles into apartment buildings, hospitals, and schools? Perhaps those who invade countries and rip off resources so greedily the indigenous children die of starvation before the age of five? Maybe those who make billions of dollars off a corrupt financial system only they understand, causing millions of people around the world to lose employment and become homeless?

Even in these cases, I would not agree the perpetrators should be humiliated, tortured, and abused, in the manner that Manning endures. Though it would help our spirits tremendously if they were brought even to the outer neighborhood of justice. I believe more than ever in the dignity of life itself, and that it is a profoundly mysterious gift. It is no one's place to knowingly and willfully degrade it.

In 2008, Barack Obama said something heartening about the role of whistleblowers: "Government whistleblowers are part of a healthy democracy and must be protected from reprisal. . . ." What happens when our leaders make such statements is that our young people believe them. Perhaps Bradley Manning thought an Obama administration would understand the need to expose the secret machinations of governments that keep so much of the world in error and darkness. Perhaps he hoped "We are the ones we have been waiting for" applied to him, in his role as sharer of what has turned out to be a Pandora's box of plagues and evils. But also of transformation and healing.

In any case, what are we to do about Bradley Manning, "canned" as he is in his tiny dungeon of a cell? Are we to let him languish there? Lose his mind there? There have been reports that his health and mental faculties are declining. Who are we if we let this happen?

Does it matter?

Have we reached a point where violence and abuse of naked, helpless people is applauded, not just in Abu Ghraib, but in Virginia?

The 4 percent of the human population of Earth deemed sociopathic may well have no problem with the inhumane treatment of Bradley Manning (and it distresses me that the officer in charge of Manning's "discipline" is a woman); perhaps to those who have no capacity for compassion the thought of this young man's torture (and not a very large or strong-looking young man either) causes no disturbance. For the rest of us, however, there must be at least a moment of considering alternatives.

We know that we—most of us, hopefully—worship freedom and love justice. We would like to see both, along with compassion and kindness, brought more forcefully into the world. We would be grateful also for tenderness and simple love. While we dream of these things that our world so desperately needs—a world awash in weapons and wars of all kinds, alas—let us cultivate within ourselves, and in all the horrid and repressive systems Bradley, Assange, and DeChristopher are likely to endure, the one gift each of us might hope to receive on our own darkest day: mercy.

Mercy, to be extended especially to Bradley Manning. Mercy, extended also to his grieving mother. For her suffering, as for that of Julian Assange's mother, there can be no final balm except exoneration and freedom for their sons. Justice for their sons, who, one instinctively feels, have fabulous moms.

It is a sad culture that punishes its children for doing what they have been taught, and believe, to be right. Perhaps Manning was taught long ago to love and protect his neighbor. To love the world and the people who inhabit it; to despise the lies that cause their suffering and destruction around the globe.

If so, he was not alone in learning this.

If he is, himself, our neighbor, what then? What are we called to do? This is the question whispered always in the ears of those who would be both merciful and just.

EVOLUTION

June 30, 2009

Dedicated to the Honorable Cynthia McKinney and everyone from the Free Gaza 21 movement now incarcerated in an Israeli jail. Your bodies are imprisoned but you demonstrate to the entire planet the joy and wonder of minds and hearts as free as the finch parents below, whose caring for their young reminds me this morning so much of what you are doing for the world. I send this to you through the air, a meditation on peace and the possibility of coexistence, with all my love and respect. May we all be free. May we all speak our truth. May we begin to know, whatever the hardship, that punishment is sometimes part of our reward.

WHEN WE ARRIVED AT OUR PLACE in the country this summer we discovered a family of house finches had made a nest in my old Kikuyu market basket that hangs on a nail beside the back door. When I was in Kenya in the midsixties I practiced carrying things in such a bag, made of raffia or sisal, the way the market women did: suspended by long straps from my forehead. This didn't work for me, and later when I bought the one I have now, in the seventies, I made sure it had shorter straps that meant I could wear it as a shoulder bag. I used it that way, off and on, for over thirty years. Carrying lip gloss, keys, sunglasses, shopping lists, and candy bars, all the trivia of the handbag, in its capacious elegance. Gradually its vibrant colors faded but it seemed as sound as ever, so I continued to use it to carry books and a portable typewriter, journals and lunches, finally even my first computer. Eventually, in its old age, I found the perfect use. Because it is light and sturdy, with leather straps as firmly attached as when it was made, I was able, by placing my arms through the straps, the bag on my back, to use it as a backpack. As a backpack it is ideal for going down to the garden for a quick collection of whatever's ready to pick, and then an energetic climb back up the hill to prepare whatever I've found for lunch or dinner. Or even for breakfast, since I enjoy spinach and collard greens in my morning smoothie.

I had counted on being able to use it this summer too. But no. It is occupied. The first day here, as we dragged out the deck furniture and snapped the tablecloth onto the table, I thought I heard an unusual amount of chirps and cheeps. I noticed two adult finches across from where I stood, watching me closely, hopping up and down, running back and forth, and shrilly calling each other's attention to the fact of intruders. I have to say that alarmed birds always make me feel outlandishly huge. I soon realized I must be between them and their nest. But where was it? Years ago barn swallows had made a nest just above the door, raising a family and eating at all hours of the day and night; their droppings made a grayish pile just as one stepped outside and so we all stepped quickly, coming in and out, hoping not to be hit. Understanding they preferred their location, I had a platform built for their nest that made a kind of porch, hoping that would catch the droppings. Instead, they were insulted by my gesture and, after they'd hatched their brood, never chose that spot again. It took a moment to realize the finches had found, for them, the perfect spot to hatch their eggs and raise their brood until they are big enough to fly away: my old market basket, hanging faithfully there on its nail, where it had hung throughout the winter. Sure enough, peeking in, and I'm sure giving their parents an awful fright, my companion and I saw a ragged little nest made of mud and straw at the bottom of my basket and in it, several pebble-size birds.

We decided to wait them out, and made an elaborate show of disinterest in the doings of the hatching basket. My cat, Surprise, was of course very interested, and was caught more than once too close for comfort to the basket, her watchful tail doing its slow, about-to-pounce dance. We moved the table, and the chairs, to a distance she could not negotiate. We were more concerned then about the safety of the tiny parent birds who were forever bringing food to their young. Hardworking and wary, they would hover for a long time, waiting for a chance to bring food to their babies, while Surprise was obviously thinking about bird chops for herself. Miles the dog was not a problem. He seemed to enjoy watching the parent birds and other visitors that came to drink water from a fountain shaped like a woman holding a bowl of overflowing water in her arms. We refer to her as the Goddess, and sometimes she is surrounded by dog, cat, hummingbirds, lizards, and dragonflies, as She, Goddess incarnate, benignly smiles and holds out her bowl of everflowing water to whoever comes.

One evening we noticed a wonderful quiet. Next morning, too. The baby birds have been taken by their parents, we said, peeking into the empty basket. They have flown away! We were happy for them. I was happy for me. Now I could have my basket back. Two days passed, cold days that made going down to the garden uninviting. On the third day we saw our old friends, the finch parents. Were they the same parents, or different parents? We couldn't tell. They were parents. They had that look of anxious industry we remembered from years ago, rearing our own young.

Oh oh, we said. Sure enough, when we peeked into the basket, another set of eggs!

I didn't think this was possible, my companion said.

I didn't think it was likely. But there they were. A second set of eggs.

And today, lots of cheeps and chirps, which means another set of baby birds. And there are the parents hopping onto the railing every five minutes with another bit of seed or wriggling creature in their beaks. We have been so hospitable, too hospitable, maybe. Yet, I really like it. That they've found my market basket hanging empty and made themselves a home in it. The air feels filled with flying creatures that take us for granted as part of their landscape; involved in their own dramas and journeys, they aren't particularly bothered by us. Maybe this is what coexistence feels like.

Cynthia McKinney and the Free Gaza 21 were released from jail in Israel and deported July 5, 2009.

BURSTING INTO LOVE

WHILE I WAS READING THIS I found myself swallowing tears, trying to hold in an impulse to burst into . . . total Love. I failed. It is the oddest, most stirring sensation to think of Mumia with his arms unchained and free enough to hug his wife, and later these two visitors. The whole day that he was scheduled to hug his wife, after thirty years, I kept bumping into things, imagining what that would feel like: thirty years! I am someone who loves to cuddle any and every hour of the day. Hard to fathom the cruelty of a sentence demanding this punishment. What it says about the punishers.

Who will hold them close? Who would dare?

And so, here is the latest report I've heard, and a photo. Mumia standing between two beautiful, hugging sisters. He does look young. He still has his locks and his smile, a smile from the inside.

Our work continues. *Besos y abrazos* to Mumia, A light in the darkness.

MUMIA ABU-JAMAL celebrates his move off of death row and to the general population at SCI Mahanoy in Frackville, Pennsylvania, with the executive director of the National Lawyers Guild, HEIDI BOGHOSIAN (right) and DR. JOHANNA FERNANDEZ of Baruch College, CUNY (left), on February 2, 2012. This was Mumia's second contact visit in thirty years. The first took place days earlier with his wife, Wadiya Jamal. Mumia's transfer to general population came after the Supreme Court allowed to stand, in October 2011, the decision of four federal judges whose past rulings declared Mumia's death sentence unconstitutional. Since this photograph was taken, officials at SCI Mahanoy have banned the use of hand "gestures" or "symbols" in photographs of inmates and their visitors. They have also banned the use of any "props" in photographs, such as the holding of a notebook.

LIFE LESSONS: GRATITUDE IS MY ONLY PRAYER

JULY 27, 2011

MANY YEARS AGO I WAS DRUBBED by a mysterious illness (later self-diagnosed as Lyme disease) that brought me to my knees. At the same time critics pilloried me: my work, it appeared, severely offended them. Moreover, my love life crashed around my feet. Still, one day, after years of being under a cloud of sickness and censor, I realized I was not only rising from my ashes, but shining. From that time to this I've lost the need for lengthy prayers. I have only one, but it is constant. Thank you, I say, before eating, working, moving. Loving. Thank you. It is enough.

These are other "life lessons" that have helped clear my path.

If you love doing it, it isn't "work."
I have written over thirty books, yet looking back I hardly remember the work it took to create them because I enjoyed writing them so much. It's the same with everything: I can spend two hours grubbing about in my garden, dazed with pleasure and intent, and it feels like five minutes. Therefore, before I embark on any new venture, I ask myself: will the joy of doing this make me lose track of any concern for time? If the answer is yes, I proceed!

A bad mood is temporary. So is depression.

I learned this when I was much younger. I used to be depressed quite often, a chemical imbalance made intolerable by my monthly cycle. I used to want to do away with myself. Somehow I managed to keep a journal during these periods, tracking every weird turn in my emotional life. Over months—possibly years—I discerned something quite interesting: my moods and depressions had a beginning, middle, and end. Aha, I thought, I need only learn to witness them and wait them out. This I began to do until, by my thirties, they were mostly gone.

To have peace of mind is to be wealthy.
(Also to know when you have enough!)

When I was much younger I thought people were made happy by the things they possessed. I also wanted things. I now have lots of things, and I enjoy them. But if they were taken away I could still be quite happy, though I might miss them. I've learned that things are not what make happiness, but rather a calm stability of Being and serenity of spirit. The peace I experience in my own mind is my most prized possession.

Love everyone and everything you can!
(They don't even have to know about it.)

I used to think the most important thing about love was to receive it. Now I understand it is more important to feel and to give it. That the good feeling we associate with love is generated by us, not by a lover of us. Their love is very nice, and I welcome it, but the feeling of actually generating love within one's self is so exquisite it almost leaves being loved by another in the dust! My greatest joy comes from loving everything and everyone I can. And it is amazing how big this can get! Daffodils, coconuts, frogs, catamarans, indie movies, dogs, bougainvillea, tribal art, snowstorms, old people, the Alps, chickens, my various "children," regardless of what they think of me, and so on.

When in doubt, find a nice hammock.

People who work hard often work too hard. I've learned to take time out and swing in one of the many hammocks I have wherever I live. From a hammock the world seems quite doable, especially if one is

listening to a good audiobook and having lemonade. From my hammock I send out good wishes to all of human- and animal- and plant-
kind. May we learn to honor the hammock, the siesta, the nap and the
pause in all its forms. May peace prevail.

This piece was written for a magazine in the Middle East.

WANDERING

THE UNIVERSE
BELONGS TO
EVERYONE

NOTHING MAKES ME MORE HOPEFUL than discovering another human being to admire. My wonder at the life of Celia Sánchez, a revolutionary Cuban woman virtually unknown to most North Americans, has left me almost speechless. In hindsight, loving and admiring her was bound to happen, once I knew her story. Like Frida Kahlo, Zora Neale Hurston, Rosa Luxemburg, Agnes Smedley, Fannie Lou Hamer, Josephine Baker, Harriet Tubman, or Aung San Suu Kyi, Celia Sánchez was that extraordinary expression of life that can, every so often, give humanity a very good name.

Thirty-odd years ago, I saw a photograph of Celia taken just after she and her fellow revolutionaries became the official Cuban government. She was in the uniform of the Cuban rebel army, thin as a rail, her dark hair cut very short. Her face was gray and drawn, and I believe she was smoking a cigarette, which I thought might account for the fact that she was frowning. After reading this biography I realized that lung cancer killed her.

I sat down to read *One Day in December* with little notion that it would affect me so deeply. I read it through, then immediately turned to the first page and read the entire, more than four-hundred-page manuscript again. I had the sensation I experienced the first time I saw a Frida Kahlo painting, probably the self-portrait of Frida wearing the necklace of thorns with a dead hummingbird attached to it: I knew life for women, and for a certain kind of creative rebel, whether female or male, a suffering, creative, and utterly devoted-to-life rebel, would never be the same. This book about Celia Sánchez is like that. Filled with amazing revelations and documentations of a revolutionary woman whose life, it seems to me, is exactly the *medicina* our desperately flailing societies and countries are crying for. A clear vision of what balanced female leadership can be, and, even more to the point, what a truly equalitarian revolutionary leadership between female and male partners might look like.

Yes, the male we're talking about here is El Jéfe. Fidel Castro. Revealed in this book to be brave and conscientious, also almost comically naïve at times, but unfaltering in his devotion and service to the people of Cuba. The most telling aspect of this was his adoption, along with Celia Sánchez, of numerous Cuban children, some of whom lost their parents during the revolutionary wars. Not only did they adopt these children but, during long years of assassination attempts and other social and political dramas of the most hair-raising sort, they managed to raise them. Amazingly Fidel and Celia worked together long before they ever met (sending covert messages to each other detailing the work to be done); when they did meet they remained inseparable (for the most part) until the day of her death. But were they lovers?

This is the question that obsessed Cubans and non-Cubans alike, while Celia lived. Reading this book one sees something so fascinating, so precious, so good for us, that the question loses all meaning. We are headed somewhere else (other than conventional marriage, for instance) in most of our relationships with each other (very good news in my opinion) and these two offer a model of a revolutionary partnership that actually *thrived*. Fidel and Celia were not "lovers" as this is traditionally thought about, though what they did in moments of privacy is their affair: he proposed at least twice and she seems never to have responded, except to build yet another lovely private space for him, attached to *her* domain. They were *beloveds*. Soul mates, *compañeros*, buddies, who reveled in each other and, together, devoted their lives to the cause of freeing the Cuban people from a brutal dictatorship while envisioning and working toward the creation of the New Person (sometimes referred to as "the New Man") and the New Society.

For much of the world Cuba already represents the future, if in fact there's one to be had. It has taught the world, especially the poor and First World–dominated countries, what it means to bear, over decades, the brunt of implacable, unrelenting, and lethal hatred—coming, unfortunately, in Cuba's case, from its nearest neighbor, the United States—and how to move steadily forward guided by one's own understanding of one's needs, even so.

The people in this book who were tortured, assassinated, and disappeared left me yearning for and missing them. The death of Frank País, for instance, a young schoolteacher of twenty who was the other commandanté, equal to Fidel in guiding the overthrow of the dictator Batista, and who was Celia's primary contact in the early days of the revolution, was murdered by Batista's police a month after his younger brother Josué was killed by them. Rosario, their mother, who claimed their bodies, is now dead herself, but I am still able to feel some of her agony. Or the two indomitable rebel women Clodomira and Lidia, who were tortured sadistically before they died in the custody of the police. Cuba has suffered so much I sometimes think of it as the country whose greatest wealth is the people's collective experience of deeply shared emotion. All those who struggled so bravely and died sometimes so horribly were passionately loved and appreciated by the revolutionaries they left behind. I believe it is the glue of this mutually endured history of so much suffering and loss, in the hope of creating a free and healthy Cuba, that, even today, holds the country together. In this book we see some of the cost of seeking to live one's own way, charting and being drawn by one's own destiny. Much of the world continues to grieve the loss to humanity of Che Guevara, assassinated so young and with so much still to offer, but he is far from the only astonishing person that is missing. These fallen heroes, women and men, young and old, many of them revealed for the first time in this book, are also cause to mourn.

Reading this story we see precisely why Fidel Castro adored Celia Sánchez and why Che and Celia were good friends. All three of these revolutionaries were persons of the highest moral character and integrity; deeply human also in their transgressions and imperfections, they were equals of the fiercest sort. There was also a price on all their heads. We see something else as well: that it can be said that the women of Cuba were equal participants in the revolution and perhaps its co-instigators. It was in fact Celia and Haydée Santamaria who, early on and with other women, took up arms to fight the dictatorship because poor children were being kidnapped for the "pleasure" of pedophiles, who were permitted and encouraged to flock to Havana to enjoy the spoils of a conquered and degraded society. In further reading, I learned that one such child, a ten-year-old girl, whom Celia had known, was raped to death. Celia, the daughter of a doctor, who frequently helped her father in his attendance on the poor, had no doubt seen evidence of this kind of abuse of children all her life; she was not prepared to endure more of it. This society girl, this high school beauty queen who moved to a little, out-of-the-way town (Pilon, Cuba), this woman who wore red lipstick, wide skirts, high heels (and would later wear high heels when she felt like it with her rebel army uniform), took to the Sierra Maestra mountains with Fidel and Ché and other revolutionaries no less brave but far less known, and placed her life against the killing machine of wealth and depravity that so insulted and wounded her beloved country.

I love this book: biographer Nancy Stout is to be congratulated for her insightful, mature, and sometimes droll exploration of a profoundly liberated, adventuresome, and driven personality. I love the life of Celia Sánchez, a life that was singular, sui generis, and true to its time of revolution and change in Cuban society, but also archetypal in its impact and relevance to all times of social struggle and revolt, including this one, in which Cuba's archenemy, the government of the United States of America, is also experiencing transformation. Such an intrepid woman warrior would have to exist in order to fight the demons that have overtaken us, and to lead the world back to its senses: a Durga. A Kali. A Celia.

Did we meet? I remember visiting Cuba for the first time in 1978. Celia would have been very ill by then; she died in 1980. I do recall a visit to the Federation of Cuban Women and, if I'm not mistaken, I met Vilma Espin, another remarkable revolutionary, and perhaps Haydée Santamaria, whom I had "met" in the story of the torture and murder of her brother Abel, one of those captured after the attack on the Moncada Barracks in 1953. I remember loving and admiring her for her reply to the guard who brought her one of her brother's eyes: *If he would not talk, nor can I.* Santamaria committed suicide shortly after Celia died: it is said that her grief over losing her dearest *compañera* was intolerable. I long to learn the story of these women, so beloved of each other, so trusted and so true. This story will no doubt be another medicine for our time: how to be completely trustworthy in times of battle; how to set out together, as women, to change the world, with men beside us (happily) or without them.

I wrote the poem that follows during the Arab Spring, when the people of Egypt rose up to begin the necessary change of their own corrupt society. It is dedicated to the Egyptian people. It applies to Cuba, as well, a country rich in martyrs. Celia, too, was a martyr, though she lived for nearly sixty years and died of "natural" causes, if cancer can ever be considered natural. I believe the deeply harrowing and stressful work she did as a revolutionary, including protecting Fidel, whom she loved, and whom she understood to be Cuba's rightful and destined leader, a leader always under attack, consumed her, as well as the grief she had to repress when certain other catastrophes occurred in her personal life.

OUR MARTYRS

When the people
have won a victory
whether small
or large
do you ever wonder
at that moment
where the martyrs
might be?
They who sacrificed
themselves
to bring to life
something unknown
though nonetheless more precious
than their blood.
I like to think of them
hovering over us
wherever we have gathered
to weep and to rejoice;
smiling and laughing,
actually slapping each other's palms
in glee.

Their blood has dried
and become rose petals.
What you feel brushing your cheek
is not only your tears
but these.
Martyrs never regret
what they have done
having done it.
Amazing too
in memory
they never frown.
It is all so mysterious
the way they remain
above us
beside us
within us;
how they beam
a human sunrise
and are so proud.

May the example of Celia Sánchez's extraordinary life strengthen and encourage us. She kept records of everything that others around her did during the revolution. In a way it is through this selfless wisdom, her caring about future rebels she saw coming to the place Cuba pioneered, that we most clearly see her.

12 QUESTIONS: KOREAN WOMEN'S SOUL QUESTIONS

By Alice Walker and Hyun Kyung Chung

October 7, 2008

Before going to South Korea, a few years ago, my friend Hyun Kyung Chung and I were asked twelve questions by South Korean feminists. Our responses became a book, *The High Spirit Love of Hyun Kyung and Alice*, that was a bestseller in Seoul. Women in South Korea were on fire to find solutions to their deeply challenging situation under what felt like a crushing patriarchy. I have chosen to leave our exchanges just as they occurred, because I see and feel the beauty of our collaboration, just as it happened. I have not yet seen what Hyun Kyung's responses were, though years have passed. Hers were written and published in Korean. It is my guess that women all over the planet are having similar questions put to them, and are questioning each other, about the direction we must now, as a gender, as a planet, take.

Dear Alice,
It was so wonderful to talk with you. I love your spirit!
   Here are the questions. I am going to translate them literally (and roughly due to time limit). Korean women (IFTOPIA) asked us to answer following twelve questions from our own life experiences and perspectives. Each question with twelve double-spaced page answers. They want to publish this book called Gift *on our big performance day. They want to spread this book as a*

conversation piece to open the dialogue between Korean women
in Korea and us. (Women from other stars.)
Fasten your seat belt and let us fly.
Hyun Kyung

1.

Let me ask you directly, can a feminist woman become a soul friend
with a man? I am becoming despaired. I do not think I can in this patriarchal world. Logs also weep like me in the fireplace.

Her ancient eyes look into my eyes. Yes, you can. I can see some men
evolve slowly everyday. I can see a man among them coming to you.
    From Hyun Kyung's poem "Alice Walker."

Can we become soul friend with men? Women anguish and cry out
that good men are hard to find. Do we have to lower our standard to
have a relationship with men? Do we have to make a big compromise
to stay with men? Or, should we change our direction and love and play
with women?

AW: Yes, it is possible. However, nothing, not even soul friendship, is
forever. I think women must look at relationships with men more real-
istically and less romantically than they have in the past. There are
good men in the world; many have been, as women have been, damaged by patriarchy. Most men are afraid to be who they really are, just
as women are. The imbalance of power stems from men's greater
physical strength; otherwise women are easily as powerful as men, if
not more so. I would say, in fact, that they are more powerful, because
women are endowed with strengths stemming from their ability to con-
ceive the progeny of the human race within their bodies. Women nurture and sustain the life force itself, using vast creative resources that
don't seem apparent in even the most developed men. Women can
think and give milk. How astonishing and powerful is that!
    We must learn to play with men. And to consider more of our rela-
tionships with men in this light. Women have been far too serious. I
myself have always been happiest with men who liked to play. After I
had a child in a marriage that lasted ten years, I was saddened to discover the playfulness, that I so loved, had gradually begun to disappear.

Looking back on that marriage, I saw that the first five years were a delight; the next two were okay, and the last three were unbearably tedious and boring. Even though we had a child together, I could not imagine continuing to live in a situation in which I felt suffocated. After that marriage I was in a relationship with another man who liked to play as much as I did: walking, talking, dancing, swimming, traveling, reading, and writing poetry to each other. We could spend entire days doing nothing but being together, washing and brushing each other's hair, bathing each other, eating together, going to the movies, going camping. It seemed we lived under the stars! This way of life suited my soul. The freedom of it meant I could continue to create, to write my books, and to be a more generous parent to my child. It was a joy to see this man grow, spiritually, intellectually, emotionally. He deepened wonderfully. Unlike in my marriage, we did not live together. This made all the difference. We tried living together for one week and saw it was impossible. So, for the next thirteen years we lived in separate houses. I am not convinced that men and women were ever meant to share the same house, though some people can do it beautifully. I was able to do it for five of the ten years of my marriage.

At the end of thirteen years, and after a lifetime of relating intimately with men, I knew I did not wish to continue my life without the experience of loving women. The man I was with was evolved enough to understand this; he loved women very much himself. However, when I became involved with a woman I found I did not want to dilute the experience by attempting to divide my time between them. Loving women, making love with women, was for me a spiritual calling. It was worship of the Life Force, of Creation, of the Great Mother, the Holy Feminine. It was also, of course, highly erotic and amazingly easy. Which I had not expected. In fact, once I got over the nervousness involved in making such a seemingly drastic change, I was shocked to discover how like breathing it was. I began to be lovers with women at the end of my fortieth decade. Throughout my fifties I had women lovers. I was very happy. Toward the end of my fifties, I once again loved a man. My most amusing discovery re: women vs. men lovers is that lovemaking, whether with a man or with a woman, is essentially the same. Women might have an edge, because we know our own bodies better; but men can be very subtle and knowledgeable, well beyond the stereotype of what makes a good male lover.

I have never compromised myself for long, whether with men or women. I have relied on my inner guide to help me preserve integrity and faithfulness to myself. Myself: this creation of the Universe who was made in the special form and Beingness of me. In my experience, fluidity is all. Study water, how it flows. Water goes here, water goes there, it retains and enjoys its essence in all settings. Women can be like that; in fact, I think we are, essentially, like that. We give birth to male children and female children. We love both, very easily. We tend to easily love our parents, who are male and female. It is this ease of relating to both sexes, and knowing both sexes come from our bodies, that makes having both male and female lovers feel completely ordinary and natural.

2.

It's so simple. Anybody who believes these two things, they are feminist: First, do you accept that women are oppressed in some way? Second, do you want to work with us to solve that oppression? Why do you make simple things so complicated?
From Hyun Kyung's poem "Sexiest Nun Alive."

Why do you want to live as a feminist? When you come out as a public feminist, people (especially men) avoid you and consider you as a problem. They call you fighting hen or troublemaker. There are so many women who cannot utter the word "feminist," because they do not want to be ostracized and alienated from their community. How long do we have to live this life under fear? Do we have to raise our voices in spite of this ostracizing?

AW: I created the word womanist for women of color, especially women of African descent (and actually, because Africa is the birthplace of humanity, all women are of African descent!). Specifically women who are culturally African American. I created it because I believe every culture has its own word for a woman who objects to her own oppression. A woman who believes women are human beings and deserve all the rights due human beings. A woman who raises her voice and her energies to fight oppression, whether in school or in the marketplace, in the bedroom or the theatre. Is there a word in Korean for such a woman? Sometimes it feels better to use the tool our foremothers, or we ourselves, have created. A word that is strictly ours, taken from our own culture. Not an import.

Having said that, however, I also affirm the right of Korean women to call themselves whatever they like, including feminist. Feminism after all is a word readily recognized around the world, and easily connects Korean women with other women no matter how far away they live.

In my own life, I have been severely criticized no matter what! If criticism can stop women, if being ostracized can stop women, then we have no chance of changing our societies. If even violence can stop women, we have no hope.

I think we must believe so deeply in the rights of women, believe so completely that our mothers deserved to be free, believe so deeply that our great-grandmothers should have been able to live their own lives, believe so deeply that our daughters must be strong and free, that we are willing to sacrifice our reputations, such as they are, in the eyes of people who deliberately misunderstand and berate us. Why would a woman wish to be with a man who avoids her for saying she wants to be treated as an equal and not as a servant?

3.
Leave Seoul.
Leave Korea.
Go to some other place in this planet
where you can reconnect with the star you came from.
From Hyun Kyung's poem "Sophia."

So many women in Korea have allergic reaction to Korea and Korean men. What is the remedy for this allergy? Is there any cure? Shall we leave Korea? Shall we get involved with men from other country? We want to hear from women like both of you who made an exodus from their own community to reconnect with their star. We also want to hear from you what you want to say to sisters like us who cannot leave, women without choice.

AW: I think it is fatal to assume we are created solely for the men (or women) of our own culture. I have spent many happy years with African American men, as lovers and friends. However, I have spent many happy years with men and women who were not African American. Life is rich! Life is varied! Life is alive! And as far as I am concerned, that is one of the miracles we are placed on Earth to discover.

The Korean women I've met are exquisite. How could they not be worshipped by Korean men? That is the question. As women, creators and carriers of life, I feel much worship is due. Instead, what we get, whatever the continent, is disparagement, diminishment, and abuse. We must turn away from this behavior, regardless of what turning away will mean. At the very least it will mean an increase in self-respect.

Also, when you realize that a loving, equal relationship with women is possible, there is an enormous feeling of plentitude, not scarcity. There are millions and millions of women in the world, just as there are men. To be limited in one's imagination to men is to me a great sadness. Meanwhile, life ticks by. Women, wonderful women, full and juicy (!) are left sitting prettily on the shelf. Men stroll by, disrespectfully, glance at the women on the shelf, talk with each other about how the women don't have the right color, hair, shape, speaking voice, height, nose, lips, odor, shoe size, etc. And the women of the world have been reduced to such beggary that they sit there on that shelf and begin with knives, scissors, bleaching creams, hair dye, deodorant, voice lessons, and so forth, to reshape themselves. Women must WAKE UP!

Men are not worth our suffering. And indeed, this suffering that has befallen women is not wanted by Creation itself. It is the absence of a strong feminine that is leading to Earth's destruction. We have become too weak and too preoccupied with the petty opinions of men to take proper care of Her.

4.

Why do you look so sad? You look
like someone else.
He has another woman.
I have been crying day and night.
Her compassionate wings embrace me.
Her oracles comfort me.

Romance and true love are different.
True love is only possible

When you do not need men for your happiness.
All my ex-lovers are my family now.
From Hyun Kyung's poem "Gloria."

So many women are melancholic because they can't have lover. And when they finally find lover and loving him, they are still melancholic. They marry, still melancholic, divorced, still melancholic. They choose to have a single life, but still melancholic. What are we doing wrong here? How is True Love possible where we can find true satisfaction and fullness of life?

AW: I feel I was put in the world to Be in and with the world. That the true relationship is between me and Creation, not me and a man. I think relationships between lovers are wonderful for their contribution to growth, but they should not obscure the fact that there are other kinds of relationships.

Once, a woman I adored had to leave me. Knowing I would be lonely, I went (with her) to purchase a puppy. On the night she left, I began to toilet train this puppy. I began to learn the behavior of this puppy. I began to feed and take care of this puppy. I missed the woman with all my heart, yet part of me was immersed in my growing affection for this little black puppy. Now that puppy is a huge one-hundred-pound dog. When I am home, we are inseparable. She is my friend, my companion, my teacher. I cannot imagine life without her. I talk to her; I take walks with her; she sleeps under the table when my friends come for supper. She snores through my Women's Council meetings. She eats snacks off the table when Sangha is held at my house. Everyone responds to her, knows her. Most people like or love her. How loving of my departed woman friend, I often think, to help me acquire her.

My dog is symbolic of all the connections that are possible. I also garden, passionately. I am deeply fulfilled by growing abundant crops of the plants I ate as a child. I love giving away large, platter-sized leaves of a special plant, the collard, that sustained African American people during and after enslavement in the American South. I now grow these plants to a size and a flavor that exceeds anything I've ever grown before. I am ecstatic that I can do this, even though, unlike my farmer parents, I was educated in literature, philosophy and the arts. I live a life that feels whole and circular. I am constantly in companionship with ancestors, many of them also gardeners and farmers. When I cook the food they planted and ate, I eat it using the taste buds of a dozen generations. It is exciting!

And I have women friends with whom I can discuss anything. For intense sensual connectedness to the Divine I have a vibrator. For cuddling I have enjoyed spending time with a big, warm-bodied man friend who wants to be the new man who loves women and is sensitive to their ways. This is a celibate relationship, and contentedly so.

The news around the world of men infecting women with AIDS should alert women to the need to create other kinds of relationships with men. Celibacy can be an excellent choice and can contain much sensual and erotic pleasure that is at the same time safe.

5.
Freedom is privilege of lonely women. Can you
endure loneliness?
I don't know.

When you receive the letter from future, you
become lonely.

But, aunt.
You do what makes your heart leap. You are right.
That's why my heart breaks so often.
From Hyun Kyung's "Price of Freedom."

Now many women refused to get married and decided to have a single life. But single life is not cool at all in Korea. Many women cannot endure their loneliness, a price of freedom, and go into marriage unwillingly. What is the nature of loneliness and true freedom? Please give us some advice for happy, solid single life.

AW: Sometimes my house has been my companion. Sometimes my dog has been. Sometimes the moon has been. Sometimes a single wildflower. Fortunately I have always cherished solitude. I was surprised to discover my own loneliness, which I felt most keenly when I was married and the marriage was not alive. Loneliness is; but it is not forever. It comes and goes like every other feeling. If you meditate, which I recommend, you can see this easily. Then its arrival will not frighten you. You say: Oh, Loneliness, there you are again. Come in. Have a seat by the fire. I was just wondering what to do with myself. And so you sit or walk or read or sing it out. It will not necessarily be lifted just because another person, especially a husband (!) is present. It is worthwhile for women to learn to be creative during periods of loneliness. I have made beautiful quilts when I was lonely. And sometimes the quilts turned into stories, or novels. Sometimes, sewing, I discovered a world unknown to me, revealed now in daydreams. Do not underestimate your own inner fertility! Do not overlook the richness of your own company! We are, as human beings, far more wealthy, in everything, than we know.

Once, in my fifties, I decided to study plant medicine. I have always loved plants and it seemed to me right that they should be able to speak to us and to help us heal our woundedness. We breathe because of them, after all! I sought out a shaman and began to practice listening to a particular combination of plants called ayahuasca. This medicine has been used by Indians, indigenous people of South America, since time immemorial. Imagine my surprise when, after taking this medicine, an entire world revealed itself inside me, and a teacher appeared, the voice of the plants (!), that immediately began to teach me incredible things about life. My outer world disappeared as if I was wearing lightproof dark glasses and the inner one bore no resemblance to it. Eventually I wrote a novel using some of this experience and the central idea is: there is no end to wonder! Women must take back their sons from the patriarchal death trap that thinks natural wonders are to be tampered with or destroyed. For the human race to survive, much effort must be expended by everyone to take back our children, daughters and sons, from a fatal vision of conquest of Life itself.

6.

I have a dream.

I gather all the people crazy
about life

and make one big household.

we do not have to live together everyday we do not
ask others to live for us.

pumpkin flower blooms beautifully as pumpkin flower. rose blooms
gloriously as rose
we all say truth of my own

but they do not become poison to others, heart we all eat
from our heart's content

but we do not make anybody poor.
From Hyun Kyung's "Gaia House."

When we are lost in every day's demands, we lose our imagination. We
do not like our everyday mundane life but alternative seems like a far
away story. It does not look realistic or easily come. We need to recover
our ability to dream again. Please share with us something about your
imagination of feminist Utopia.

AW: Amazingly, this poem, "Gaia House" by Hyun Kyung, is exactly
the plan I set out to implement after I left my marriage. I think this is
absolutely the right dream for women and I believe it is doable! I
bought a house with three stories. It was a small house, only twelve feet
wide. I invited my lesbian cousin to live on the top floor; I invited other
friends and relatives to visit us. My daughter had her room. Eventually
we would have added a dog and/or a cat. In fact, all my houses have
been roomy enough to accommodate many others, because I believe
we can share households in an equalitarian way. One of my oldest
friends from college days lives in such a cooperative household. She is
a single woman, and happy. What happened to my own cooperative
household? I became famous. After becoming famous in America it is
difficult to plan anything with others. All of one's energy goes into
staying connected to the source of one's life, one's creativity and joy.
   Today I am part of a Women's Council that meets each equinox and
full moon. We have been meeting for five years. I am part of a Sangha
(a Buddhist support group). This has met for three years. Out of these
two groups could easily come candidates for a cooperative household.
This may well happen, as we get older.

I would suggest beginning a circle of women. Meet regularly. Don't have an agenda. Get together simply to Be Together. Eat, drink, be merry. Dance if you feel like it. Lie about on cushions. Tell stories. Share secrets. Teach each other how to garden, how to build fires. But definitely do not plan what you are going to discuss or do. Whatever work needs to be done will be done without your trying to make it happen. This is one of the discoveries made when associating with other women.

7.

As women, we have more compassion for our mothers than our fathers. For some of us, our mothers are victims and our fathers are oppressors, a sad dualism. We also say, I will never live my mother's life! Many of us are wounded by growing up witnessing our mothers' suffering. What is the mother-daughter relationship? What can we do to make this relationship healed?

AW: My mother was wonderful, not perfect. She had her off days like any other woman. She suffered a great deal, hormonally and emotionally, from PMS, a condition I inherited. She was magical. She could grow any plant under the sun. She had an affinity for all that is natural and creative. My father had this also, to some extent. I have learned to have more compassion for my father as I've understood how men are crushed under patriarchy. He also had many tender feelings that he was not able to entertain or express. The feminine was suppressed in him. But not at the time he and my mother married. During their first years, when they had four of their eight children, my father was more mothering of their children than my mother. He loved to bathe them, sing to them, cuddle them, cook for them. But under the dual oppression of race and class oppression (being a poor black man under white supremacy) and under patriarchy, my father became more rigid and closed and masculine.

Lucky for me, my mother was physically strong. When my father tried to dominate her, she was able to stand her ground. She could fight, just as a man would fight, to ensure protection for her children and her own liberty. This characteristically self-respecting behavior deeply impacted my life. So much so that it is hard to imagine a lover or husband even thinking about abusing me. Whenever a partner has

disrespected me and no one has ever dared to lift his hand, I have, sometimes tearfully, changed my relationship to her/him. This is my mother's
legacy.

My daughter and I have inherited some of the problems carried over
from my relationship with my mother. When I was small, my mother's
condition was little better than a slave's. She had enormous fields to
sow, to weed, to harvest. Sometimes with my father, sometimes alone.
If she took me with her, I would be an infant crawling around in the
grass and dirt, where there were snakes, and other dangers. She sent me
to school when I was four. I missed her terribly. Later, in order to pay for
my needs in school, she held other depressing jobs that took her away
from home. She left home before sunrise and returned after sunset. I
could not complain of missing her because I could see she was doing
her best; telling her my feelings would have burdened her even more. In
my life, I have spent too much time away from my daughter; she has
missed me, just as I missed my own mother. This has created pain between us. For many years we barely spoke. Now we have committed
ourselves to speaking openly with each other about our sorrow. This is
the beginning of the process we hope will heal all the generations of
mothers and daughters in our family.

8.

Women have put tremendous effort to be beautiful. In Korea, going
out of your house without makeup takes enormous courage. Inner
beauty is considered as ugly women's excuse. Media bombards us to
become beautiful in some specific and acceptable way (cosmetic surgery, makeup, fashion, etc.). We all long to become beautiful. How can
we truly become beautiful?

AW: Happiness is beauty. Beauty is happiness. That is the true meaning of inner beauty. Women must unplug from the media. Shut off the
television, which is toxic. Shut out the billboards. Shut out all com-
mercials that seek to sell a better you. There is no better you that can
be sold to you by someone else. You are already the best, and how to
improve on this is a wisdom that grows from silence. Quiet time when
you can appreciate your essence, is essential. In the circle of women of
which I am a part we reflect each other's beauty. We treat each other
with dignity and cherishing. It is easy to see our delight in each other.

If someone took a photograph of us our radiance would be obvious. This circle is a foundation for each of our lives. No matter what happens to us in the larger society, there is a place where we are seen for who we truly are: women who have survived many terrible things; women who have created homes and families; women who are capable of protecting and sustaining not only ourselves but parts of our communities and parts of the world. We are women who speak up and speak out. Women who dance under the moon. Women who hike the hills. Women who swim the rivers. Women who honor the strength of women and understand the importance of having time together. Women who will fly thousands of miles to be present for Women's Council. We are our priority. Simply knowing this makes the whole world feel safer for human life. And not only human life, but plant and animal life, as well.

It is worthwhile to know, and love, your natural face. Your natural hair. To present your natural self to the world. The honesty of this is a tonic, a medicine, for society, even if it is attacked. The young especially need to see people who are not frightened by their own looks. Whenever one is tempted to hurt oneself in an attempt to be more beautiful, think of the teenagers in the West who are mutilating their faces and bodies through cosmetic surgery in an effort to look beautiful before their features and bodies have even fully formed. This is a madness that will spread throughout the world unless adults model gratitude for having a human body and deep appreciation and respect.

9.

What is the true meaning of women's independence?

AW: It is vital that women earn their own living. That money is understood to be important to a woman's freedom. To this end we must educate our daughters even more rigorously than our sons. We must have a material foundation that allows us, in any situation, to speak our minds. Only when women around the world feel confident enough to speak out will the world have a possibility of being saved. Women hold the key to everything; it is our voicelessness, which is tied to our lack of material wealth, that permits the degradation and destruction of planet life. We must awaken to the strength we have already: the strength to bond together as women; the strength to bring up our daughters to be articulate and aware; the strength to raise our voices wherever we are able to raise them, if that is only at the supermarket. Which is an important place, indeed, since most of us shop there and that is where most of our families' food comes from. Women are not powerless. We must cease to think of ourselves that way.

When we can speak, write, act from our hearts; when we can comment on any activity or person or behavior anywhere in the world; when we are not afraid to follow, with action, our ideas about how things should be; then we are independent, we are free.

On International Women's Day a year ago, I was arrested, along with twenty-two other women, in front of the White House. We were protesting the president's impending war against Iraq, which we opposed. Not only was this a vibrant political experience, it was also a deeply holy, sacred one. Just to be able to say NO! in this way was wonderful; NO to the bombing of human beings and animals and rivers and cities; NO to the terrorizing of children and their families. It was an extremely happy day, to be free enough, independent enough, to say NO to an atrocity which all the women knew would be a calamity for everyone on the ground in Iraq. This is the kind of happiness that can blossom when women cease limiting their activity to concerns about men and reach out to care for and embrace the whole world.

10.

Women's lives are filled with trauma, stress, and impasse. We are harassed by men in the subways, in our workplaces, and by life itself, etc. How can we get out of our trauma, stress, and impasse?

AW: It is time for women to remember who it was that gave birth to the first human being and then gave birth to all the humans who followed. Who foraged for food with her digging stick. Who later began agriculture so that humankind might continue to eat, even when the climate and the weather changed. We know how to improve a bad situation. It begins by gathering together, which is why feminism, Womanism, is so important. If there are dangerous places women must go, go in a group. Learn to meditate, learn to exercise. Become strong. Believe with all your heart that life, happiness, joy, this world, all of it belongs to you. Begin to walk with that conviction in every step.

11.

Most of the mythology we know of is about patriarchal God. Where are all these powerful and beautiful Goddesses hidden? Where can we find them? How can we discover Goddesses within us? Please tell us Goddess story.

AW: We ourselves are the Goddess.

I will tell you the story of how I finally understood what it was that I so loved about my mother. Whenever she was home, the energy in our house completely changed. Even the plants raised their heads; the cat was happier and stretched itself more. The dog was more peaceful. It was because she went from one place in the house and yard to another, touching this, whispering to that. Singing, humming, stroking. Often she carried a pitcher of water, which she poured wherever water was needed. And now I am able to feel this force in myself, in my own house. Some days I move about my house and garden, enchanted. For I am able to feel the Goddess in myself. She Who Brings Sounds of Reassurance; She Who Brings Sustenance; She Who Brings Peace. Whenever we, with love, tend to the world, whether that is our room or our garden or our children or our lovers, we become the Goddess. If you want to see Her, look in the mirror.

12.

AW: The title of my book is Anything *We Love Can Be Saved*, not Everything *We Love Can Be Saved*. It is a book that grew out of my forty years of activism. It means that if human beings can collectively love the planet, we can save it. Encouraging others to love nature, to respect other human beings and animals, to adore this earth, is part of my work in the world. Sometimes all that can be saved is one's sanity. Or, sometimes, all that can be saved is a precious open pollinated seed, a seed that will continue to produce plants because it has not been genetically engineered to self-destruct. Under male rule, much of life has been compartmentalized and separated. Our children grow up without understanding their connectedness to all the other children of the world. They have no feeling connection to animals or to plants. They are taught that torture of plants and animals is okay. They are taught to think human beings deserve to dominate the rest of Earth life. We must work to change this. It is essential that humans learn to love the entire planet as passionately as they love their own gardens. We must persevere in our appreciation of this wonderful place, Earth. We must never despair of Earth because there is bad behavior almost everywhere we look. If we look closely we see that spring continues to arrive. Winter comes with its refreshing snow. Summer stuffs us with its fruits, and its smells of sweetness and plenty. Autumn prepares us for rest. No bad behavior by any human being has ever stopped the changing of the seasons and their incomparable gifts to us. We must begin to affirm our good fortune, rather than our misfortune. The person who stands in front of us is the person we change the world with. We need never go very far. Beginning with our own selves is always the right place to start. Sit down, take a deep breath. Then another, and another. How can we save us, this world, in the madness of injustice, hatred, greed, and violence we witness every day?

The peace that the world needs can only come if we bring it within ourselves.

It will be a great trip to Korea. I can't wait. We will spread Goddess Spell according to Alice and Hyun Kyung to Korea. Be well and celebrate your beautiful self!

Love,
Hyun Kyung

ADOPTING AN
ORPHANAGE

October 12, 2009

ALICE THINKS AFRICA IS a magical and worthy Mother of Humanity, whatever may be happening there; and she has had the honor, and the pain, of experiencing Mother Africa in some of its most challenging situations. She has ceased trying to explain, even to herself, why the eyes and smiles of African children never leave her, or why the quiet strength and tender wisdom of African elders stir her emotions. Or why her friends, the writers and artists, musicians and dancers of Africa strike her as human miracles. Like so many contemporary people, Alice's ancestry is mixed—African, Native American, European—and yet it is Africa that seems to have a permanent call to her heart.

Alice went to Africa for the first time as a college student, in 1964, under the auspices of The Experiment in International Living. In a remote village in Kenya, she and her companions built a school for the local children out of sisal stalks, the only material available. Later she would return to Africa to research the practice of female genital mutilation (FGM), which led to a novel, *Possessing the Secret of Joy*; a film, *Warrior Marks: The Sexual Blinding of Women* (directed by Pratibha Parmar); and a book by the same name. She would return many times to monitor the advance of the abolition of FGM and to visit her friends.

Alice's belief in education is total, having been raised in a poor, highly intelligent family in which education was prized almost as much as food. Her parents led the effort to build the first school for black children in their community: it was immediately burned to the ground by descendants of slave owners who wished to keep tenant farming families ignorant. She has understood, since her first visit to Africa, how the West has used African labor and resources to enrich its own people, while leaving Africa with less than it needs to support and sustain itself. The "mystery" of Africa's poverty, its lack of a strong, well-educated middle class, has never been mysterious to her.

Alice has found the reality of upwards of 12 million orphans in Africa, whose parents have died of AIDS, especially hard to wrap her mind around. For a while she thought her obligation was to adopt at least one, possibly two, of these children. However, thinking rationally, this did not seem feasible, given Alice's age and her great distraction of mind, which has often been pointed out to her. Once, while in Rwanda, she met a young boy, David, whose mother, Vestine, she was supporting through the organization Women for Women International. Vestine's family had been murdered; Vestine has AIDS. There were four children living in a mud apartment whose dust was so thick that Alice, having spent only an hour inside, coughed for weeks afterward. David was twelve years old but looked five. He had never had enough food to eat. He was, in spite of all this, gorgeous, and he and Alice took to each other immediately. He owned only one toy, a truck so tiny it fit his hand; he could close his fingers around it. This toy made him happy, as did walking with Alice to the vehicle that carried her away from him. Take me with you, he cried. Alice didn't know how to take him with her, nor how she would manage to take care of him, if the Rwanda government would let him go. His voice, however, haunted her. It does still. It always will.

What to do?

Maybe instead of adopting an orphan, she finally thought, I can adopt an orphanage. And she tried a couple on for size. What was missing, in each case, was a sense of connection with the adults running the orphanage as well as with the children. At one orphanage in Kigali she was sent a bank number, for deposits, but no word of how she might learn the day-to-day activities of the children. Or see pictures of them. At another, pretty much the same. It was only when she met Kwamboka Okari, whose niece was already a friend of Alice's in Berkeley, and they talked over dinner, that she realized that, perhaps, she had found her orphanage. The Margaret Okari Children's Foundation.

Alice realizes that Earth is in dire straits, and that there is everything to be done, but she also knows the Earth is forgiving and very willing. If everyone does even a little, all that needs to be done will be done. This is clear to her from her own life as one small being from one small place in the world, but with a belief in service inherited from her parents, and a deep love of people, and a faith in them, that she apparently brought in at birth.

Adopting an orphan still appeals to her. After all, as we say these days: sixty-five is the new fifty. If one appears, she will receive it with joy. But if one does not, she is happy to be Auntie to any number of children in orphanages, having adopted the institution itself as guardian of the child.

COMING TO SEE YOU SINCE
I WAS FIVE YEARS OLD:
AN AMERICAN POET'S
CONNECTION TO THE
SOUTH AFRICAN SOUL

The Eleventh Annual Steve Biko Memorial Lecture:
University of Cape Town, Cape Town, South Africa

SEPTEMBER 9, 2010

Note: This written talk has been edited and amended to include
the names of additional writers I wish to honor. Also, it appears
there is more than one official way to spell Nkosi Sikeleli Afrika.
I have used the phonetic spelling based on the sound I learned as
a five-year-old.

Steve Biko:
I have spent most of the early morning thinking of what I want to say
to you: there is so much. First of all I want to say that I am in your
country, have been drawn to your country, the beautiful South Africa,
which for some years in our own struggle we referred to as Azania,
because of a deep love of you, of your heroines and heroes, of your
long, long struggle toward positive humanity for yourselves and for all
oppressed people on the planet. You have been a great inspiration to
all people on Earth who are interested in and devoted to justice, peace,
and happiness.

I was asked to provide a title for my talk and this is what came to me: "Coming to See You Since I Was Five Years Old: a Poet's Connection to the South African Soul." The reason I have been coming your way for over sixty years is because when I was five years old my eldest sister, Mamie Lee Walker, all of seventeen years old herself, came home from college her freshman year and taught my eleven-year-old sister and myself your national anthem, "Nkosi Sikeleli Afrika." (Sung.) We were the only children of any color who were taught this song in our tiny, totally segregated town in the Deep South of the United States, in Georgia; the somber, intense passion and dignity of the melody entered my heart. It has lodged there for the last sixty years.

It did not just lodge there, it propelled me into the deepest of curiosities about who Africans might truly be. Because, in the deeply racist United States of the forties and fifties, when I was born, Africa was shrouded in the most profound mists of distortion, racially motivated misperceptions, gross exploitation, and lies.

Africans were almost cheerfully despised.

Considered to be savages. Certainly.

And yet, for me, and for my sister Ruth, there was our sister coming home from college, whose fees my materially poor parents sweated to pay; there was the sound of "Nkosi Sikeleli Afrika." (Sung). "God Bless Mother Africa" was sung so earnestly by her loving sons and daughters, her horribly abused children, that it made an impression on our psyches never to be erased.

Here is part of the poem that goes with this awakening to Africa. In the poem I changed my sister Mamie's name to Molly.

FOR MY SISTER MOLLY
Who in the fifties knew Hamlet well and read into the night
And coached me in my songs of Africa
A continent I never knew but
learned to love
Because "they" she said could carry
A tune
And spoke in accents never heard

In Eatonton. [Our small town where we didn't actually live. We lived in the outlying countryside of Putnam County, which was far more beautiful.]

When I myself went off to college it was that song, "Nkosi Sikeleli Afrika"(Sung), that sound of so much humility, love, devotion, and trust that led me to the most important friendship I encountered during my student years—my friendship with an African woman named Constance Nabwire who hailed from Uganda.

From that friendship, and the understanding that Constance and I were sisters, developed my deep interest in and concern for Africa and its peoples, its animals, its rain forests, and its diverse cultures. Through the writing of Africans both male and female I began to encounter an intellectual and moral thoughtfulness that bordered on, and often embodied, the most astonishing profundity. I remember reading *The Concubine* by Elechi Amadi and *The Radiance of the King* by Camara Laye, for instance, and just being stunned. I would go on to read Ama Ata Aidoo, Buchi Emecheta, the great, troubling Bessie Head, the Ugandan poet Okot p'Bitek (part of whose masterpiece *Song of Lawino* would preface my first novel), Ngugi wa Thiong'o of Kenya, and of course the incomparable author of *Two Thousand Seasons*, Ayi Kwei Armah, who, years into the future, would become a friend.

It should not have been surprising that as soon as I found a way to do so, when I was around twenty, I made my way to East Africa, to the land of Constance Nabwire's birth, to discover for myself what made her such a wonderful person, wise and gentle beyond her years and certainly beyond that of most of the other girls at our school. I am happy to say I encountered a Uganda that bears little resemblance to the one we see today.

Uganda was referred to by Winston Churchill as the Japan of Africa, because of the people's courtesy and kindliness. This was a colonialist view, but even so. It was also a land of the greenest hills and valleys, where there was a palpable feeling of peace and patience with the stranger.

I was taken in immediately by a Ugandan family who sheltered and cared for me during my visit, dispelling forever any sense I might have had that I would not be recognized as one of Africa's children.

From this encounter in Africa, and later in Kenya, where I joined others in beginning the construction of a school, I followed my curiosity about the African continent in many of my works.

It was in Kenya that I first learned of female genital cutting. I was so shocked that I hid from this subject for many years. And then, because by now I knew I loved Africa, whatever was going on there, I set out to learn all that I could about this practice and then I set out to write about it as fully as I could. This I did in a novel called *Possessing the Secret of Joy*.

I was driven to find the answer to the question: why would any parents who loved them willingly hurt their children?

One of the things I began to understand about oppression, as I worked on this issue, was how the oppressor, whoever it is, will happily steal everything we have, but they will leave us our self-inflicted suffering. They will leave us, gladly leave us, our scars. And they will then help others define us by the wounds and scars we give ourselves. They will take all our land, our water, our minerals, and our dances even, and they will feel justified in doing so, but they will leave us with visibly very little, except that which is gruesome to outsiders and painful to those of us who must suffer it.

The resonance of "Nkosi Sikeleli Afrika" (Sung) is also deeply embedded in *The Color Purple*. Half of that novel is set in colonial Africa, among Africans, and explores what happens to the Africans as their land is confiscated by foreign rubber plantation owners/thieves. The discovery that Africans are enslaved on their own land is of grave concern to the African American missionaries who come to understand that they, too, in America, have been stolen from the African people and the African continent in the same way that the land has been. This is a horrifying realization and sends them into intense pain and grief. They are also awakened to the sham of their missionary mission to uplift the hapless natives.

Many readers fail to realize this, but *The Color Purple* is a theological text. It is about the reclamation of one's original God: the earth and nature. It is about reexamining that word that most colonized people are taught to loathe: pagan.

One who loves and worships nature, venerates and protects Mother Earth; one who cares for all of Her creatures with a degree of acceptance and tolerance. There is a built-in humility toward Nature that means it is respected for the very wonder of its being and that if a tree must be cut down, for example, one must beg its pardon.

This respect for nature is one of the biggest losses to African and other indigenous peoples since our domination and colonization by people who think about Nature entirely differently than we do—those unfortunate sufferers, in the northern part of the globe, from the ravages and hardships of the last Ice Age.

Nkosi Sikeleli Afrika (Sung), God Bless Mother Africa.

Hearing this song, learning this song, hearing your heart and soul coming through it, even as a five-year-old, how could I ever leave you?

And so I have taken you, your spirit, the spirit of Steve Biko, of Winnie Mandela, of Nelson Mandela, of the children of Sharpeville, completely into the very marrow of my bones.

In our own struggles to end American apartheid you have been with us.

In our struggles against nuclear weapons that threaten to end all of our lives, your struggle has encouraged us.

In the infinitely long struggle to affirm the rights of women, your example of never giving up, sustains us. For we have seen in your struggle the completely complementary nature of male and female solidarity in the pursuit of the common objective: freedom.

In my ongoing befriending of the other animals of the planet, it is your struggle that is part of my passionate defense of them. For who knows better than black South Africans what it has meant to be treated as if one did not deserve to live.

Another poem, from my very first visit to East Africa: when I didn't yet understand that while the white man was wantonly slaughtering almost all the buffalo in my country, he was also busily destroying the animals of Africa. I saw this in a shop window in Nairobi, but naïve as I was, I did not understand what I was seeing.

It is a short poem; if you blink you could miss it. Only this, a haiku:

Elephant legs
In a store
To hold
Umbrellas.

And today, when I write about Aung San Suu Kyi in Burma (Myanmar) or visit Gaza to see the devastation caused by the Israeli assault on a people under present-day apartheid laws, it is as if a tiny recording of "Nkosi Sikeleli Afrika" (Sung) is lodged in my brain.

And because it is there never ceasing, just as your desire to be free never stopped, I know that whatever disaster I am witnessing will have an end. The people of Palestine, like the people of South Africa, have a right to their land, their resources, their freedom. I know, from the world's gradual embracing of the South African struggle, that the same will be the fate of the Palestinians. And the why of it is simple: no lie will live forever. And when a lie is exposed—that Africans are merely savages, that Palestinians are merely terrorists, that women are basically servants of men or whores—there in the bright glare of our collective awareness it dies. When lies die, people live.

And that brings us to consciousness. And to Steve Biko.

Stephen Bantu Biko is known as the father of Black Consciousness in South Africa. He taught that black people must investigate and validate their own existence, irrespective of other people's opinions of them. That they must see themselves in the warm light of their own genius—the unique gift that they come into the world carrying to deliver to all of humankind. That they must have faith that they are made perfectly for the singular expression of the Divine that they are.

This is why one reveres Stephen Biko. Because, in short, he fully understood that the foundation of any true liberation is self-love.

And that reminds me of an earlier poem that I wrote about missing things like car keys, glasses, and where one parked the car. That short poem, in my book *Absolute Trust in the Goodness of the Earth*, is titled: "Where Is That Nail File? Where Are My Glasses? Have You Seen My Car Keys?" It is very short and goes like this:

Nothing is ever lost
It is only
Misplaced
If we look
We can find
It
Again
Human
Kindness.

There is also a lovely phrase from poet Galway Kinnell that comes to mind here: that "sometimes it is necessary to reteach a thing its loveliness."

This is perhaps where South Africans are, many of them, at the moment. Needing the rest of us who have been so deeply inspired and imprinted by your courage, dignity, and beauty of soul and body, to remind you of all this; to remind you of who you are.

It is with so much sadness that one reads about South Africa in recent news. As an activist, a revolutionary, a poet and writer, and yes, for all my daughter's criticism of me, as a mother, I am unable to comprehend how you now have a president who has three wives and twenty-odd children. A president who has been accused of atrocious acts and who seems to have little of the restraint in his personal life that would mean more dignity and respect accorded to his people.

I am by no means the only person in the world scratching my head over this.

I have been in your country for three or four days. Each day has brought a new disclosure in the news of rampant greed and materialism that quite takes one's breath away. There is news about the desperation of the poor. News of violence and despair. A lack of faith in the persons guiding the country. The feeling that perhaps people have lost the will to guide themselves.

Was it all for this? Was Mandela's incarceration for nearly three decades and Steve Biko's death from torture, for this?

For people fighting over mines they own not simply in South Africa but in battered and bleeding countries—i.e., the Congo, for instance—far, but not that far, away?

Perhaps my heart is heaviest regarding the Congo because I was recently there. As you know it has become known as the worst place on Earth to be a woman. And indeed, while I was there I witnessed what is happening to our brothers and sisters because of the greed that is devouring their land. On a level almost too horrible to contemplate, the people themselves are being devoured, sometimes literally.

I know I am not the only one in this room who remembers the beauty and dignity, the grace and eloquence, of Patrice Lumumba. That last view of him, his hands tied behind his back, his torturers attempting to force something into his mouth. His proud refusal to open to whatever it was. Then, the news later, that he had been tortured, had been killed. His body thrown from a plane. And then later, the colonialists placed another African in his place who was not bothered by the rape of his country. In fact, he profited from it. Is this to be the fate of South Africa?

Nkosi Sikeleli Afrika. (Sung.) (Sadly.)

South Africans of that era, as well as black activists in the United States, saw exactly what was going on, and we wept for the dream of Africa for Africans that we witnessed being lost.

All true revolutionaries, like Lumumba, love us. They want us to have abundant, joyful life. Tenderness, said Ché Guevara, is at root what revolution is about. Caring for each other, honoring the other in ourselves. Ourselves in the other. *Namasté.*

I have seen the hovels, the shacks, the unpaved roads, the unkempt children on one side of Johannesburg. And the mansions behind the highest walls I've ever seen around dwellings, on another. What to make of this? What to make of the words of your constitution where you profess such an understanding of the unique sufferings of the poor?

What to make of the stories one sets outside one's mind; they are so troubling: The young woman stoned, years ago, for admitting she had AIDS? The rampant rape and other brutality against women and children that appeared everywhere in the news? The disdain, often, for those who have fallen ill with a disease? The documented homophobia? The turning away of the "human face" Stephen Biko wanted us all to have?

And also there is this: my love for Winnie Mandela, whose voice throughout the apartheid years kept alive for millions of us in the United States the reality of the South African struggle. What happened there? we in the United States ask ourselves. Can it be that if she is guilty at all of any bad behavior it is because, being human, and having been treated, under apartheid misrule, worse than many of us can even imagine, she broke? And after giving us all of her love and substance for so many years, what was the new South Africa's response to her? If we cannot extend compassion to those whose lives prove their devotion and love, who are we that Life should smile on our stinginess of heart?

We do not understand, nor will our children ever understand, why a country does not have both its parents: its father, yes, but also its mother. Neither of them perfect, but both of them necessary for our birth.

It was deeply disturbing to many of us in the United States to see that Bill Clinton (who could not respond to the genocide of 800,000 Rwandans) and even de Klerk are going down in history as more honorable, more smiled upon by many South Africans, than Winnie Mandela. How can this be?

When I was shown the house where the Mandela family lived I was struck by the fact that this woman, this soldier, this "man among men," as Abraham Lincoln once said of the indomitable freedom fighter Harriet Tubman, is portrayed ironing. I have nothing against ironing—I don't do very much of it. But it seems a strange choice, lovely as Winnie Mandela looks while ironing, for someone who spent so much time harassed, firebombed, jailed, stuck in solitary confinement—200 days. Whose every move was monitored and contested brutally by white supremacist, Nazi/Fascist police.

It was outside what was formerly the Mandela home in Johannesburg that I heard a version of "Nkosi Sikeleli Afrika" (Sung) I'd never heard before. It came from the mouths of young men who were making a condescending parody of it while holding out their hands for money. Knowing that moment would live forever in my consciousness, I felt I, and the South African struggle, had lost enormous ground.

The African way with woman leaves much to be desired, and I am not faulting only the men. Some women are content to be potted plants. Here and elsewhere. But most are not.

I have a poem about this:

A WOMAN IS NOT A POTTED PLANT

A woman is not a potted plant
Her roots bound

To the confines
Of her house

A woman is not
A potted plant

Her leaves trimmed
To the contours
Of her sex

A woman is not a potted plant
Her branches

Espaliered
Against the fences

Of her race
Her country
Her mother
Her man
Her trained blossom
Turning this way
And that
To follow the sun
Of whoever feeds

And waters
Her

A woman is wilderness
Unbounded
Holding the future

Between each breath
Walking the earth
Only because she is free
And not creeper vine
Or tree.

Nor even honeysuckle
Or bee.

These stories of coldness, cruelty, and lack of compassion would make anyone doubt their people's loveliness. And yet, Nkosi Sikeleli Afrika (Sung), you are so lovely. It is this loveliness, who you deeply are. But you have forgotten, as so many of us have forgotten, that we are beautiful, and it is not all our own fault.

We have entered a period of such instability and impoverishment of spirit that even though they are charged with our soul care, our ministers, our teachers, our spiritual guides are in a state of fright themselves.

Never before has humanity faced losing the Earth itself, which is exactly what we are losing as global warming increases, and greater climate disasters affect us, worldwide. We are, all of us on some level, living with a degree of terror that humanity has never experienced before.

It is not so surprising therefore that there are those who feel the need to protect themselves behind vast barriers of wealth.

But such "protection" is an illusion. Mother Nature presents a very different kind of army than the ones we are used to fighting: the armies of poverty, colonization, weapons of all kinds; media doublespeak that keeps us confused. In fact, what is so chilling about Mother Nature is how indifferent She can be to who should be punished for the crimes committed against her. We are all being punished. And this is because we have forgotten one of the most basic of the things that made us beautiful: that we must never fail to have respect for her. And we must cease, at once, taking more than she is willing to give.

And here I will insert another poem from my collection *Her Blue Body Everything We Know: Earthling Poems 1965–1990 Complete*.

WE HAVE A BEAUTIFUL MOTHER

We have a beautiful Mother
Her hills are buffaloes
Her buffaloes
Hills
We have a beautiful Mother

Her oceans are wombs
Her wombs
Oceans

We have a beautiful Mother
Her teeth

The white stones
At the edge
Of the water

The summer grasses
Her plentiful hair

We have a beautiful Mother
Her green lap
Immense
Her brown embrace

Eternal
Her Blue Body
Everything
We know.

Nkosi Sikeleli Afrika: (Sung) God Bless Mother Africa.

I would remind you that this beautiful Mother of whom you sing and of whom I write, is not an intellectual idea. She is real and She is Nature. She is Earth. She is this world. She is the cosmos, the moon, and the stars. Grass and planets. She is your lions and elephants just as She is our buffalo and bears. She is the Everything of Life, our Mother. Our Goddess and God. It is this Everything of Life we must return to, bow to, protect, and nurture. It is largely because we have forgotten the beauty of our Mother that we have forgotten the beauty and wonder of ourselves, for we are one.

On a practical level, what is to be done?

I realized, during the Bush years in the United States, which were all but unbearable for many of us to endure, that we must in no instance rely totally on external leadership. That each of us has a leader within us; it is our conscience. One of the ways of developing this leader within is to sit during some portion of the day in meditation. Or in contemplation, if the thought of meditation seems too far-fetched. This is the time, all the old Africans knew, when the soul is permitted to catch up to the runaway body and the speedy, chattering mind.

During this state of inner development it is sometimes revealed not only that we are all connected to one another but that, indeed, we are one another. Our separation is largely illusion. Realizing this, there develops the intention of caring for the totality of Life, not just for our selves.

I have been a political, social, and spiritual activist for most of my life, and feel connected to peoples and struggles all over the globe. The foundation for this work, as an adult, lies in the circle of women (at times including men) I have instigated or joined. And this is the medicine, today, that I bring to you.

That at the moment, from what I read in the papers, your government is not listening to your cries for a new and better way to exist. That "democracy" of which much has been said, is still radically unclear to the people who still hunger and thirst. As well, the old methods of protest have left a great weariness and disappointment.

It is time to circle.

I advise that every one of you in this room call up between seven and eleven of your staunchest, smartest, and most thoughtful friends, and that you create of yourselves a circle that meets at least once a month in each other's homes. There, in the safety and privacy of that sacred space, enter thoroughly into dialogue about what you wish for and will work for in your country. There need not be a specific agenda. In fact, it will work better if there is not.

What I have found, especially with women's circles, is that when a certain number of women get together, leaving all agendas outside the door, whatever is most urgent gets addressed anyway. There appears to be magic simply in the willingness to tackle life's hardest problems from the humble position of being simply one among many in a circle of individuals caring for the common lot.

I began my writing life as a poet, went on to write seven novels, dozens of short stories and essays, volumes of poetry, children's books, etc., but now I am reembracing poetry as a priority, which is what, in my opinion, current movements for liberation and justice desperately need. Poetry is the lifeblood of rebellion, revolution, and the raising of consciousness. And it is the raising of consciousness that is the most effective way to ensure lasting change. About this Steve Biko was absolutely right. Once our consciousness changes, so does our existence.

I believe we must spread the idea of circling around the globe until all our circles merge, transforming the face of the planet organically. Making our public political leaders, those who refuse circling with the people, as obsolete as they frequently show themselves to be.

We are capable of leading ourselves if we can develop the capacity to listen to, to hear, what we ourselves believe. This will undoubtedly require releasing our attachment to many of our gadgets, which are drowning out our inner voices.

Last, I would advise you to dance.

Over a period of about a year I wrote a book of poems that will be published in the United States next month. It is called *Hard Times Require Furious Dancing*.

I believe Africans, who have suffered so grievously and who obviously have also experienced a great depth of joy (you see this sometimes in your smiles and eyes), have always known this. That this is why dance, like song, is prominent in the culture of all Africans.

In writing this book I revisited the times in recent years that my heart was heavy, nearly bursting with sorrow; times when losing family, friends, or the Earth itself, felt like more than I could bear.

And yet, just as springtime makes us forget about winter, my own love of the wonder of existence, in any condition or form, forced me to wish to celebrate Life.

And so I hired a band and a dance floor and invited friends and family to a gathering at which the only directive was: dance!

Times are hard. Everywhere. Mother Africa, also known as Mother Earth, is very irritated with us. We may be on our way to extinction as a species. I wish Her happiness in any outcome.

Hard times require furious dancing. Each of us in this very large room is the proof.

Nkosi Sikelel' iAfrika. (Sung with hope.)

And with all my love,
Alice Walker

Delivered in honor of Willie Lee Walker, father of eight, who exhibited as long as he was able, a courage and spirit like Stephen Biko's in the American apartheid South.

ST. JOHN:
THE LENNONONO GRANT
FOR PEACE CEREMONY

REYKJAVIK, ICELAND
OCTOBER 9, 2010

I HAVE AN ALTAR ABOVE the stove top in my kitchen that has been there for many years; it is the first thing I see when I make my morning tea. Frida Kahlo and Diego Rivera are on it; Amma, the hugging saint from Kerala, India, is there; also Che Guevara and Fidel Castro. B.B. King and Aung San Suu Kyi. His Holiness the Dalai Lama beams out at me, and Lakshmi, the goddess of abundance, lifts a flower; there is the face of a healthy, beautiful, caramel-colored baby girl, whose name is actually "Dream"; and photographs of Pema Chodron, the Buddhist nun, my mother—who remains my greatest inspiration and wisdom teacher—and me. Close to the center of this arrangement is a picture of John Lennon wearing sunglasses and his "I Love New York" T-shirt.

Sometimes people think he's Dustin Hoffman but I've never understood this.

In a far upper corner of my altar is a photo of Joan Crawford in her most fierce Mommy Dearest mode, just to remind me of some of the cost of everyone's hard-earned sweetness and light.

Like millions around the world I deeply loved John. I am in the habit of sainting people and I could easily saint John. I learned how to do this in Mexico. Near my retreat there, where I have spent part of each year since 1987, is a small town called San Patricio. I thought at first that this was because Mexico is a Catholic country and this designation had something to do with the church. It turns out, however, that this St. Patrick came to Mexico to fight against the Mexicans in the U.S. war's effort to take part of Mexico, which of course it did: California, New Mexico, Arizona, Colorado, Texas, Nevada, and some of Utah. (What it didn't take from Mexicans out West, it took from the Indians.) In any case, this particular St. Patrick, obviously of Irish ancestry, an Irish American, understood the unfairness of the battle and switched sides. He fought against the United States alongside the Mexicans. For this they honored him as San Patricio, a different kind of St. Patrick, and named a town after him.

To me, John Lennon was like that. Coming to consciousness, and then to activism, about the inequities in the world, not just on the various battlefields but in the homes and streets where women and children live. "Woman Is the Nigger of the World" is still indicative of a profound ability to change sides, and to see the world from the angle of the oppressed. His ability to sing his sadness and grief as well as his deep joy, especially the joy he shared with Yoko Ono, was enchanting, because in all his expressions he was so present and so pure. A true artist, yes, but also a rebel, a mystic, a sufferer, and a revolutionary. He seemed to understand completely that if we truly sing "the core" of ourselves we will reach the core of "the other" that is identical to our own, for all "the other's" tendency to hide. We hear this in the song "Mother," which, along with "Working Class Hero" is a cherished song of mine.

In addition to this, it was John who got me over my residual resistance to the possibility that a white man can be permitted permanent lodging in the nonwhite heart. When he was killed, my grief took me below my knees. I suffered well-deserved remorse that I had ever imagined John as someone whose whiteness might keep him outside my heart, when in fact all along, because of his courage, his irrepressible freedom and fun-loving spirit, his loving-kindness, not to mention his devotion to truth, he was fully ensconced.

I have written about this gift of realization John Lennon gave me in an essay. Such is the way of time that I cannot remember which essay or exactly when I wrote it.

I have also written about John and Yoko in a poem, "These Days," dedicated to "people I think of as friends." For, without ever meeting them, I have felt the sustaining friendship of John and Yoko. In their courageous living out of their unique and spirited lives, they have made a profound offering to the world.

Reminding us to live in freedom and joy, in love and surprise. To move forward with humor and hope. Making our own inimitable music and dancing as much as we can.

This is the poem, whose refrain is "Surely the earth can be saved. . . ." It is from *Horses Make a Landscape Look More Beautiful* and is in my collected poems, *Her Blue Body Everything We Know: Earthling Poems 1965–1990 Complete*. It is a joy to be able to read it aloud during this ceremony that marks what would have been John's seventieth birthday.

> These days I think of John, Yoko and Sean Lennon.
> Whenever I listen
> to "Working Class Hero,"
> I laugh: because John says "fucking"
> twice,
> and it is always such a surprise
> though I know the record by heart.
> I like to imagine him putting Sean to bed
> or exchanging his own hard, ass-kicking boots
> for sneakers.
>
> I like to imagine Yoko
> making this white boy deal with the word NO for the first time,
> and the word YES forever. I like to think of this brave and honest
> new age family
> that dared to sing itself
> even as anger, fear, sadness and death squeezed its vocal cords.
>
> Yoko knows the sounds of a woman coming are finer by far than
> those of a B52
> on a bombing raid.
> And a Kotex plastered across a man's forehead at dinner can
> indicate serenity.

Hold on world
World hold on
It's gonna be all right
You gonna see the light
(Ohh) when you're one
Really one
You get things done
Like they never been done
*So hold on.**

(Sung).
Surely the earth can be saved
by all the people
who insist
on love.

Surely the earth can be saved for us.

I did not mention this at the LennonOno Grant for Peace Ceremony in Reykjavik, Iceland, on John Lennon's and Sean Lennon's birthday, October 9, but my award will be donated to the Margaret Okari Children's Foundation that educates AIDS orphans in Kisii, Kenya. It will help with many necessary things: transportation, drinking water, school uniforms, the building of classrooms and dormitories, clothing, and food. What will the world receive for this gift? The beautiful smiles of some of the most beautiful and precious children on the planet.

I also failed to mention other spirits gracing my kitchen stove altar: Kwan Yin, the goddess of compassion in her most androgynous aspect, whose observation that "Tranquility has no boundaries" seems to me the essence of cool. A small porcelain Buddha lifting his robe to reveal underneath it dozens of little Buddhas in the making! Sekhmet, ancient lion-headed goddess of African Egypt: protector of Justice and of Healers. Emma Goldman! Who reminds us to dance as we revolutionize. There is also an Earth goddess, formed serenely by Earth of her own red clay, and surrounded by stones and bells.

---

*From "Hold On John," by John Lennon.

ABOUT AUNG SAN SUU KYI, MEDITATOR AND TEACHER

December 13, 2009

To paraphrase our beloved James Baldwin: the world is held together, really the world is held together by the love and compassion and clarity of thought of a very few individuals. Though this idea may be frightening, the world being in such distress, it is also comforting. At least there are a few people who can be counted on to lead us in a proper direction for survival as humans, and for thriving as a species. Aung San Suu Kyi is at the top of the list. That is really the reason she is jailed and on her way to being imprisoned in Insein Prison, in Burma, where conditions are notoriously horrific and from which inmates often emerge, if indeed they do emerge alive, broken, and in need of things like wheelchairs. What can we do?

My parents grew up in a society very much like Burma's, in the Southern United States of North America. Repression of every kind, for people of color, was the order of the day. They taught their children to hold an inner dignity as the highest possible sign of human development, and they taught us to believe in education. These are things that, when I traveled in Burma recently, I recognized immediately in the Burmese people. These people, like the Palestinians who suffer a fate remarkably similar to theirs under Israeli occupation, are holding a sacred thread, not unlike the thread of Ariadne, which we can use, if we lend our whole selves to the effort, to lead us out of the labyrinth of confusion, and away from the people-eating Minotaur that has turned out to be human greed. It is as astonishing as it is fascinating to see so clearly that it is our own greed that is eating us.

In Burma it is the greed of a faceless mob of generals who dream up ways every day to further ransack and impoverish the Burmese population and the land of Burma itself. Selling its precious woods, gems, and minerals, and routinely enslaving its people to work on "public projects" designed to enrich those in power. I am sure the junta viewed a recent film made in Burma by unbelievably courageous journalists, journalists with cameras, called *Burma VJ: Reporting from a Closed Country*, that thoroughly exposes their implacable brutality. In graphic detail it shows the relentless attempt by the generals to dominate and destroy the Burmese people. It depicts the soul-stirring solidarity of common people with the monks and nuns who rise in defense of them, and the slaughter of monks whose very chants, as they're bludgeoned or shot down, remind the Burmese people of their nonnegotiable belief in Non-Harming. This is one of the places I suggest we start: viewing and widely distributing and discussing this film. From the point of view that everyone on Earth is Burmese. Greed knows no nationality or boundary, and if we wait for things to change in Burma of their own accord, we will have abandoned what is most threatened in all of us: our human dignity and our freedom to pursue the life we choose for ourselves; in other words, democracy. Indeed, true democracy is what Americans, from all the Americas, are working toward. Largely because of centuries of greed and theft, we are far from the goal.

When I returned from Burma in February 2009, I wrote a long letter to Aung San Suu Kyi. I understood she might never see it; the point was to send it as a postcard for the world to read, for those who knew nothing or little of her situation, of Burma's situation, to have a quick study in preparation for the struggle to free her and to give her country back to her, and to the people who love it. As an offering to a contemporary view of a tiny part of Burma, by a North American, that I was able to grasp in less than two weeks, I offer this letter/postcard to anyone who wishes to read it.

There is also an Aung San Suu Kyi web page where one can find suggestions for actions. There is a petition that asks the United Nations to intervene. There are suggestions for places to contact and people to write. I personally feel we as a world have almost passed the following point, but I will offer it: it is time for people to descend en masse in places like Burma and Palestine and to . . . well, show up. Do I know how to get hundreds and thousands of people on this journey? No, I don't. But somebody does; it has been done before. People showed up en masse in Mississippi decades ago, and changed the direction of the world. Without the Mississippi struggle there would be no Obama, for starters; there would be no possibility of Americans, black and white, feeling the freedom and joy in each other's being that is so frequently the most pleasant and astounding surprise of the recent quarter century.

What makes Aung San Suu Kyi so very special—and Buddhists will yawn—is that she is a meditator. This means her mind is well trained to grasp the implications of actions, especially violent ones, too many of our world leaders seem clueless about. They talk about annihilating, obliterating, beggaring, starving, impoverishing, raping, and pillaging other human beings as if this behavior has no consequences to themselves or to those they represent. This is an incredibly antique way of looking at our problems: that we can bomb them away. War is a dead end, literally. And, what is more, we simply can't afford it. Not morally, and not financially. How long will it take the citizens of the United States, one wonders, to recognize that the house their country bombed in Iraq is the same one they were living in until it was foreclosed? We see, if we care to look, that everything really is connected, and not only connected, it is the same thing. Aung San Suu Kyi gets this, which is why she renounces violence in the face of one of the most violent regimes in the world, while at the same time not condemning those who, driven to desperate measures by their mistreatment by the regime, resort to violence in an attempt to defend themselves.

I can't think of anything more important than Aung San Suu Kyi's struggle, which she is waging so brilliantly. She has proved she is not afraid of death, and one feels imprisonment will be to her as being jailed was for Martin Luther King—simply part of a necessary pilgrimage of the soul. I am not as concerned about her, to be honest, as I am about the rest of us. We need Aung San Suu Kyi. We need her example of integrity, courage, a raging and revolutionary loving kindness that has kept her steady in her long years under house arrest. It is amazing to think of the discipline she has taught herself over these years: to see through the masks of even the most brutal dictators, and to discern the confused, unwell, frightened persons behind the masks.

To say, even after years of house arrest: I would hope one day to be friends. I would sit down and talk with them.

This is a rare being. But not too rare for this world. It was this world and the Burmese culture and life in India and England, and her own special spirit, that produced her. A spirit, for all its rareness, not of "heaven" but of Earth. Reading her thoughts, one finds nothing vaporous or otherworldly; she is among the most practical of people. Aung San Suu Kyi and the people of Burma are world treasures; if we lose them, we lose knowledge of a human capacity for wisdom, and an instinct for understanding our human responsibility for the gift of life, that will mean we may never know what, on this endlessly giving and radiant planet, a planet that bows to us every single day, we are doing here.

It is up to the citizens of the world to free Aung San Suu Kyi and all Burma's political prisoners, as well as the country of Burma itself. Our governments, bogged down with the accumulated mistakes of the past, and burdened by their own entanglement in greed, are not likely to be sufficient help, even when they are willing. We must remember as we look about the planet at people like ourselves who are oppressed and discouraged, that we are the majority. Sometimes the feeling of being very small in so large a scheme of suffering hinders us. But, take heart. Before the ice at the polar caps completely melts and we are all submerged, along with our dreams, we can do a lot. Especially if we can commit to do even a little. Once someone pointed out to Sojourner Truth how insignificant she was: a black person, a woman, recently enslaved. To paraphrase her acerbic rejoinder: If I'm only a flea on the back of the stubbornest mule on Earth, by God I intend to keep him scratching.

That we can do. Somebody who reads this, perhaps in China, Cambodia, Thailand, or Burma, will know how to be a flea on the backs of the generals in Rangoon. Somebody in Washington, D.C., may know how to do this. Each of us must find our own mule. Meanwhile, we cheer you on!

With metta, and in solidarity with Aung San Suu Kyi, and the brave people of Burma, especially the monks and the journalists!

SOLIDARITY

Letters

A LETTER FROM ALICE WALKER TO AUNG SAN SUU KYI: SO LONG A LETTER

DECEMBER 16, 2009

To Aung San Suu Kyi
Prisoner No. 1 of Thousands and Millions
Rangoon, Burma

From Alice Walker
In a Country With Its Own Afflictions
The United States of America

February 15, 2009

Dear Aung San Suu Kyi,
Two weeks ago my partner, Garrett Kaleo Larson, and I were in Rangoon, on your street, and passed by your gate. We looked over the barricade, constructed of wood and bamboo and barbed wire, at an upper-story corner of one of your buildings. We noted the sentries manning guardposts in the street on either side of your entrance, blockading your compound. We wondered where you were. I especially wanted to see you. Not even to say hello, but simply to see that you are well. It has been almost twenty years since you were really free, though the junta appears to let you out from time to time, simply to see if you have learned to behave. You haven't.

We had been in your country for a couple of weeks, traveling as pilgrims, bringing aid to those most harmed by Cyclone Nargis. We traveled also with Jack Kornfield, a teacher of Buddhism, who studied Burmese Buddhism in Southeast Asia many years ago. Jack is a member of my Women of Color sangha and a personal friend. Until recently he was the only nonblack person, the only male. He is a marvelous teacher, great storyteller, and, as shown by his willingness to sit with us for nearly ten years, a courageous human being. It was on his invitation that we traveled to Burma. Our group of fourteen visited numerous clinics, hospitals, and schools; we visited even more numerous monasteries and pagodas. I had no idea such treasures, for the inspiration and reassurance of humanity, existed.

On the way to Burma I had stopped in Washington, D.C., for the inauguration of our new president, Barack Obama. And while there, I co-hosted a program for radio and television called *Democracy Now! The War and Peace Report*. The goal of this show is to explore what is happening to democratic movements around the world, with emphasis on the challenges faced. Its host, Amy Goodman, had said to me when I mentioned going to Burma, that the junta had refused to let your British husband, Michael Aris, visit you during the last years of his life, and that when he fell ill with prostate cancer you could not go to him in England because this would have been used as an excuse to expel you permanently from your country. He died without seeing you and without your having a chance to hold him close in gratitude for what he meant to your life. I hadn't known about the cruelty of this separation, nor had I understood your decision to sacrifice the years you might have had with your children, who were young when you were detained in the eighties, and who are tall and handsome young men now. And yet, entering Rangoon, I began to see. And that is why I had to come to where you are. You are invisible in the streets—though my partner and I joked that some day Burma will be awash in Aung San Suu Kyi T-shirts—and you are everywhere.

We had been warned not to mention your name. Not because of what could happen to us—expulsion would likely be the worst of it, but because of what might happen to whomever we were talking to. As you know, your country is a place of spies and intrigues and sudden arrests and disappearances and is perhaps the most notorious country on Earth for arresting peaceful demonstrators, torturing them, and forcing them into slave labor, building roads and bridges and edifices the junta thinks will increase profits from its tourism scheme. It is also known for its illegal government's mowing down of peaceful, loving people, including students, monks, and nuns, who object to the rampant rape and pillage of the country and the Gestapo-like atmosphere that stifles all freedom to follow paths of creative activity and thought. Burma, with its fifty million incessantly monitored inhabitants, is sometimes referred to as the largest prison in the world. Not mentioning your name was difficult, but I accepted it as a practice. Having read that you lived on a lake, I noted two lakes on the ride in from the airport. I wondered if your house was across the water I was seeing and if you, that very moment, might not be gazing out on it too. Later I would see photographs of the part of your house that faces the lake and see that enormous rolls of barbed wire physically cut you off from it. As we drove down the streets of Rangoon I thought of you walking there, many years ago, when you were little, and going places with your brothers, or with your mother, Daw Khin Kyi. I was very moved to learn of how you returned to Burma, from your quite pleasant life in England: Daw Khin Kyi became ill, and would later die. You went home to be with her. I loved my own mother very much, and supported her during her declining years, but I never went back to the small country town where she lived to stay with her. A part of me will always regret this and see it as a failing, which makes what you did all the more remarkable to me. And then, Life caught you there. The Burmese daughter who'd strayed to democratic India and then to the West, never dreaming that in your country's time of greatest trial and need, you would be the one called to the test.

The junta has changed the names of places: Rangoon is now Yangon. Burma is now Myanmar. At first I thought I was resisting these new names because I encountered Burma, as a student, in the fiction of George Orwell, when Burma was Burma and Rangoon was Rangoon. But then I thought of other dictatorships, for instance in the Congo, when for a brief period it became Zaire: to blot out or cover over centuries of horrific murder and theft by changing the name of the place as if this then changed what had transpired. I was glad to understand, during our visit, that the people of Burma, not having been consulted about the change of names, tried to avoid using them, as most of us in our group did as well. I was struck by something the junta hasn't

changed: your father's tomb. You will understand that, as a visitor being driven through the streets of Rangoon, I rarely had a clue what
I was looking at. Still, the small statue of a person I took to be your
father caught my eye. I thought: who is that figure? Why does he seem
so solitary, here where the Buddhas might be taller than a house, and
where sometimes, as in the Shwedagon Pagoda, there might be whole
families of Buddhas. Your father in life, as in death, seems to have been
of a bravely independent spirit, impatient for an independent and uni-
fied Burma. He was an Aquarian, like Abraham Lincoln and other
leaders eager to live in a future that is at least fifty years away. When he
was assassinated, along with six of the other top leaders of the country's movement for unification and freedom from British colonial rule,
your country was dealt a blow as severe as that felt by your mother and
her children. Though you were only two when this happened, I imagine you could feel the loss through your mother's workaholic sadness
and heaviness of spirit. That she kept going in spite of her loss, that
she refused even to weep in public, says a lot about your parents and
what they were willing to endure for you.

When I think of Burma now, having returned home to the United
States, I am overwhelmed by the fact of its existence. It is such an unusual experience, being in your country, that there are almost no words
for it. And of course we traveled in what I consider the best way: putting ourselves at the service of those most in need, meditating at least
once a day in circle, visiting farmers and fisherpeople and listening to
the stories of their lives, enjoying their kindness and the deep humanity in their eyes, visiting monasteries and hearing teachings from ab-
bots and monks, and of course, shopping! I had not expected such
huge, amazing markets in which everything imaginable is on display.
Being Westerners we gravitated toward the clothing: old, colorful
pieces made by the hill tribespeople. So beautiful we were reminded of
our own Native American and African roots. Some items, like the
silver coin helmets the women wear, so striking we could not fathom—
assuming we bought them—on just what occasion we might put
them on.

I will just tell you of a few profound moments for me: the first was
in Mandalay. Mandalay is a word most Westerners recall from having
read Kipling a hundred years ago. But Daw Suu Kyi, as you well know,
it is real and it is still there! We had a room just above a moat that sur-

rounded a thick stone wall that enclosed the ruins of a palace. One day, leaving this idyllic perch—the moat is broad and green and a mile long on each of its four sides—we went to visit the over seven hundred pages of the Buddha's teachings. Each page, nearly as tall as I am, carved in stone, and in its own pagoda. So, hundreds of identical white pagodas! I think it was here, walking into one of the unlocked pagodas, and running my fingers over the Pali script carved in stone, I felt who the Burmese people are. A people who deeply value the Buddha's teachings, and hundreds of years ago made the decision to leave his precise words of wisdom for coming generations, ensuring guidance for all those sure to show up eventually, clueless and in need of help. Ah, I said to my friend Jack, who appeared to explore an open pagoda with me, the Burmese people are a people of devotion. In a group like ours, from all walks of life and from many kinds of trials and suffering, there was always somebody shedding a tear; this was my moment. My own connection with ancestors is one of my most treasured relationships—it is always my sense that, to the best of their abilities, they are looking out for us. To see this tender concern carved in stone, this blatant and enduring love for generations of spiritual descendants to come, got to me. I recognized myself as one of those provided for.

And then there was the visit to the countryside by way of the Irrawaddy River. Leaving our boat we trudged along a sandy track to the homes of local farmers who live in houses made of bamboo. First of all, imagine. We were a troupe of strangers, the majority of us white, suddenly appearing in their front yards. I tried to imagine my own response if such a group showed up at my door. We stood around looking at everything, speaking through our Burmese guide (who thankfully had arranged our visit, I learned later) and admiring their drying crop of peanuts—a favorite nut of mine—and their exquisitely beautiful cows! Each household had at least one cow and a bullock, used to pull the bullock cart that stood nearby. A cart artfully carved along its sides and with lovely spoked wheels that seemed unchanged since the Buddha's day. I rode back to the boat in one of these, marveling at the spontaneous gift of a single peanut a young girl had given me when she saw my admiring glance at the peanuts, as they dried in huge circles on the bare ground in their yard. I had not been so happy to see one of our group scoop up a whole handful and eat them, as if these farmers, so resembling my own family who were farmers, could easily afford to lose whatever he took. It was a Western moment, when our lack of awareness and even more of home training showed itself. I had noticed that Burmese people in general are very thin, but did not yet know that many are starving, or subsisting on one meal of rice or one glass of rice milk a day. My partner and I spoke with joy about the sense of presence we experienced in the cows. They were self-possessed; indeed, they appeared thoughtful and curious, sleek and vibrant and well cared for as they are. Their owners too seemed sincerely appreciative of them: a farmer, when asked to pose with his team, aligned himself next to them with pride. I was enchanted by their look of dignity and calm. We do not have cows like that any longer in my country. The cows here have all heard of hamburger and the billions sold. They've experienced the rush to become huge and saleable, they know about the slaughterhouses in action around the clock. May all sentient beings be free from fear, hunger, cold, and maltreatment of any sort: so the Buddha taught. And so we witnessed the contentment and sense of family human beings might have with the nonhuman animals, who share, and benefit, their lives.

It is sometimes difficult, enjoying an experience while traveling, and at the same time critiquing it. We were up very early one morning to go hot air ballooning over one of the most astonishing places on Earth: the ancient city of Bagan. In four gigantic balloons, operated by Englishmen, we gently floated up into the sky as the sun was coming up, gasping at the splendor of temples and pagodas in their thousands revealing themselves below us in the morning mist. First over a community of small bamboo houses, the people in them just waking up, glancing up at us and waving, then north toward the flat, blue, Irrawaddy River, the people's gardens stretched out along its banks: corn, peanuts, squash, maybe eggplant. Again I thought: how happy would I be to have strangers floating over my house, over my head? My honest answer: not very. I said to my partner how odd it seemed that the community over which we drifted had not a single pagoda; how worrisome, actually, that this should be so. One would ideally want the ancient ruins to be surrounded by people: children, goats, oxcarts, houses, the works. Separated, both the people's community and the historical monuments seemed deprived of life. This was before I learned the junta had forcibly removed the people from around their holy sites, to make the ancient city, many of whose shrines were built in the eleventh century, more scenic to tourists.

I thought of Mexico and its Day of the Dead, a time when attention is deliberately turned on the ancestors, and what they have accomplished is celebrated. I thought of the nights spent in the cemeteries, eating, drinking, praying, making music, being with one's dead. Showing by one's remembrance that one lives in perpetual gratitude. I would want this someday for the people of Bagan. That even a junta so greedy and unfeeling as the one they endure will not separate them forever from a major source of their inherited strength. Part of inherited strength is knowing who one is, whether the news is bad or good.

Imagine, Daw Suu Kyi, if you knew nothing of your father's heroism, your mother's fortitude.

The inauguration of our new president was glorious. It was also very cold. It would amuse you to hear of some of our trials getting into various balls, changing from warm clothing to ball clothing (I am not a ball gown kind of woman) in a tiny bathroom, not being able to find the right door of the building for the Green Ball and thereby missing my chance to introduce a wonderful man and writer, Van Jones, who has written a book called *The Green Collar Economy.* A book that is of major importance in getting our own failed economy on its feet, and, as I traveled through your country, I thought it might well have relevance to Burma. Your economy, as you know, is in ruin, as is ours, and has been for an even longer time. People need meaningful work; the country itself needs restoration and restructuring. The soil and water need protection. There isn't likely to be petroleum to fuel any of this. That leaves sun and wind. Water. The mighty Irrawaddy. When you are free, you will no doubt face this crisis, which Jones demonstrates is, in fact, an opportunity. I would send you a copy of his book if I knew how. We were happy to arrive safely at the Peace Ball, and it was wonderful to see so many faces of the U.S. peace movement still glowing after all these years. You will know of Joan Baez, who was there, still singing beautifully. Sweet Honey in the Rock, of whom you probably don't know, a favorite black women's group of mine, also sang. Harry Belafonte was there and Dick Gregory. I did not see Pete Seeger, the grandfather of the peace song, but maybe he was there. It's possible that none of these names will ring a bell, but these people and dozens more have carried the flag of peace, through song and story, art, poetry, and activism for many, many years. I felt honored to be among them.

Our new president is beloved by many, as you are. We know he is a mere human being, though a singularly courageous and sensible one, and not a magician. The United States is in serious trouble. It is not, however, in more trouble than much of the world has been in for a much longer time. One of the things I like about Obama is that he has lived in many places and he knows this. Which means he also knows the resiliency of humans, their ability to move when they have to, their courage to deal with dangers known and unknown. There are so many things to love about our country, though because of its racist and fascist past it has been hard to see them. Like millions around the world, my partner and I watched Obama and his family with much tenderness on that day of his swearing in. It has been a long haul for African Americans, as for you Burmese. And it is not over, just because an African American is president. In fact, walking by the bay near my own neighborhood in California days after returning from Burma, I encountered my first racist verbal assault on the West Coast. It was so unexpected I had walked on several paces before I truly heard it. In a neighborhood not far from mine a young black man was shot to death by a white policeman while lying face down, helpless, on a public commuter train platform. In Texas, white men with whom he had been drinking dragged another black man to death. Which is to say racist behavior is alive still in the United States. In some ways, because we are of different colors, there is a greater sense, I think, of knowing what we're working with. I can only imagine the struggle it must be to endure rabid, sadistic, sociopathic abuse by people who are Burmese, just like you, and claim to be Buddhist as well.

Because we had stayed in Washington for the inauguration, we missed our group's experiences in Rangoon. By the time we arrived in Rangoon, they were already in Mandalay. One of the places my friend Jack had not wanted us to miss was the Shwendagon Pagoda, where, in 1988, you announced your political party's candidacy for leadership of your country. (Later, when your party won the election, you and its leaders were arrested.) However, so much travel, so many time zones, and so much winter chill had left me with no energy to see it, except in the distance. That and Scott's market were crossed off the list! How-

ever, on our return, and just before leaving Burma, we once again had
an opportunity to visit this place. And that is where I saw some of
what I think you see when you look into the faces of your people. Our
people, for I would claim them too. With its sixty tons of gold for a
roof (which I suspect the junta will try to steal some day), its hundreds of Buddhas, its giant tree that guards the inner sanctum of the
shrine, the Shwendagon Pagoda is best described as a dream. I did not
remotely imagine such a place existed. Could exist. Nor will I attempt
to describe it further (and of course you know it well) except to say it
was as if all the temples one has read about or visited in all the ancient
lands on Earth were still fully functioning: people walking, meditating, praying, gazing at the Buddhas, bowing. Some people lying pros-
trate, their foreheads touching the floor. I will always remember Jack
disappearing for a few minutes and then returning with an armful of
roses, to offer to the innumerable Buddhas, each with a distinctly different face. You are so right to love your people and your country, Daw
Suu Kyi. Both are beautiful and rare and completely worthy of your
sacrifice.

And then, returning home, and reading your words: you do not consider what you are doing—holding the light for democracy in Burma
at such cost to yourself—a sacrifice. You consider it a choice! You
know how, when reading someone, you begin to cherish him or her?
That has been happening, as I read you. Like Gandhi, Martin Luther
King, the Dalai Lama, Amma, Fidel Castro, Wangari Maathai, Rigo-
berta Menchu, Desmond Tutu, and Nelson Mandela among others, you
are a tremendous mentor and teacher for this time. I must not leave Che
Guevara off the list, because, until the Aung San Suu Kyi T-shirt comes
into prominence in Burma, T-shirts with his likeness appear to hold a
liberated mental space for Burmese youth. We saw them everywhere. I
imagine it will be a matter of time before the junta recognizes Che's
face as a signal of resistance, and perhaps will jail wearers of these
shirts. It was also a delight to us to receive the elation, high fives, and
smiles at the election of Barack Obama as president of the United
States. If we had brought Obama T-shirts they would have been
donned immediately. Just as my partner and I immediately donned, on
arrival in Mandalay, the Burmese longyi, the wrapped and folded cloth
kilt or skirt that Burmese men and women wear. I had a couple of hilarious efforts getting mine to hang right: I thought the opening was in

back, not in front. My partner on the other hand wore his with dignity and grace from the very first. Because he is Eurasian he blended in quite well, in Burma, until he began to blow his trumpet one day at the tiny, dusty airport in Bagan, while we were waiting for it to open and our plane to arrive. There is something so American, and black, about the trumpet, especially when one is a lover of Charlie Parker, Miles Davis, bebop in general, and improvisational jazz, as he is. Our musical trio, that included a singer and guitarist, stopped the locals in their tracks. Frowning sometimes in wonder or bewilderment, their enchanted faces made us smile.

For a factual, easy-to-read overview of your life, I've studied *Aung San Suu Kyi, Fearless Voice of Burma*, by Whitney Stewart. I was glad to have the photographs of you and your brother as children and the handsome photo of your parents at the time of their marriage. They were incredibly good-looking. The courage you so gracefully exhibit as you confront the dictatorship is seen in the way your parents sit. The second book I've read, going back many times to immerse myself in its spiritual wisdom, is *The Voice of Hope: Aung San Suu Kyi, Leader of Burma's Struggle for Democracy: Conversations With Alan Clements*. I congratulate you on collaborating with Clements, a monk who has lived in Burma, someone deep and confident enough himself, and well versed in Buddhism, to draw from your depths a thoroughness and clarity that makes your conversations flow with political and spiritual nourishment. Every leader on the planet should read this book at least once.

On the radio this morning I heard the voices of Burmese refugees in India calling for your release and that of the thousands of political prisoners in Burma. Recently, as you know, the junta sentenced peaceful protesters to as many as forty-five years in prison. In response to the urgency in the refugees' voices, I decided to send this part of your letter now, since it is already quite long. I will send a second part later. There is still so much to "discuss" with you: why, for instance, do you not consider yourself a feminist? (I consider myself a "Womanist," or feminist of color.) What must humanity do with the recently acquired information that 4 percent of the human race is born without a conscience and is therefore incapable of feeling compassion? Do you agree with me that some of these people become the world's most brutal dictators? What is the remedy for the "hungry ghost" syndrome that is behind the raping of the planet: people who cannot, no matter how much they consume, feel they have enough? What role does the eating of curry play in a country that has at times very little food? This last may seem a frivolous question but I sense it is not, and made sure to be told how to make a good Burmese curry while I was in Rangoon, by a young man who drove us between hotel and airport.

I also hope "Daw" is the appropriate word to use in addressing you. I understand it is something akin to "Madame" or "Lady." And is a title of respect. I trust this is correct. We are nearly the same age, you are one year younger; it isn't likely, if we ever met, we'd call each other "Madame" or "Lady" but let's hope Life gives us the opportunity to see what we would do.

You will win your struggle for democracy and freedom, because you must, and in the process teach the world the useful, highly desirable, political and spiritual truths you have found, and that world leaders, especially, need to know. In the second part of my letter to you, I will focus more closely on your spiritual and political thoughts, which are priceless.

In gratitude and solidarity,
Alice Walker

Reading Amy Tan's novel Saving Fish from Drowning *is the most elegant way to bring most English-speaking readers up to speed on the ongoing situation in Burma. It is masterful, wise, sometimes outrageously funny, while remaining as serious as a heart attack.*

A LETTER ABOUT NATURE
FROM 2005

MARCH 23, 2010

A letter that offers thoughts on Nature. Perhaps it can be of use to those who, fearing earthquakes, floods, blizzards, and storms of all kinds, now find Nature less of a comfort and far less beautiful. I discovered it as I was clearing my computer of old files. Please overlook the writer's shoptalk.

Karla Simcikova
Mongolska 1427/14
70800 Ostrava—Poruba
Czech Republic

August 12, 2005

Dear Karla Simcikova:

At first I thought your name was difficult to pronounce, because it was unfamiliar to me. Now I see it is quite easy after I have carefully looked at it several times. That is how it is, I think.

Thank you so much for your fine book, for which you must feel no nervousness. It is beautiful and explores my work in just the way I have wanted someone to explore it. It is hard for some people, academics and reviewers especially, to let one grow, move on, remain alive. For many, *The Color Purple* is all they wish to consider. While for me, *The*

Color Purple, whose characters I love because many were inspired by my grandparents' and parents' lives, was a gift to ancestors whose gift back to me was *The Temple of My Familiar*, a novel much closer to my own ways and time, as you clearly grasp. And that, too, is the way it is. There is a circle always happening between life and "art." And one is forever being moved and moving one's self along the spiral.

I have only a few comments: Of course nature is "violent"—in the sense of frequently causing pain, destruction, or suffering—but my sense is that this "violence" is unintentional and more an expression of Nature's completeness than anything else. (I can feel this in my own being, when I wound or injure something or someone, not by design, but in the process of being me.) I would not become angry at a tree in the forest if a tree limb fell on me; at a bear that mauled me in the park; at a shark that bit me in the ocean, etc. Or if I froze to death in Antarctica or was done in by heat in the desert. There would be no personality for me to be angry at. Only an indifferent force, the same force that makes lilies and pecans. (Which I enjoy.) That is closer to what I mean. I accept all of it because all of it is so magnificent and amazing. Such a gift. And I try to avoid falling tree limbs. Renegade bears. Etc. When I was a child I was shot and partially blinded, by my brother, two years older. My parents (gentle, nonviolent people; though of necessity killing animals for food) bought the gun, knowing what guns do. He shot it, knowing what guns do. Unlike humans, Nature just goes on Being (a kind of ceaseless blooming), it seems to me, without any premeditation or inclination to behave outside its own Way. Does a snowstorm think about us? No, and it may wreak havoc and be sublimely beautiful. The freedom of this behavior awes me. (And is what it means, I think, to be God/Goddess.) My "insistence" on the "goodness" of nature is more correctly my insistence on my love of Nature. The truth is that I don't really care what it is doing—flooding, quaking, storming, freezing, wild things killing and eating each other, ticks biting—I still adore it. And I adore myself as part of it. I wish more people, all people, could feel this. When I see a windstorm I think: one day I'll be the wind in the storm! It's clear to me I'm not leaving the cosmos. I am home. The deep comfort of this, I believe, is what earlier mystics referred to as ecstasy.

I think the last line, "Let's all have faith in Walker," is not right. The tone is wrong for all that's gone before. Perhaps simply delete it? The faith we must have is in ourselves, and if after all this writing and thinking we're counseled to have faith in someone else, other than ourselves, then what I am attempting to share about my journey has not been understood.

I would only add for your consideration, though your book seems finished, that my greatest spiritual teacher was my mother. I believe this is true for most people on Earth; male dominant religions have been created to obscure this reality. I have been especially pleased that the Dalai Lama, almost alone among world spiritual leaders, credits his mother with being his primary teacher of compassion. My mother was of African, English, Native American ancestry, possibly also Irish and Scottish. So I could see race as defined under American apartheid was senseless. She was moreover capable of creating something out of nothing, or so it seemed to me, which made her a goddess even before I understood there could be such a thing. And like Buddha, when asked about the meaning of "this," meaning Creation, she pointed to her flowers. When one grows up, as I did, virtually wrapped in Nature, finding solace and freedom there, one does not have to learn to be a pagan, one has only to discover the word later in life. And so my spiritual journey has seemed to me to be about remembering what I already knew, which is how Buddha says it is! A huge comfort, that one.

If you don't mind, I will keep, for my archives, your manuscript. Or, do you wish it returned? I am in the country, having a wonderful summer, but can bring it down and mail it by September.

Blessed be,
AW

AN OPEN LETTER TO
NAWAL EL SAADAWI

FEBRUARY 3, 2011

Dear Nawal El Saadawi,
Remember when we met in Amsterdam many years ago? I was ecstatic
to meet you because at last I would be talking with an African woman,
a doctor, about the troubling practice of female genital mutilation occurring over much of the continent. A subject you had spent years of
your life courageously addressing.

Thank you so much for agreeing to meet with me then; we met as
sisters. Your thoughts on the subject, your books, your novels, your essays and articles, your biographical writing, all shed light on the North
African/Egyptian/African culture that for so many of us was quite mys-
tifying. Many people remain mystified, actually, and some will no doubt
wonder why I am suggesting Egypt is in Africa. It is simply astonishing
what propaganda can accomplish!

And that is what we're in for now. There will be attempts to tell the
world we did not even witness what we just saw: the most spectacular
demonstration of a leaderless and peaceful revolution the world has ever
seen. Our world, at any rate. A glorious illustration to all of us that we
can lead ourselves, irrespective of our leaders, and that as climate change
crashes down upon us, this is probably our only hope. While we freeze,
drown, fry, and/or starve, our leaders are likely to be in whatever their
version is of Sharm el Sheikh.

I have been so happy to hear news of the people forming brigades, joining hands to keep the area of protest clear of trash. That there is active recycling! We can of course carry this forward into political life: organizing ourselves, block by block, street by street, kitchen table by kitchen table. Because, really, we have no choice. If in fact we wish to truly live and not simply to exist.

I am humbled to think of your courage and inspired to think of your joy, which I heard ringing in your voice in an interview with Amy Goodman of *Democracy Now!* You are eighty, you say, with so much delight! This is the kind of view our world is pining for, as its people, men and women, who feel helpless to change the planetary spiral into violence, greed, and meaninglessness, turn instead to whittling on and camouflaging themselves. Like Mubarak, raven haired, who wishes he were not eighty-two years old apparently. Yet, as you demonstrate, what better time is there for someone to be actively, genuinely, beautifully old? And proud of it!

It's true I worry about you, out there on the streets of Cairo, in Liberation Square. But I understand too that you and the Egyptian people are aware that what you are doing, challenging a brutal dictatorship, is inherently risky, inherently dangerous. It hurts me to think you may not have seen the last of Egyptian jails, prisons, death threats, and periods of exile. I love, though, as you must, the feeling of solidarity with others who wish to live deeply, joyously, completely. All those who have dared to risk everything, in order to show up for the biggest moment of their lives: the moment of wakefulness. I too had begun to think the peoples of the world had fallen asleep. That they had been beaten down so far sleep seemed the best bet until actual death, eternal sleep. But no, we are awake. The planet itself, in my view, has awakened us. Mohamed Bouazizi is like the Universe's messenger, the planetary messenger, alerting us to the fact that we must move. And quickly. Without any kind of delay.

Earth itself is calling us to protect it. But how can we if we're set upon, held down, and oppressed by thugs?

On that day in Amsterdam, we clasped each other's hands, knowing we were embarking on a long journey into many kinds of darkness. And today, I again hold both your hands in my hands, and stretch them out as well to all those around you in Liberation Square. You are standing up for the collective, not just for Egypt, not just for Tunisia and Yemen and the Arab world; you are standing for us all who believe a better world is possible and that we have a right to experience it before we die. And before our planet loses all patience with humans and concludes it has had quite enough of us.

In solidarity and with much admiration, love, and respect,
Alice

TO WHOM IT MAY CONCERN: WITH SPECIAL ATTENTION TO THE PRIME MINISTER, ATTORNEY GENERAL, AND SPEAKER OF THE KNESSET IN ISRAEL

November 10, 2011

To Whom It May Concern
With Special Attention to:
1. The prime minister of Israel
2. The attorney general of Israel
3. MK Reuven Rivlin, speaker of the Knesset

From Alice Walker, American author and jurist for the Russell Tribunal
Cape Town, South Africa

November 10, 2011
It is with grave concern for MK Haneen Zoabi that I write to you today. It is my understanding that Ms. Zoabi is being threatened with the loss of her Israeli citizenship, even though she is an indigenous Arab who has lived in what is now Israel for all of her life. This does not appear democratic in the least, especially since this punishment is to be

meted out for the simple reason that Ms. Zoabi has expressed her human right to oppose oppression and destruction of the Palestinian people by Israel; and to speak publicly on their—and her own—behalf. Which she has done previously by joining the Freedom Flotilla to Gaza and more recently by appearing as a witness at the Russell Tribunal on Palestine in Cape Town, South Africa, November 6, 2011.

It is also appalling that the party, the National Democratic Assembly (BALAD) that would represent Arabs living in Israel, is banned. In what way is this silencing of over a million Arab citizens in Israel democratic?

The members of the Russell Tribunal on Palestine that met last week in Cape Town, South Africa, heard testimony from many people who oppose Israel's apartheid and persecution against the Palestinian people. It is chilling: the history of Israel's brutality against the people whose land constitutes the foundation of the state of Israel. The over 26,000 house demolitions, the countless assassinations, the huge number of murders, the theft of water and land, the arrogance and racism that I have personally witnessed on travels through the West Bank. Not to mention the devastation of Gaza which I also witnessed shortly after the twenty-two days of bombing by Israel in 2008–2009.

I was moved by Ms. Zoabi's testimony as well as the testimony of other Israelis, both Jewish and Palestinian.

Though it may well go unheard, I ask you to take care in your treatment of Ms. Zoabi and others of the witnesses from Israel. They are clearly some of your best citizens whose voices will be needed to steer a course for Israel away from its dishonorable course of apartheid and persecution of people primarily guilty of being in Israel's way to becoming a state that denies the rights of others while disingenuously and selfishly seeking to name and control everything for itself.

The world has awakened to what is actually happening, and has happened, in Israel/Palestine and people of the world are no longer mesmerized and held hostage by Israel's clever defense and mythologizing of its behaviors. We who were witness to the courage, righteousness, and passion of Ms. Zoabi as she testified before the Tribunal recognize her greatness. It would be to your advantage, if you wish to build a secure nation in which you honor all your citizens, to recognize this also. She loves her country and her countrypeople, both Arab and Jew. This she expressed with so much openness and beauty that many of us on the Tribunal were stunned. One of the things she said that stayed with us all is that what is of most importance to her is not a one-state or a two-state "solution" but that everyone, Arab and Jew, have the freedom to fully express who they are: that this might be the democracy suitable to both peoples after such a long and bitter and unequal struggle.

We were privileged to hold this session of the Russell Tribunal in South Africa, home of so much sadness in the past. Now struggling, imperfectly of course, to affirm its belief in a democracy that works for all its people. We received the supreme blessing of hope from the South Africans joining us at the Tribunal. Black, white, and colored. Their stories were no less horrific than those of the Palestinians testifying: the difference was that theirs are in the past. And, on their faces, one sees the peace of having won, at least to this point, a chance to work for a country that is just.

For the justice and peace all humans hunger for,
Alice Walker

SOLIDARITY

On Palestine

WE CAN OFFER
WHAT WE ARE

Headed to Gaza With
CODEPINK

DURING THE RECENT RUTHLESS ASSAULT on the people of Gaza when so many people were injured or murdered, I lost my own sister; she had been ill for many years. The loss of this one person, whose death was anticipated, was such a blow, that when I considered the losses to the people of Gaza—of mothers, children, fathers, brothers, uncles, cousins, and friends, I wondered how the anguish of so much tragic loss could be sustained. Housing, hospitals, nurseries, libraries, schools were also lost. Surely the blow to the human spirit would be intolerable for many, and there would seem little reason for continuing to live.

Going to Gaza is our opportunity (my partner Garrett Kaleo Larson's and mine) to express solidarity with the people there. To demonstrate the concern we feel each day for the suffering endured. To remind the people of Gaza and ourselves that we belong to the same world: the world where grief is not only acknowledged, but shared; where we see injustice and call it by its name; where we see suffering and know the one who stands and sees is also harmed, but not nearly so much as the one who stands and sees and says and does nothing. We can bring our witness, one of life's strongest gifts, as others have come to our side, witnessing our struggle, when life appeared impossible to bear. When all is lost, or nearly lost, tenderness remains, or could. We can offer what we are.

BOYCOTTS MUST HAPPEN
IN THE HEART

December 17, 2009

As a writer born in the South, both black and a woman, I've had my share of disagreements with the legendary white male writer William Faulkner, who, in the sixties, was quoted as saying if it came to that, he'd join the white Southerners refusing integration in the South and "shoot down n——s in the street." He was an astonishing writer, with the same intense fidelity to the psychic history of his terrain in Mississippi as Gabriel García Márquez has to his, in Colombia, South America. It was incredibly painful, and disappointing, to think of him in this light. I consider this disappointment, oddly, as I sign on to the boycott of the current International Film Festival in Toronto, which intends to showcase Israeli films in a celebration of Tel Aviv's one hundred years of existence, as if Gaza was not recently besieged and bombed, and as if no Palestinians ever lived in Tel Aviv.

Occasionally I visit black churches (for the infusion of color and culture from my Southern childhood) and I hear the same stories I heard as a child: of the Hebrew children, a.k.a. Israelites, still told with admiration to our young people in order to help them along Life's way. To be devoted, as Ruth was to her mother-in-law, to be brave and loving as were Jonathan and David, to trust in "God" and Moses and any number of characters whose stories were drilled into the consciousness of a captive slave population that was forbidden to read. It amazes me, in these churches, that there is no discussion of the fact that the other behavior we learned about in the Bible stories: the rapes, the murders, the pillaging, the enslavement of the conquered, the confiscation of land, the brutal domination and colonization of all "others," is still front and center in Israel's behavior today. I'm always struck by it, myself. In fact, going into Gaza recently to celebrate International Women's Day felt like entering that part of the Bible that I think frightens every child: the bloody part that everybody accepts because "God" tells them they have to, and any back talker is likely to be struck by lightning. Or turned into a seasoning.

When I perceive the knottiness in people's thinking that any discussion of Israel's behavior causes, I understand a deep battle is occurring re: denial and acceptance: denial of copiously documented crimes against humanity, on Israel's part, and acceptance of who many of today's Hebrew children, whose ancestors are so lovingly studied and relied upon by countless generations all over the globe, have turned out to be. As with my experience of William Faulkner, we are seeing a deeply disturbing side of the very people we've been taught to admire, and it is hard to separate actions we deplore from our feelings of familiarity, gratitude, and solidarity. Indeed, it has felt too far to many people who choose to remain silent in these grim times as if they are losing mentors and spiritual guides, as if they are losing friends. So effective has been the weekly indoctrination from our churches; so effective have been the centuries of propaganda.

However, over fifty years—roughly the amount of time it has taken to destroy most of Palestine and to replace it with Israel—is too long a period to indulge in moral fence straddling. It is bad for our health. Something must be done; and it must be done without bloodshed and without, hopefully, sowing more dragons' teeth. Which is to say, making more bombers, besiegers, and "warriors." Saying no to complicity, with a spirit that acknowledges suffering of everyone involved, is a good start. Boycotts were made for this.

What is good to grasp is that boycotts, to be effective, must happen in the heart. That is why, when the empty buses rolled through the streets of Montgomery, Alabama, in the late fifties and early sixties, and no black persons showed any interest in being on them, those of us who heard about it or saw the photographs wept. We realized we were one. A people. When the white supremacists arrested Rosa Parks, we felt her love of us. At that moment it was the strongest nutrient for our growth we could have imagined. We were young and seemingly weak, but we saw that we were cared about and represented, by her bravery, in the adult world, our value sanctioned. When Martin Luther King and Ralph David Abernathy and Coretta Scott King and others joined hands and said, You know what? We can do without whatever it is you're selling that is harmful to us, we were filled with joy. There is a connection that happens, when we make a stand; of that we can be sure. It is fueled by sacrifice, but the sacrifice is, ultimately, liberating. It is fueled by love, which is infectious. It is ignited by our determination not to lead the young into gray areas where it is easier to smoke a joint than to figure out why grown-ups don't speak out about wrongs that are apparent to everyone.

A Boycott Story: The Beautiful Israeli Sandals That Fit Me and Looked Great.

There they were; I was trying them on. They were fantastic. However, I live in Northern California where political consciousness is quite high and is likely to bring you down to earth when you least expect it. The saleswoman said apropos of nothing: Yes, they look wonderful on you. (Pause.) They were made in Israel. Oops. Who came to mind when she said that? Ariel Sharon? Netanyahu? Tzipi Livni? No. No Israelis at all. Who came to mind was a young Palestinian woman I had recently learned about; she had been arrested eight years ago and held in solitary confinement, in an Israeli prison, ever since. Never charged with anything. What did this woman do with her days? I thought. Could she possibly be the person who, in her cell, made these shoes? Suddenly, I could see her there in her cell. It felt cold. It felt barren. It felt lonely. She was all of these things, and more. Seeing her there, torn away from her world, made so strong an impression I lost all interest in the sandals. I could not even bear to look at them. I noticed her cell had a metal door and that there was a huge lock. I could never have purchased anything that would keep her there. I could only wish with all my heart to become a key.

I ended up buying a really boring pair of sandals made in Germany, and the irony of this didn't escape me either.

I walked out of the shoe store strengthened in some indefinable way; I had kept faith with the part of my spirit that knows what is right to do. As the people of the Toronto film festival know what is right to do. In fact, almost everyone knows what festivals in the past, festivals leading up to World War II, for instance, were used to accomplish. A slanting of the story to make the bully look respectable. History will repeat itself until we stop it.

The attempt to "brand" Israel/Tel Aviv as a benign place, through the propaganda of an International Film Festival celebration, is like pouring deodorant over a smell that has already escaped to the four corners of the world. In any case, I for one will never forget the smell of Gaza. Where the children, at this moment, are playing in the white phosphorous–covered rubble left after Israel's bombardment of their playgrounds for twenty-two days. I am thankful I cannot forget. Because, as Native American writer Paula Gunn Allen writes: "The root of all oppression is the loss of memory." If this is true, health for humanity will come from never doing to others what we wish to forget.

Faulkner will always have a place in my heart, for his extraordinary novels and stories, and his exceptionally long sentences. I will not permit him to take all of himself away from me because of words he allegedly said that are so unworthy of him. I prefer to remember that he also warned us that there are some things so harmful to the human spirit that we must not only refuse to accept them, but refuse to bear them, entirely.

Though I am unable to verify the information about the Palestinian female detainee mentioned earlier, which is worrisome to the journalist in me, there is an organization dedicated to keeping a record of Palestinian prisoners: the Palestinian Prisoners Society. The following is their report about another woman being held, without charge, in solitary confinement. I am especially grateful that this woman has a name.

Female Detainee in Solitary Confinement Since 2005
Thursday, July 23, 2009, 00:42
by Saed Bannoura, IMEMC News

The Palestinian Prisoners Society (PPS) reported that female detainee Mariam Tarabeen, a [female detainee] from Jericho, is still in solitary confinement in an Israeli detention facility for more than four years without any justification.

Tarabeen was kidnapped by the Israeli forces in 2005, and was sentenced to eight years, the Palestinian Prisoners Society (PPS) reported.

The PPS said that one of its lawyers visited Tarabeen, and that she reported that she is subjected to ongoing violations and harsh treatment by the guards.

She has been in solitary confinement for nearly four and a half years. The Israeli Prison Administration hasn't provided any justification for keeping her under solitary confinement.

There are an estimated 11,000 Palestinian prisoners in Israeli jails and prisons. There are reports of widespread torture of prisoners, women and men, covering decades of abuse. There is the placing of individuals in grave-like boxes for extraordinary lengths of time, beatings and denial of sustenance, and the forcing of prisoners to remain naked, among other horrors. For women there is a double bind: it is sometimes fatal for women in Muslim cultures to admit to certain "violations" of their persons, because, no matter the circumstance, they are blamed and severely punished for their own misfortune. By their own folks. This is almost unbearable to realize. The karma for this injustice for the entire culture is, to my mind, reflected in the suffering we witness in places where women have few or no personal sovereignty rights. And where men of conscience are too traumatized to stand beside women. Or where the men themselves are punished for taking a stand. To change all this will require all the courage the world can muster. But change it we must.

"YOU WILL HAVE
NO PROTECTION"

*Supporting BDS (Boycott, Divestment,
and Sanctions)*

JUNE 3, 2010

*The quote in the title is from a statement by Medgar Evers to civil
rights activists in Mississippi, shortly before he was assassinated,
June 12, 1963.*

MY HEART IS BREAKING; BUT I DO NOT MIND.

For one thing, as soon as I wrote those words I was able to weep. Which I had not been able to do since learning of the attack by armed Israeli commandos on defenseless peace activists carrying aid to Gaza who tried to fend them off using chairs and sticks. I am thankful to know what it means to be good; I know that the people of the Freedom Flotilla are/were in some cases, some of the best people on Earth. They have not stood silently by and watched the destruction of others, brutally sustained, without offering themselves, weaponless except for their bodies, to the situation. I am thankful to have a long history of knowing people like this from my earliest years, beginning in my student days of marches and demonstrations: for peace, for nonseparation among peoples, for justice for women, for people of color, for Cubans, for animals, for Indians, and for Her, the planet.

I am weeping for the truth of Medgar's statement; so brave and so true. I weep for him gunned down in his carport, not far from where I would eventually live in Mississippi, with a box of T-shirts in his arms that said: "Jim Crow Must Go." Though trained in the United States military under racist treatment one cringes to imagine, he remained a peaceful soldier in the army of liberation to the end. I weep and will always weep, even through the widest smiles, for the beautiful young wife, Myrlie Evers, he left behind, herself still strong and focused on the truth of struggle; and for their children, who lost their father to a fate they could not possibly, at the time, understand. I don't think any of us could imagine during that particular phase of the struggle for justice that we risked losing not just our lives, which we were prepared to give, but also our children, who we were not.

Nothing protected Medgar, nor will anything protect any of us; nothing but our love for ourselves and for others whom we recognize unfailingly as also ourselves. Nothing can protect us but our lives. How we have lived them; what battles, with love and compassion our only shield, we have engaged. And yet, the moment of realizing we are truly alone, that in the ultimate crisis of our existence our government is not there for us, is one of shock. Especially if we have had the illusion of a system behind us to which we truly belong. Thankfully I have never had opportunity to have this illusion. And so, every peaceful witnessing, every nonviolent confrontation has been a pure offering. I do not regret this at all.

When I was in Cairo last December to support CODEPINK's efforts to carry aid into Gaza I was unfortunately ill with the flu and could not offer very much. I lay in bed in the hotel room and listened to other activists report on what was happening around the city as Egypt refused entry to Gaza to the 1,400 people who had come for the accompanying freedom march. I heard many distressing things, but only one made me feel not exactly envy but something close; it was that the French activists had shown up, en masse, in front of their embassy and that their ambassador had come out to talk to them and to try to make them comfortable as they set up camp outside the building. This small gesture of compassion for his country's activists in a strange land touched me profoundly, as I was touched decades ago when someone in John Kennedy's White House (maybe the cook) sent out cups of hot coffee to our line of freezing student and teacher demonstrators as we tried, with our signs and slogans and songs, to protect a vulnerable neighbor, Cuba.

Where have the Israelis put our friends? I thought about this all night. Those whom they assassinated on the ship and those they injured? Is "my" government capable of insisting on respect for their dead bodies? Can it demand that those who are injured but alive be treated with care? Not only with care, but with the tenderness and honor they deserve? If it cannot do this, such a simple, decent thing, of what use is it to the protection and healing of the planet? I heard a spokesman for the United States opine at the United Nations (not an exact quote) that the Freedom Flotilla activists should have gone through other, more proper, channels, not been confrontational with their attempt to bring aid to the distressed. This is almost exactly what college administrators advised half a century ago when students were trying to bring down apartheid in the South and getting bullets, nooses, bombings, and burnings for our efforts. I felt embarrassed (to the degree one can permit embarrassment by another) to be even vaguely represented by this man: a useless voice from the far past. One had hoped.

The Israeli spin on the massacre, that the commandos were under attack by the peace activists and that the whole thing was like "a lynching" of the armed attackers, reminds me of a Redd Foxx joke. I loved Redd Foxx, for all his vulgarity. A wife caught her husband in bed with another woman, flagrant, in the act, skin to skin. The husband said, probably through pants of aroused sexual exertion: All right, go ahead and believe your lying eyes! It would be fun, were it not tragic, to compare the various ways the Israeli government and our media will attempt to blame the victims of this unconscionable attack for their own imprisonment, wounds, and deaths.

So what to do? Rosa Parks sat down in the front of the bus. Martin Luther King followed her act of courage with many of his own, and using his ringing, compassionate voice he aroused the people of Montgomery, Alabama, to commit to a sustained boycott of the bus company—a company that refused to allow people of color to sit in the front of the bus, even if it was empty. It is time for us, en masse, to show up in front of our conscience, and sit down in the front of the only bus we have: our very lives.

What would that look like, be like, today, in this situation between Palestine and Israel? This "impasse" that has dragged on for decades. This "conflict" that would have ended in a week if humanity as a whole had acted in defense of justice everywhere on the globe. Which maybe we are learning! It would look like the granddaughter of Rosa Parks, the grandson of Martin Luther King. It would look like spending our money only where we can spend our lives in peace and happiness, freely sharing whatever we have with our friends.

It would be to support boycott, divestment, and sanctions (BDS) against Israel to end the occupation of Gaza and the West Bank (Google for details) and by this effort begin to soothe the pain and attend to the sorrows of a people wrongly treated for generations. This action would also remind Israel that we have seen it lose its way and have called to it, often with love, and we have not been heard. In fact, we have reached out to it only to encounter slander, insult, and, too frequently, bodily harm.

Disengage, avoid, and withhold support from whatever abuses, degrades, and humiliates humanity.

This we can do. We the people, who ultimately hold all the power. We the people, who must never forget to believe we can win.

We the people.

It has always been about us, as we watch governments come and go. It always will be.

WHAT CHANGES THE WORLD? BEARING WITNESS TO THE TRUTH

Introduction to Palestine Inside Out:
An Everyday Occupation
by Saree Makdisi
(Norton paperback release, 2010).

JUNE 25, 2010

I CANNOT BEGIN MY SHORT prefatory note to this book without offering a silent bow of thanks to writers like Charles Dickens, Harriet Beecher Stowe, Frederick Douglass, Victor Hugo, and others who, like Saree Makdisi, have had the courage, patience, will, and love for humanity to endure the suffering of knowing what is happening to horrifically abused people in dire need of the world's attention, and to write about them. It has seemed to me, reading *Palestine Inside Out: An Everyday Occupation*, that only a saint could bear to contemplate such cruelty and diabolical torture as Palestinians undergo on a daily basis under Israeli military rule, and only a warrior of compassion, a bodhisattva in fact, one who vows never to leave the Earth until every suffering being is relieved, who could bring this knowledge to the conscience of the global community. It is a heavy burden of caring about millions of dispossessed and outrageously wronged people that Makdisi has delivered. It will be a mark of our own humanity if we step forward to help him, and others who care about the body and soul of our species, to carry it.

There were many times, reading this book, that I had to put it aside. It brought up too many memories of being black and living in the United States under American-style apartheid. The daily insults to one's sense of being human. Not just the separate toilets and water fountains with their blatantly unequal lettering and quality of paint, but the apparent determination of the white population, every moment, at every turn, to remind any person of color, no matter how well spoken or well dressed, or how well educated or in what position of authority in the black community, that they were niggers, objects of ridicule, contempt, and possible violent abuse. My parents dealt with this daily assault on who they were as human beings by rarely speaking of white people at all; this was their effort to protect their children from the most poisonous effect of an unpredictable and lethal domination, internalized hatred, which, they feared, might grow in their children as suicidal or homicidal violence, eventually turning on their parents, their communities, and themselves.

After four hundred years of enslavement followed by over a century of brutal harassment and soul thrashing by white supremacists who had all along wanted only our labor or our land (when we, African or Native American people, possessed land), this internalized self-hatred kept people of color in the United States timid and bowed down with feelings of unworthiness and shame. Like the Palestinians of the last sixty years, since the coming of European Jews to settle in Palestine after Hitler and the Holocaust in the thirties and forties, or like the indigenous people of South Africa (or Africa in general), my people (African, Native American, and poor European) could not fathom, for the longest time, what had hit them. After all, who could imagine it? There you are sitting by your own fire, living peacefully with your family and clan, never having harmed anyone (for the most part), praising and worshiping your own peculiar god. In comes a trickle, and then a flood, of strangers. First, you feed them, offer them a seat by your fire. Let them admire your little ones. Perhaps you generously teach them how to plant whatever grows around your compound. Perhaps you give them a turkey to keep them from starving in what they persist in calling "the wilderness." Perhaps you lend them a starter set of goats. Living in the lap of generous nature, speaking generally, there is a certain kind of greed and stinginess that is quite beyond your understanding.

Way back in Europe, though, your "guests" have come up with a plan to assuage their hunger for more—more land, more money, more crops, more food, more things to buy and sell—and drawn maps that have your "territory" on it like a large pie, and they are busy dividing up slices of it. You, sitting by your fire, your little ones clamoring for a bedtime story or another mango, date, olive, or fig, are not on the map at all. Coming back to your fire, the strangers smile at you, learn your language, as if respecting it, admire your culture. But you notice they've brought strange gadgets that they use to measure things. At first you and your neighbors laugh: these crazy people, you say to each other, why, they would measure even the sky! But soon you do not laugh, because they have measured a road that goes right through your living room. They have destroyed all the villages on one side of yours, already. You did not know, because you couldn't imagine anyone doing such a thing, and besides, you do not understand their language, though they, many of them now, certainly understand yours. Why should you learn the language of your guests, you think. For a long time it doesn't make sense to make the effort. And when you begin to understand that your guests are your enemies, it seems horrible to you to try to learn to speak their wicked tongue.

However, speaking and comprehending the language of your enemy, and that of your enemy's friends, turns out to be the key factor in this frightening drama, wherever it unfolds on the globe. And it seems to be unfolding, or already has unfolded, on every continent, everywhere. That is a key reason Western universities demand foreign language studies in their curriculums.

I think of my people: black people, red people, white people; none of them handled "the king's English" for a very long time. The Africans were not even able to speak their own languages to each other: members of the same tribe were never permitted to live together. No wonder they made a hash of English, which they no doubt hated entirely. The Indians, as eloquent as the Africans in their own languages, were assaulted with such ferocity that, even in boarding schools where they were forbidden to speak their own languages and forced to learn and speak English, they unconsciously mangled it, feeling it to be foreign and wooden in their mouths. The poor Europeans, though, to save themselves, learned to speak proper English, supported as they were by a system that favored whites. Advancement for them, as for the

Jewish settlers in Palestine, was unlimited, if they could blend in, accepting the spoils of war against the indigenous and enslaved, with those in power.

This is an old, old story, and it is a terrifying one. Can people who hunger so desperately for what other people have ever have enough? One thinks of Hitler, of course, and Napoleon; of the American generals who fought wars of conquest against Mexico and Cuba and the Philippines. Guatemala. Iraq. Afghanistan. And countless other places we may never hear of. Countless other peoples ground into the dust because their tent or hut, their children and their goats, sit on top of "resources" they've never imagined existed in the earth beneath them. The mapmakers have laid out the "territory" for their plantations: oranges, olives, peanuts, coconuts, rubber trees, cocoa. They've discovered where there's gold, or diamonds, or coltan. They've hired militia to see that you don't give them any trouble. They teach their soldiers to understand you are not really human, that they can do whatever they want with you, since what is really desired is your disappearance.

We must really ask, as humans, what is to be done about this hunger for more, this greed that is self-blinding. It isn't as if stealing from, humiliating, and murdering others means you have a lovely future for yourself. Far from it. The reason the scripture says "Do unto others as you would have them do unto you" is because our species, like other creatures in Nature, learns its behavior from each other. It's that simple. If the behavior that we use is abusive, violent, and cruel, then that is the behavior that will eventually come round again to us. That is why the world is encircled with wars, small and large, and why so many humans are mistaken in the belief that they can be happy having raped, pillaged, murdered, or destroyed someone else.

Happiness is what we really want, most of us anyhow. Peace. The ability and reason to feel joy. This cannot be had except by living these qualities internally, infusing them into our social structures and relationships. One has to decide, I think, what one's task is on the planet, now that we know the planet is sick of our abuse of it and can continue quite well without our ungrateful presence. And that is what this book demands of us: that we make a decision.

It is a hard read, make no mistake. You will think, while reading it: I did not know this! How could this be! Why didn't someone tell me! I was blissfully happy without such knowledge! And then too, I didn't realize I was paying—with my taxes (over a trillion dollars since 1948)—for so much suffering in a part of the world I never think about! You will think: Well, there's nothing I can do! It is too tangled, too insane, too entrenched, too threatening to my own sense of who I am and who "they" are! Holy shit, you may declare, this is more than one person can contemplate!

And you are right. Lone contemplation of any of the world's problems is passé. We must now contemplate everything that matters collectively. What is required, however, is that we bear witness to the truth of what has happened to us as humans: witness to the deformity of humanity that we see all around us on the globe, witness to the patterns of destruction whose roots are in our own construction as human beings, witness to the story of the mother's or father's or child's hurt and grief that will never make national headlines. This will require enormous belief in us as children of this Paradise, otherwise known as Earth. That we do, in fact, belong here, and have a right to be here, unmolested and protected in our homes, churches, mosques, synagogues, temples of whatever sort, and schools.

We are designed, I believe, us human beings, to instinctively wish to protect and cherish each other. We must be taught—those who are not born sociopathic—how to be stonily unmerciful. Bearing witness to the truth, however distressing, can be done by anyone, in whatever fashion this can be expressed. Out of that witnessing, which Makdisi's book allows any reader to do, will come something: a sharing, a thought, an effort, who knows what? But it will add to the energy we need to shift humanity back on a track that once seemed perfectly clear: that human life is a supreme gift, no matter whose life it is, and must be appreciated, defended, and honored at all costs.

NOTHING IS STRONGER
THAN A CIRCLE

Thoughts on the Russell Tribunal re:
International Corporate Complicity in
the Destruction of the People of Palestine

November 19, 2010

IN MANY OF MY TALKS TO YOUNG PEOPLE, to women, to peace activists, etc., I advocate that in these times of planetary disasters and instability people everywhere should gather together in circles of friends, in each other's homes, on a regular basis, to talk through the fears and challenges with which we, as a world, are faced: more frightening events at this time than at any period in human history. It is time to circle, I advise, with the hope that eventually our diverse circles will engage each other, merge, and organically transform the Earth.

I think of the Russell Tribunal as one of these circles, perhaps the most important, though its members may consider themselves strangers to each other. That they are not strangers is evident by their appearance, as a group, to take on the Tribunal's exacting and highly essential work: to cast the light of conscience on the behaviors of powerful interests and destructive players in the world community. This is a duty that calls out to those who understand how important it is to end our common silence about abuse and atrocities committed in our names, and who also realize that we must be determined in our efforts to care for the maligned and traumatized and oppressed of the Earth. That this caring signifies our awareness of membership in the same clan, the same family. The family of humankind—of which any oppressed person is the brother or sister, the mother or father, the child or grandparent—that is, at one point or another, of our lives, also our own self.

It has been an honor to be invited to join the present session as part of a jury hearing testimony on international corporate complicity in the destruction of the Palestinian people, who, since I visited Gaza a year and a half ago, have become part of the Earth's peoples to whom I have felt duty-bound to show up for. What has happened to them has of course happened to countless others. Including my own tribes: African, Native American, European immigrant. It is because I recognize the brutality with which my own multibranched ancestors have been treated that I can identify the despicable, lawless, cruel, and sadistic behavior that has characterized Israel's attempts to erase a people, the Palestinians, from their own land. For isn't this what the U.S. military was ordered to do to the "Indians" of America? Did not the British burn out communities of Scottish people and horrifically oppress the Irish? Did not wealthy and powerful whites, generally, for a time, rape, kill, capture, and/or enslave Africans? And are not some of their descendants, at this very moment, stealing and confiscating African and Indian and poor white land, and harming people and other life-forms, using many of their ancestors' ancient tools of brute force and deceit?

It grieves me that I am unable to be in this circle of brave and compassionate people for this occasion because of a mundane yet tenacious visitor: the flu. Which condition, as I recover, I can almost consider absurd. Since college I have admired the pacifist Bertrand Russell, the founder of the Tribunal, and also Jean-Paul Sartre and Simone de Beauvoir, early members. James Baldwin, as well, a person of such laser-like intelligence and moral integrity that it would have been a joy to sit in his symbolic chair.

But the Tribunal will go on: because it is a living part of all of us. That part that knows what is right. That part that really does not appreciate wrong. That part that is not blind. Not deaf. The part that hears the cries of others in distress because those cries echo our own internal expressions of shame, horror, dejection, and despair.

The Russell Tribunal is rare and precious and glorious, because it reminds us to act for ourselves, to follow our own conscience. To join with our fellow humans who are also awake. Or at least beginning to stretch and yawn. It is a treasure that makes the world not only more safe, but infinitely richer.

I bow to its belief in justice, fairness, and international standards of decency and law. The ability of humans to acknowledge and defend what is right and to do the work of holding the light in a world that seems at times to be sliding inexorably into the darkness. All that is ever needed to challenge that darkness is one light. May each of us, following the Tribunal's example, be that light, however small and flickering, wherever we find ourselves.

Postscript: The First Day of Spring, 2011
Northern California

And when we bring our flickering candles together, what happens?

Like much of the world I watched with intense hope and emotion the unfolding of the Egyptian uprising that began January 25, 2011. Would the people stand their ground in the face of a cruel dictator's efforts to frighten, batter, torture, and destroy them? Would they look at the bodies falling around them and, sickened and afraid, fade back into the shadows? Shadows with which all oppressed people are familiar: the backstreets of nonbelonging, nonbeing; the dark corners of being hungry, insufficiently housed and clothed; the dim corners of being denied education and therefore intellectual stature and light; the literal dungeons of underground torture chambers.

There were moments when it was almost unbearable to watch the Egyptian people's sincere and principled revolt that has, by its example of peacefulness and dignity, transformed and renewed the spirit of creative resistance around the globe. I did watch and listen, however, to every sight, every sound, relying especially on the guidance of a young Egyptian American broadcast journalist, Sharif Abdel Kouddous, who was inspiring in his courageous determination to do justice to the unfolding drama of the Egyptian people in perhaps their finest hour, and who is a member of the astonishingly thorough and savvy team of journalists and producers at *Democracy Now!* in the United States. Many times I could not hold back tears of joy, to see so many people, sick of their own oppression, get off their knees, climb out of the shadows, and rise.

I felt I knew them. Their willingness to sacrifice themselves for the future of their children, culture, and country felt familiar to me. I have seen this same courage among African Americans, in our struggle for dignity and equal rights; I have seen it in the lives of Native Americans, whose long struggle not only to free themselves but also Mother Earth from aggression and defilement has been a life-enhancing example for me. The images of people praying, singing, weeping, suffering, dying: these are now, thanks to the people of Egypt, relics to be referred to, touched, reviewed, cherished, to give us strength for the road ahead.

I think of events like this uprising as "a human sunrise." My faith is always in the people and in our ability to create this. In that spirit I offer poems. For it is poetry that, like music, dance, theatre, and art, generally, can send us beyond the edge of our fear. These poems encourage us to look deeply into what kind of world it is we wish to construct, as we rightfully demolish the old one.

I wrote the first three poems decades ago to commemorate what can happen when hope is lost and a revolution in the making begins, for whatever reasons, to sour. The soured revolution is unfortunately common; mistrust, greed, internecine squabbling, and warfare usually produce it. Also the age-old dilemma for the masculine of what to do with the feminine after political change is made and woman clearly intends to remain by man's revolutionary side. Then too, there is the revolutionary leader who loses the way and turns a wrathful face to the people that frightens them into backwardness and submission.

It is well, I think, to consider these things and to recognize them as they are happening.

THE QPP

The quietly pacifist peaceful always
die

to make room for men who shout.
Who tell lies to

children, and crush the corners off of old
men's dreams.

And now I find your name,
scrawled large in someone's blood, on this
survival list.

HE SAID COME

He said come
Let me exploit you;
Somebody must do it
And wouldn't you
Prefer a brother?
Come, show me your Face,

All scarred with tears;
Unburden your heart
Before the opportunity
Passes away.

ENDING

I so admired you then; before the
bloody ending
of the story cured your
life of all belief.

I would have wished you alive

still. Or even killed.

Before this thing we got, with
flailing arms

and venomous face took our
love away.

A soured revolution is one of the saddest disasters that can befall humanity. For it comes after so much hope, and suffering, and loss. So much pain and sacrifice. So much dashed belief; in ourselves and in others who have appeared so beautiful and magical, brave, and compassionate to us.

What can help prevent it? That is what is considered in the following poems, written in response to the unfolding of uprisings and revolts in Tunisia and Egypt and the Middle East generally, but in many other parts of the world as well. Parts of the world that remain unseen and therefore uncared about by much of the global community.

"Blessed Are the poor in spirit (*for theirs is the kingdom of heaven*)"

Did you ever understand this?

If my spirit was poor, how could I enter heaven? Was I depressed?

But now I see the power of editing;

and how a comma, removed or inserted with careful plan,

can change everything.

I learned this, anew, when a poor young man in Tunisia

desperate and humiliated
set himself ablaze

and I felt uncomfortably warm as if scalded by
his shame.
I do not have to sell vegetables from a cart as he did

or live in narrow rooms too small for spacious thought; and, at this late date,
I do not worry that someone will remove every
single opportunity for me to thrive.

Still, I am connected to, inseparable from, this young man.

Blessed are the poor, in spirit, for theirs is the kingdom of heaven.
Jesus. (Commas restored).

Jesus was as usual talking about solidarity: about how we join with
others and, in spirit, feel the
world the same as them.

This is the kingdom of knowing the other as self, the self as other;
it is this challenge,
overcome, that transforms grief into

peace and light.

I, and you, might enter the heaven of right here
through this door.

In this spirit, knowing we are blessed, we might remain
poor.

TO CHANGE THE WORLD ENOUGH

To change the world enough you must cease to
be afraid of the poor.

We experience your fear as the least pardonable of humiliations; in
the past

it has sent us scurrying off daunted and
ashamed into the shadows.

Now,
the world ending

the only one all of us have known we seek the same

fresh light you do:

the same high place and ample table.
The poor always believe there is room enough for all of us;

the very rich never seem to have heard of this.
In us there is wisdom of how to share loaves and fishes

however few;

we do this everyday. Learn from us,

we ask you.
We enter now the dreaded location of Earth's reckoning;
no longer far off

or hidden in books that claim to disclose revelations;

it is here.

We must walk together without fear.
There is no path without us.

OUR MARTYRS
For the Egyptian people, February 11, 2011.

When the people have won a victory whether small
or large
do you ever wonder at that moment where the martyrs might be?

They who sacrificed
themselves

to bring to life something
unknown
though nonetheless more precious than their
blood.

I like to think of them hovering
over us

wherever we have gathered to weep
and to rejoice; smiling and laughing,

actually slapping each other's palms in glee.

Their blood has dried and become
rose petals.
What you feel brushing your cheek is not only
your tears
but these.

Martyrs never regret what they
have done having done it.

Amazing too they never
frown.

It is all so mysterious the way
they remain above us

beside us within us; how
they beam

a human sunrise and are so
proud.

I will never get over the fact that human beings are sometimes willing to
die for each other, for their dreams, and for a future that is only dimly
imagined. Nothing moves me more deeply than this sacrifice; it makes
me wonder, often, if this isn't part of the reason we are born, to recognize ourselves in others, in the planet itself: in grass and trees and
children and turtles, and to die for all of it, that all of it, of us, might
live.

In any case, my response to the human sunrise is always the same,
as shown by this poem:

MAY IT BE SAID OF ME

May it be said of me
That when I saw
Your mud hut
I remembered
My shack.
That when I tasted your
Pebble filled beans
I recalled
My salt pork.
That when I saw
Your twisted
Limbs
I embraced
My wounded
Sight.
That when you
Rose from your knees
And stood
Like women
And men
Of this Earth—
As promised to us
As to anyone:
Without regrets
Of any kind
I joined you—
Singing.

From The World Will Follow Joy: Turning Madness into Flowers ©
2011 by Alice Walker. This piece is the foreword to the book Corporate
Complicity in Israel's Occupation: Evidence from the London Session
of the Russell Tribunal on Palestine. *Edited by Frank Barat (November
2011).*

THE PEACE OF NONVIOLENT RESISTANCE

Report from the West Bank
(Palestine)

APRIL 19, 2011

I HAVE BEEN IN PALESTINE for five days. It has been amazing. Deeply distressing and sad in many ways, but also filled with joy, with creativity, exuberance, and hope. Who knew there was so much life left in Palestine? That people are in love with literature and poetry? That young people are on fire about the novels and short stories they're reading in their classes? As well as about the revolutions shaking the Arab world? That despite the hardships of occupation there is a sense among Palestinians that the world is changing and is at last capable of hearing them. And not just hearing them, but responding. And not only to their tragic and hair-raising reports of the lethal Israeli occupation, an occupation as pathological as any ever to afflict humankind. No, the thought in the air around here resembles the brilliant red poppy one sees glowing between massive rocks, its roots somehow not crushed, that sings: Oh yes, I am still here, still red, still blooming as me, in spite of everything!

And guess what? I have no desire to resemble these rocks that sit on top of me.

This is the peace of nonviolent revolt which entails a radical dedication to nonabandonment of the peaceful self.

Long live all of us, and especially the Palestinian people: tenacious, like the red poppy. Waving bright hope in the smallest wind. Blooming, joyful, retaining our humor and generosity to the stranger, but also our love of green grass and spring.

Each of Earth's peoples teaches the rest of us something: you demonstrate steadfastness—how to hold on, through lies, murder, brutal repression, breathtaking theft, unbearable despair, until at last, singing our own outraged and wild poppy song, we come to join you.

Ramallah, Palestine

AUNTIE, I SIMPLY CAN'T IMAGINE IT!

Joining the Freedom Flotilla II to Gaza

Mendocino, California
June 10, 2011

I

Why am I going on the Freedom Flotilla II to Gaza? I ask myself this, even though the answer is: what else would I do? I am in my sixty-seventh year, having lived already a long and fruitful life, one with which I am content. It seems to me that during this period of eldering it is good to reap the harvest of one's understanding of what is important, and to share this, especially with the young. How are they to learn, otherwise?

Some of this narrative I have written before, but in the interest of completion, I will reiterate here: On December 27, 2008, one of my two sisters died, just as the Israeli military began massively bombing the Gaza Strip, an assault that would continue for twenty-two days and nights. She was older than me, and had been sick practically all her life. Stress of many kinds had separated our spirits, though love remained. Even with so much distance between us I felt, when she died, as if I'd lost part of myself. It was amazing, the grief. And then I learned, that same day, of a woman in Gaza who had lost five of her daughters to the bombing; she herself was unconscious. Immediately I felt: I must go to her and tell her that even though I am an American and paid with my taxes for some of the grotesque weapons of mass destruction rained on her family, I did not sanction devastation of her life, or, if she survived, her grief.

That was my first trip to the Israeli-dominated territories of Palestine.

What I found left me speechless and helped inspire a small book: *Overcoming Speechlessness: A Poet Encounters the Horror in Rwanda, Eastern Congo, and Palestine/Israel.* For months I found it impossible to talk about what it had felt like to walk among the rubble of what had been people's homes, hospitals, libraries, and schools. I found old people sitting in the pulverized remains of homes they'd sacrificed generations of labor and love to create, and was told of people wounded so badly they were rotting (from the tungsten DIME contained in the bombs) from the inside out. The water system had been destroyed, the sewer system also. What remained of the American School was a mountain of rubble. I sat there in its ruins, in despair. Five things besides people and animals one must never assault, I believe, are: water, homes, schools, hospitals, and the land. The Israeli military had deliberately destroyed, or made impossible for the Palestinian people to use, all of these.

About a year later, I was on my way to Gaza a second time. In Cairo I accompanied Jodie Evans of CODEPINK to talk to an official of the Red Crescent. We begged this official to permit entry to Gaza of the 1,400 people who had come from all over the world to march for peace with the Palestinian people, who had been "put on a diet" by the Israeli government and denied food and medicine or the ability to escape their confinement on the tiny Gaza Strip. The official was a nice man, a good man, I felt. I don't think it was easy for him to tell us we could send only a few dozen of the 1,400 people into Gaza, one bus, and very little of the millions of dollars' worth of humanitarian aid CODE-PINK and other organizations had gathered. Though the children of Gaza are dangerously malnourished (those who haven't died) because of the years-long siege and blockade, we were not allowed to send much sustenance to them, including items such as milk or juices, "because," we were told, "they are liquid."

This year, watching news of the spring uprising at Tahrir Square in downtown Cairo, I've often wondered if our man from the Red Crescent was there; whether he recalled our visit: Jodie Evans's relentless haggling to be permitted to help a sick and desperate people, whose children were being destroyed before their eyes, as well as before the eyes of the informed world. I hoped he was one of those who rallied in the street, and who testified later, after the deposition and arrest of Hosni Mubarak, that, yes, indeed, we must open the (Egyptian) Rafah gate (the only exit from Palestine not controlled by Israel) and let the people out.

How are the people to rebuild their bodies and their homes, their hospitals, schools, apartment buildings, ministries, water systems, sewerage systems, their greenhouses if they are denied materials sent to them from people outside their prison? That is the question. Illegally controlling the waters of the Mediterranean approaching the Gaza Strip, the Israeli military, against all international law, unilaterally attacks boats and people trying to break the embargo of goods and materials.

My last visit to the Palestinian people was in April 2011, when I was invited to speak at a TEDxRamallah program that took place in Bethlehem. After this astonishing daylong event of meeting and listening to Palestinian activists and artists, available, I believe, on YouTube, I joined PalFest, the Palestine Festival of Literature that takes place each year, bussing a caravan of writers, poets, musicians, artists from town to town in the occupied West Bank to interact with whoever shows up. As I did this, I was almost returned to speechlessness by what I experienced there.

First of all, my partner, G. Kaleo Larson, and I entered Palestine (which one can only officially do by going through Israel) by way of Jordan. Already, in Amman, in our hotel, my computer mysteriously vanished: it would be returned to me later, while I was in Ramallah, with all references to future activity regarding Israel removed. Then there was the experience of the Allenby Bridge border crossing. There, as we approached the first checkpoint with our Arab driver, we felt the change. He became more cautious and tense. Sure enough, he was coldly informed by one of the armed soldiers that he could not drive us, and our bags, to the bus waiting on the other side of the building that would take us hopefully into Palestine, but must put us out on the street. Which meant we had to drag quite heavy bags a good distance, without our driver's help or guidance. We had no idea where we were exactly or even what we were to do next. However, we did know that if we ever visited Palestine again, and it was still not liberated from Israeli control, we would not bring suitcases but backpacks.

II

I have a niece who startled me once by saying: Auntie, I simply can't imagine what you all went through, under segregation. She and her husband live in the American South, apparently in peace, in an integrated neighborhood that would have been unthinkable only forty years ago. They are blissfully the parents of twins, recently born, and, with the exception of floods, droughts, tornadoes, and windstorms, life appears to be vastly different and better for black people, now that Jim Crow laws are history, than it was when I was young.

However, beginning at the Allenby Bridge crossing, on our way into Occupied Palestine, I began to want my niece, bogged to the neck with her twins as she is, to observe the scene with me. Because it was tantamount to stepping back into our own past of segregation (United States apartheid) with its, for us people of color, rigidly enforced brutality and fifth-class "citizenship."

First of all, we quickly realized we had somehow chosen the entry into Israel's occupied "territories" that primarily Arabs use. We, being among them, were not to hear or see a kind word or look for the next many hours. We were treated immediately as if we were stupid if we didn't understand whatever they were speaking: for a long time Hebrew and Arabic were indistinguishable to us. We were pointed here to this window, there to that window, by women and men who spoke to us in snarls and barks. All of these windows extracted cash. Finally, we made it to the bus that had been waiting for quite a while already, there in the hot sun, motor idling, people sitting inside fanning, some of them with small children. No place for the children to pee, if they had to, either, the mother in me noted.

After a long, inexplicable wait, the bus moved. It proceeded through no fewer than six checkpoints, stopping each time to be inspected, before cruising slowly to the next checkpoint until at long last we reached the terminal. Confusion. Our bags went one way, ourselves the other. If this is a bridge, where is the water? The Aquarian in me wanted to know. At some point we, and our luggage, were checked thoroughly by rude, hostile young people who also lifted from my wallet every bit of my Jordanian currency. The women especially were a shock: they yelled at the Arabs (men, women, grandparents, children, it made no difference) almost as if they'd forgotten how to speak to humans. They ordered them about in ways I hadn't seen done to people of color for a couple of generations.

With our passports already taken from us by someone on the bus, we were directed to join long lines already formed, all Arabs, before a number of windows. This we did, sitting, when we could, for about nine hours. Without Jordanian money I was unable to purchase even a bottle of water. Fortunately a Palestinian woman bought a bottle for me, and refused the American bills I asked her to take. Our wait was interrupted by fruitless attempts to understand what was being asked of us. Were we to stand here or there? Would there be a bus? A boat? (Still expecting a river since we were on a bridge.) We tried to explain that someone sent to pick us up would likely leave if we did not emerge soon. Our wait was also interrupted by four hours of interrogation.

In the Southern United States when I was a child, they would have said: Boy, or Girl, I want to talk to you. And that could mean nobody would ever see you again. Or it could mean they'd see you so badly beaten they'd wish they hadn't. Or it could mean. . . . Anyway. A young woman who had seemed attractive to me until she began harassing me (in English) about where I was going and who I was going to see, had seemed to make a sport of taking my passport here and there behind the partition that separates the waiting area from the rest of the building. I had already filled in a form that told everything I knew myself about my trip. But I had left off my e-mail address because, I thought, who around here is going to want to e-mail me? But no, an annoyed young man arrived and demanded this information. I lied: I don't have e-mail. Which I said partly to save us both the embarrassment of a woman old enough to be his grandmother having to say: I don't want to give it to you. But I needn't have worried. He commented that he had ways to get the e-mail address and didn't really need my help. I said: But why should I give my e-mail address to you? To which he replied: Because if you don't we won't let you into the country. He said this so nastily that I wondered: does his mother agree with how badly this kid was raised?

It was this "kid" who would interrogate me for four hours, waving me into a room behind the waiting area, and not telling my partner where I was being detained, which of course stressed him out. He grilled me about everything; scrolled up on his computer activist statements I'd made that even I had forgot. He reminded me a lot of a Jewish artist friend named Wendy Cadden. Dark haired and slightly built, he could be her younger brother or perhaps her son, or grandson, I thought: I concentrated on this possibility while he went on and on, more politely now, but still in charge since he had my passport and had demanded I leave everything but what I was wearing outside his office.

At some point I said to him, seeing him really as I might have seen my own (misguided) son: Don't you realize this behavior, of making old men, mothers, little children wait in long lines pleading with you to visit their families, is wrong and is bad for you? I couldn't bring myself to use the "N" word, but I did say: Don't you think this behavior—insulting, threatening, humiliating—makes you all seem rather Germanesque? I meant the old Germanesque, of the late thirties and early forties, not the current Germanesque. He didn't seem to care. Alas.

After leaving his office, and having asked his name, which was Near but pronounced Nayear, I was disdainfully waved over by another young man, this one in uniform. He held my passport and started asking me the same questions I had spent four hours answering. By now hot and hungry, I said in exasperation: You know what? I agree. You don't want me in your country and I don't want to go there. Give me my passport and I will go home. I also said: Doesn't your rudeness to a guest to your country make you ashamed? He looked about eighteen years old and appeared confused by my comment. Has the notion of shame so completely disappeared? I wondered.

Later on, it would be explained to us that all the rudeness, the waiting in long lines, the absence of water and, apparently, of toilets once one boarded the bus, the harassment and the fact that buses might wait hours before moving, was all part of a plan to keep anyone coming through that gate from ever coming back!

And I remembered Near asking me: Why didn't you go through Tel Aviv? As if I might have saved myself a bit of Arab torture. But actually I was glad we'd gone the Arab route; it was like sitting with my own parents and grandparents in segregated waiting rooms, bus and train stations all over the South. I was even glad Kaleo and I hadn't known there was a VIP lounge, which many younger, more affluent Arabs made use of. Some of them had come out to us, wanting an autograph (!) and explaining how, for a fee, we could sit with them in comfort, on sofas, inside a small room that appeared to have a snack bar.

By the time we were allowed out of the "Israeli Terminal," as Palestinian friends call the Allenby Bridge crossing, the van sent to pick us up had left. It was late at night. We climbed into a taxi and sped off. We had no idea where we were but the moon was nearly full and stunning. The moon, especially when I don't know where I am, always reminds me of Sojourner Truth, whose children were sold away from her during her enslavement: I look at the moon and you look at the moon, she said to them in her prayers, or words to that effect.

Perhaps after the Flotilla II experience, I will be able to write about the solidarity and friendship we experienced with the other poets and writers—most Arab Palestinians but also some Jews, Palestinian and American—we encountered. I like to think about some of the unusual discoveries we made: like how many Palestinian Christians there still are in "the Holy Land," and how kind some of them were to us. How extraordinary it is to see people from all over the world flocking to the spot in Bethlehem's "Manger Square" and the Church of the Nativity where Jesus is said to have been born, with little concern apparently that in the form of his present-day compatriots, Jesus, a Palestinian—is still being crucified. The tackiness of rampant commercialism makes "the Holy Land" a small area to market, and it is marketed relentlessly. Mass-produced trinkets produced in China and Taiwan flood the area. Many of the Palestinian-owned shops have been pushed away from the most lucrative sites. The land itself, from millennia of being considered the only "holy land" there is, is battered, beaten down. My heart ached for it. What a catastrophe to be so famous; a footprint on your face every minute. The true holy land is within the heart itself, is my view, as is the true Jerusalem. Not to mention that all of the Earth is holy, which means one can freely worship wherever one is. (Of course you can't make any money off of that idea!)

But I digress.

I thought of my niece as I found myself approaching "Jews Only" roads in a van filled with Palestinian Arabs. Our driver conscientiously pulled over to wait for the appropriately colored license plate (on another van, into which we moved) that would permit us to continue. The Palestinian license plate color is green, the Israeli one yellow. In fact, on the night of our arrival, we had noticed our driver had turned off the big, new American-looking highway onto a poorly constructed and congested road that in fact was blocked at the top of a steep hill. The driver, muttering, turned around on a dangerous curve and continued on the main road. Nervous, I now realized, because it was illegal for him to be on it.

Now here, I thought, was something even white Southerners had not thought to segregate: the very roads! Though I did recall how my grandparents in Georgia, in their mule-drawn wagon, when I was a very small child, had had to pull over, almost into the ditch, if a white driver in a car roared past.

Always somewhat grumpy in the early morning, I found myself our third or fourth day unable to bear conversing with a prominent Palestinian historian who sat down beside me, drinking coffee and blowing cigarette smoke. I moved to another seat. However, I soon felt very small as this same man, whose work is lauded and loved in Palestine, quietly got up, gathered his things, and moved to the front of the van to be let out. In the middle of nowhere, it seemed, by the side of the road. He explained to a poet at the front of the bus that he did not have the right permit to be allowed even to ride on a bus through the city of Jerusalem, where it seemed we were heading.

III

I think one reason it is so hard for people to deal with the Palestine/Israel issue is that so much of it is unbelievable. Even when you're standing there, in the middle of it, the mind has to struggle to grasp what is happening. What has been done for the past sixty-odd years, and what is being done now. Just as my niece finds it impossible to imagine what a segregated American South felt like, I find it hard to believe Israelis assume they can live through generations of brutally oppressing the people whose lands they occupy. The greatest, most obvious expression of their intent to do this is THE WALL.

Once when I fell in love with the works of the great Chinese writer Ding Ling I went to visit her in Beijing. She was in her eighties and magnificent, thinking fondly of her sixties as really extraordinary years, though she had been badly abused by the Cultural Revolution. While there I went with our group to visit the Great Wall of China. What I liked was that every once in a while an artist had managed to etch a flower in the wall (maybe I imagined this!) but also: it was explained to us that the wall never worked properly to keep out the invaders because many of them simply bribed the gatekeepers who, for money, let them in. *Hummm.*

The Israeli-built apartheid wall is HUGE. It is incredibly tall and thick. It must be at least twenty feet tall and sometimes it is installed atop a three- to five-foot platform that increases its height. It is also sunk several meters into the ground. It has cost so far three and a half billion dollars (a bit over the amount U.S. taxpayers send to Israel each year); it is everywhere, and it is indescribably ugly. On the Israeli side we learn it is "prettified" with tiles of various colors, but on the Palestinian side it is bare concrete. To their credit, Palestinians have given graffiti artists free reign, and there is often moving and arresting art.

One of our new friends, a poet, took us around to show us the wall in action. First, we went to a shop that sells Palestinian books and crafts. Unfortunately for the owner, a beautiful, middle-aged, stressed-out woman, her shop was "too close" to Rachel's Tomb, so the wall was built practically on her doorstep, depriving her of a view of anything except its menacing presence. The woman was so trapped by the wall she reminded me of a small animal frantic in its cage.

Our second visit was to the tiny home of a family of four: a mother, father, and two small boys. The ditch for the wall's placement was being dug while we had tea, the noise of it so powerful it shook the house. When the wall is completed, the man's house will be completely cut off from his fields, depriving him of a livelihood; his small boys will have to cross three checkpoints each day to reach their school. They were gracious to us, even cheerful, this small, isolated family, in a way that reminded me very much of the days of segregation and soul torture in the South. The boys played as if they understood nothing of their family's crisis, as we had played as children, well loved by our overburdened parents who never had the heart to tell us how viciously we were all being oppressed. (Kaleo later reminded me that the little boy I thought was playing hide and seek was actually hiding. He had been severely beaten by an Israeli soldier a few weeks before.)

The last visit was to the poet's own house, which she shares with relatives. When the wall is completed just behind her house, she will lose the sunrise. The morning sky. I will call her Fatima. Being with her was almost exactly like being with poor black people in Mississippi in the sixties: wherever she took us to look at the wall, where it was newly being constructed, where it was planned to stretch next, where it would steal another football-field-size area of farmland from her family and from other Palestinians, we were trailed by men in big white trucks, silently, slowly, menacingly, to let us know they were aware of and hostile to our presence. Instead of white sheets they have white trucks, I thought—new ones, bought no doubt with American money and, in fact, come to think of it, I believe they were American-made trucks. I noted that the machines used to dig ditches for the wall were made by Volvo. I thought of the beautiful red Volvo I'd owned when we lived in Mississippi as civil rights activists (the safest car we could find) and how I would now never own another one.

On the last day of PalFest, the Israeli military teargassed the tent in which the evening's event was to take place. My partner and I had left Palestine by then and did not experience it. Though, because we had bonded with our "tribe," as we thought of the other artists, we felt it very much. Our tribe, true to the audacity of artists, carried on, as we knew they would.

Getting out of Palestine through the Allenby Bridge exit proved as stressful as coming in had been. Though we rose early and hailed a taxi outside our hotel, and though we speedily made our way to the bridge's checkpoint, and even though there were only a few other vehicles waiting to be permitted entry, we were forced to languish for three hours as giant tourist buses were waved through on one side of the two-lane entry and those taxi or van drivers preferred by the border guards were permitted to pass ahead of us. All around us, as traffic backed up, we noted people, women and men, who were being forced to wait, emerge from their cars and vans and make use of the trees and grass to relieve themselves. Finally, exasperated but also worn down by this treatment, I felt, our driver asked my partner to appeal to the border guard to let us advance. This my partner did, though tempers by this time were so tense among all the held-up drivers that he was almost assaulted by an irate driver who felt we were being permitted to move ahead of him. He had recently arrived and had no way of knowing we had been there for hours.

Inside the terminal my partner was permitted to pass to the other side; I was held up, my passport again taken behind a partition. Again, I felt confusion about what I was supposed to do. At that point I noticed a young Jewish man who looked like the son of a former teacher of mine. I stopped him and asked what was going on. He didn't know, but he courteously showed me where I should sit until all was sorted out. My partner soon returned and eventually we were on our way. With this young man's face, dark hair and thoughtful eyes, his simple and as yet undestroyed kindness, still warming me.

IV

I have never believed in the Israeli-Palestinian peace talks. Whenever I saw the men gathering to talk about peace I was reminded of what the Indians said to the white colonizers of America who came to talk peace with them: "Where are your women?" An occasional woman has appeared to take part in the talks, but overwhelmingly the process has been male driven. I like to think if women, in equal numbers to men, had been at the table things might not have turned out so badly. But perhaps, recalling the disrespectful young Israeli women at the checkpoints, this is naïve. In any case, it is when one sees the Israeli settlements, after hearing about them for decades, that the final "Aha" moment arrives. They are colossal, and, like the wall, they are everywhere. It is obvious, looking at them, gigantic, solid, white, and towering, that they have been constructed to completely devour the rest of Palestine, and that the peace talks have been a ruse to continue their growth so that Jewish Israelis can claim the land by possession alone. Possession is nine-tenths of the law is one of the dictums I learned from my Jewish lawyer former husband. This belief might even be enshrined in the Torah. In any case it is a very old idea, and Israelis have made good use of it.

Dispossessed of land and houses, poverty-stricken, refugees in their own country since the catastrophe of 1948, when Zionist terrorists drove them from their villages, towns, and cities, Palestinian laborers have been forced to build these settlements for the Israeli settlers and, having built them, are rarely permitted inside them, except to service them. This is similar to our own history, in America: the genocide and enslavement of Native people, and the forced black and Indian labor that built so much of America, including the White House. Sometimes one wonders if this greed that devours the very substance of other human beings is part of human DNA. I don't think it is; and, in any case, I hope not!

V

Our boat, the *Audacity of Hope*, will be carrying letters to the people of Gaza. Letters expressing solidarity and love. That is all its cargo will consist of. If the Israeli military attacks us, it will be as if they attacked the mailman. This should go down hilariously in the annals of history. But if they insist on attacking us, wounding us, even murdering us, as they did some of the activists in the last flotilla, Freedom Flotilla I, what is to be done?

There is a scene in the movie *Gandhi* that is very moving to me: it is when the unarmed Indian protesters line up to confront the armed forces of the British Empire. The soldiers beat them unmercifully, but the Indians, their broken and dead lifted tenderly out of the fray, keep coming. And that is how, I suspect, it will be with us. The tide is turning on this issue that people around the world have agonized over or tried to ignore for generations, and nothing can stop the tide. Like the ocean's waves, whatever the opposition, we must retain our nonviolence (it is more beautiful than violence) and we must keep coming.

Alongside this image of brave followers of Gandhi there is for me an awareness of paying off a debt to the Jewish civil rights activists who faced death to come to the side of black people in the South in our time of need. I am especially indebted to Michael Schwerner and Andrew Goodman, who heard our calls for help—our government then as now glacially slow in providing protection to nonviolent protesters— and came to stand with us. They got as far as the truncheons and bullets of a few "good ole' boys" of Neshoba County, Mississippi, and were beaten and shot to death along with James Cheney, a young black man of formidable courage who died with them. So, even though our boat will be called the *Audacity of Hope*, it will fly the Goodman, Cheney, Schwerner flag in my own heart.

And what of the children of Palestine, who were ignored in our president's latest speech on Israel and Palestine, and whose impoverished, terrorized, segregated existence was mocked by the standing ovations recently given in the U.S. Congress to the president of Israel? I have witnessed their bravery, as they attempt to protect their communities and homes using stones, their only ammunition, against the armored Israeli tanks (American-bought) that destroy their land, neighborhoods, houses, and families, and, like much of the world, have been profoundly moved. I have noted that their arms have sometimes been broken by Israeli soldiers for throwing these stones, and that nine- and ten-year-olds have been tortured and left to become dejected and hollowed-out teenagers in prison or jail.

I see children, all children, as humanity's most precious resource, because it will be to them that the care of the planet will always be left. One child must never be set above another, even in casual conversation, not to mention in speeches that circle the globe; to do so is to extend the world's disasters. As adults, we must affirm, constantly, that the Arab child, the Muslim child, the Palestinian child, the African child, the Jewish child, the Christian child, the American child, the Chinese child, the Israeli child, the Native American child, etc., is equal to all others on the planet. We must do everything in our power to cease the behavior that makes children everywhere feel afraid.

Finally, thinking of my niece who can't imagine what segregation in the United States was like, there is the memory of my own surprise to discover, in the Southern freedom movement, what solidarity between black and white was like. Like her, I had not been able, prior to moving to Mississippi, to imagine it. This was so true that when I arrived in Jackson I was annoyed to see white people, working daily under great stress, and on our side, already there. I once asked my best friend and husband of that period, who was as staunch a defender of black people's human rights as anyone I'd ever met: How did you find your way to us, to black people, who so needed you? What force shaped your response to the great injustice facing people of color of that time? I thought he might say the speeches, the marches, the example of Martin Luther King Jr. or of others in the movement who exhibited impactful courage and grace. But no. Thinking back, he recounted an episode from his childhood that had led him, inevitably, to our struggle. He was a little boy on his way home from Yeshiva, the Jewish school he attended after regular school let out. His mother, a bookkeeper, was still at work; he was alone. He was frequently harassed by older boys from regular school, and one day two of these boys snatched his yarmulke and, taunting him, ran off with it, eventually throwing it over a fence. Two black boys appeared, saw his tears, assessed the situation, and took off after the boys who had taken his yarmulke. Chasing the boys down and catching them, they made them climb the fence, retrieve and dust off the yarmulke, and place it respectfully back on his head.

It is justice and respect that I want the world to dust off and put—without delay, and with tenderness—back on the head of the Palestinian child. It will be imperfect justice and respect because the injustice and disrespect have been so severe. But I believe we are right to try.

That is why I sail.

For insight and inspiration on this issue, I recommend: The General's Son, *by Miko Peled, a book that dispels many of the myths about the creation of Israel that have so confused the world, written by the son of an Israeli general who was a central participant, over decades, in Israel's wars. There is a short video featuring Peled on YouTube that is well worth viewing. Also, "Freedom for Palestine," a song that will make you dance, by OneWorld.*

AND SO OUR TRAILS
CONTINUE

August 4, 2011

On the boat to Gaza—as we waited day after day to sail—I met a doctor from Scandinavia who was going with us, to take care of us if we were harmed. The very thought drew me to her. I liked her calm, competent, unassuming manner, as well as her gentle smile. We talked.

I asked if she knew of the writer, Nella Larsen.

No.

I said she'd written elegant novels in the late twenties and early thirties, then gave up writing to become a nurse. She'd been unjustly accused of plagiarism, also, which undermined her confidence in her craft and deeply wounded her, but I did not mention this.

Her mother was a Dane, I said. Her father, a West Indian.

A really interesting novelist, I said. Comparable to, or perhaps compatible with, Kate Chopin and Jean Rhys, I always thought, though I did not bring up these admirable novelists, either.

You might want to read her novels, *Quicksand* (my favorite) and *Passing,* I said. Both are fascinating. There's an edge to them that's unusual in novels written by American women of that period.

Our doctor seemed interested and took down her name.

But as we talked I was reminded of something else: that Sue Bailey Thurman, the social activist and scholar, also wife of theologian Howard Thurman, gave me, toward the end of her life, in a box that contained several purple wine goblets, a small silver candlestick that leaned like a tiny tower of Pisa. She said it had belonged to Nella Larsen. I still have it.

Not long ago, in a biography of Larsen that made her seem unconvincingly shallow, I learned her Danish grandmother had given two silver candlesticks to Nella when she visited her mother's country as a young woman.

The Danes had been curious about the "exotic" Larsen and had wined and dined her, if we are to believe that her fictional character in *Quicksand*, Helga Crane, is based on Larsen's real-life experience in Denmark.

Where is the other candlestick, I now wondered? And how tiny the candle would have to be to fit. A birthday cake candle, maybe. And was she given the candlesticks partly because one of them (the one I now had) was defective? How would Nella have felt about this?

It seemed worthwhile to urge the doctor to look Larsen up on the Internet and to read her novels.

She presents an experience of Danes, of Denmark, and of course of the American South that I'm sure most Danes can't imagine. Though by now there must be many biracial Danish children who are not considered "exotic."

Oh, yes, the doctor laughed. One of them is in a boat in the flotilla. Among the Danish contingent, she added.

Sure enough, leaving the press conference in Athens, where we Americans affirmed our presence in the international flotilla to break the illegal Israeli siege of Gaza, I was warmly embraced by a handsome, golden-brown young man, whose goodness of heart and purpose of spirit shone in his bright, dark eyes.

I did not have time (we embraced in a crowded doorway) to ask if he knew of his biracial ancestor, Nella Larsen, but I imagined him discovering her one day: a previously unknown, but perhaps now a useful and illuminating, even companionable, mentor and friend.

And so our trails continue. With or without us.

OVERCOMING SPEECHLESSNESS

A Poet Encounters the Horror in Rwanda,
Eastern Congo, and Palestine/Israel

In this essay, poet Alice Walker writes of encountering "the horror" (as in Joseph Conrad's novel Heart of Darkness*) in Rwanda, Eastern Congo, and Palestine/Israel and finding her voice again after a period of speechlessness.*

Part of what has happened to human beings, she believes, is that we have, over the last century, witnessed cruel and unusually barbaric behavior that was so horrifying it literally left us speechless. We had no words to describe it even when we viewed it, nor could we easily believe human beings would fall to such levels of degradation; we have been deeply frightened. This self-imposed silence has slowed our response to the plight of those who most need us, often women and children but also men of conscience who resist evil but are outnumbered by those around them who have fallen victim to a belief in weapons, male or ethnic dominance, greed, and drugs.

Walker also envisions a one-country settlement to the ongoing crisis in Palestine/Israel.

—Editor, Seven Stories Press

Three things cannot be hidden: the sun, the moon,
and the truth.
—Buddha

1. Three years ago

Three years ago I visited Rwanda and Eastern Congo. In Kigali I paid
my respects to the hundreds of thousands of infants, toddlers, teenagers, adolescents, young engaged couples, married people, women and
men, grandmothers and grandfathers, brothers and sisters of every
facial shape and body size, who had been hacked into sometimes quite
small pieces by armed strangers, or by neighbors, or by acquaintances
and "friends" they knew. These bodies and pieces of bodies are now
neatly and respectfully buried in mass graves. Fifteen years ago, these
graves were encircled by cuttings of plants that are now sturdy blos-
soming vines that cover their iron trellises with flowers. Inside the adjacent museum there are photographs of the murdered: their open
smiles or wise and consoling eyes will remain with me always. There is
also, in the museum, a brief history of Rwanda. It tells of the long centuries Tutsi and Hutu lived together, intermarrying and raising their
children, until the coming of the Belgians in the 1800s. The Belgian
settlers determined, because they measured Hutu and Tutsi skulls, that
the Tutsi were more intelligent than the Hutu, more like Europeans,
and therefore placed the Tutsi above the Hutu. (Before the Belgians,
the territory had been colonized by the Germans.) When the Belgian
colonists left for Europe, over a hundred years later, and after many
changes to each of these groups, they left the Hutu in charge. The hatred this diabolical decision caused between these formerly coexisting
peoples festered over generations, coming to a lethal boil in the tragedy of genocide.

I had done research while in college and written a thesis of sorts
on the "Belgian" Congo, where King Leopold of Belgium introduced
the policy of cutting off the hands of enslaved Africans who didn't or
couldn't fulfill their rubber quota. They were collecting the latex for the
rubber that made tires for the new cars everyone was beginning to want,
in America and Europe. I had not known these same activities spread
into the Kingdom of Rwanda. To the Belgians, apparently, and to the
German colonialists before them, it was all one vast "empty" territory,
to be exploited without any consideration for the people living there.
Indigenous Africans didn't seem to exist, except as slaves.

While visiting the set for the film *The Color Purple*, many decades
after college, a sad older man from Africa, who had been a doctor in

the Congo, and was now hired as an extra for our film, lamented the loss of his country, his people, and his land, telling me that the Firestone Corporation had taken millions of acres of land, "leasing" it for pennies an acre, in perpetuity. The people who'd lived there since the beginning of humanity had been forced to tend the trees planted there on Firestone's vast rubber tree plantation. I immediately thought of every car I'd owned and all the tires that ran under them.

2. From Kigali

From Kigali, and meetings with survivors, witnessing their courage and fortitude, their willingness to move on and beyond unspeakable tragedy, I went to Eastern Congo. There, I met with women still victimized by the killers of Kigali who had been chased across the border into their country. These women had been the victims of rape on so large a scale—rape as one of the cruelest weapons of war—it seemed impossible they had not, in their despair, chosen to destroy themselves. Their villages had frequently turned against them, because of their abuse; if their husbands were still alive, they regularly dismissed them, refusing them shelter in their own homes.

One beautiful woman, who came to meet me wearing white and purple, had been a sex slave in the bush for over a year, forced to carry loads that bent her double, her eyes repeatedly struck to damage her vision so that she would not be able to identify her assailants, her whole body beaten until, over a year later, there was still a discernible limp when she attempted to walk with what one assumed was her former grace. We embraced each other with tears, and with joy. I was more thankful to see her radiant resurrection than I had been to witness anything in my life. She had been raped with every imaginable instrument, including machete handles and gun barrels. Thanks to you, my sisters of Women for Women International, she said, I have come through. Many of us have come through. We will not go back. We will not be slaves and beasts of burden.

Over four million* Congolese have been murdered in an endless war whose foundation rests on the mineral wealth of the Congo. One of those minerals, coltan, makes cell phone use possible. Millions of fami-

---

*This number is now estimated at over eight million.

lies are homeless and in ruin, living in the rain and heat. War continues, like a sickness that has no cure. Infectious diseases are rampant. Weapons flow into the hands of the young, even into the hands of children. How can she smile? I wonder, about my just-met Congolese sister. But she does so because she is alive, which means the Feminine is alive.

There is the work of the Mother to do.

There is the work of the Daughter to do.

This is a source of joy. We embrace, parting. She will learn how to start a business and longs to take lessons in computer use.

3. Coming home

Coming home, I found that I could talk about this woman, and, indeed, she would later come to America and talk about herself. She understood the importance of speech, speech about the unspeakable, and is a source of my ability to share the following story, which propelled me into a period of speechlessness. While in Congo we were invited to visit a young woman, just my own daughter's age at the time, thirty-six, who was in a local hospital. When we first saw Generose she was lying on a pallet on the floor in an outer passageway, waiting for us. Taking up her crutch, she led us to a quiet area at the back of the hospital where we sat circled around her, as she told her story. Her story was this: Her village had been terrorized by the Interahamwe murderers (presumably Hutu) that had been chased out of Rwanda by the Tutsi forces of Paul Kagame (now president of Rwanda); the suffering had been unbearable as people were chased from their homes at all hours of the day or night, many of them choosing to sleep in the forest or hide themselves in their fields.

She was home with her husband and two children because her husband was sick, when one evening, there was a fierce knock at the door, and gunmen who also carried machetes entered, demanding food. There was little to offer them but the staple diet: a boiled vegetable (that to my eyes, being shown it in the fields earlier, looked like okra leaves) and a few balls of steamed millet. The men ate this, but were angry and not satisfied. They went and found the husband, still in bed, and hacked him to pieces on the spot. They came back to Generose and her children and took hold of her. Holding her down, they began to cut off her leg. They cut off her leg, cut it into six pieces, and began to fry it in a pan. When some part of it seemed nearly done, they tried to force her son to take a bite of it. Strongly, beautifully, and so much the son of our dreams, he said: No, I will never eat my mother's flesh. They shot him to death without more conversation. The daughter, seeing this, watching her mother bleeding to death, knowing her father had been hacked to pieces, was now offered the same opportunity. Terrorized, she bit into a piece of her mother's body. Her mother, having crawled away, does not know what became of her. Though she does know that her assailants went next door that same evening and murdered a couple who'd been married that day, raping and mutilating the bride, and tearing out her eyes.

This was the child Generose was hoping we could help her find. Apparently she had escaped after this gruesome torture, and now, where could she be? Generose hoped for only two things from us: that we help her find her daughter (beyond our capacity, probably, though Women for Women International would try) and that we help her start a small business so that when her daughter is found she can provide a safe place for them to live. A proud woman who reminded me of a young Toni Morrison, she did not once stammer in the telling of her tale, though those of us around her felt a quaking in the heart. I have not for a moment forgotten this child who was forced to bite into her mother's flesh. Yet it has been almost impossible to speak of it.

Coming home I fell ill with the burden of this story, as I had fallen ill after reading in the *New York Times* a year or so earlier of similar torture used against the so-called "pygmies" of Africa's rain forests. That, in order to frighten them away from their homes, to ultimately make way for lumbering and mining interests located in the West, mercenaries were indoctrinating their soldiers to believe that killing them ("pygmies" because in ancient Egyptian the word means elbow-high), and the eating of their hearts, would make them invisible and capable, as these smaller people seem to be, of evading capture by blending with their environment. Reading this story I felt as if my own heart had been taken out of me, and this assault on the planetary human body that I represent brought me low.

4. Sangha

I was fortunate to have a sangha (a Buddhist circle of support) to which I could eventually turn. Sitting around me as I talked, two of our members realized I needed even more of a healing than simply being able to speak about what I had witnessed and heard of what is happening to the people of the Earth. They immediately devised a ritual for my care. Placing me on the green grass of my yard, surrounding me with flowers, stones, photographs of those who comfort us (I placed several under my blouse: John Lennon, Pema Chodron, Howard Zinn, the Dalai Lama, Amma, and Che among them) and their own loving words, they helped me shed tears of hopelessness, as I asked myself and them: What has happened to humanity? Followed by more tears of resolve. Because whatever has happened to humanity, whatever is currently happening to humanity, it is happening to all of us.

No matter how hidden the cruelty, no matter how far off the screams of pain and terror, we live in one world. We are one people. My illness proved that. As well as my understanding that Generose's lost daughter belongs to all of us. It is up to all of us to find her; it is up to us to do our best to make her whole again.

There is only one daughter, one father, one mother, one son, one aunt or uncle, one dog, one cat, donkey, monkey, or goat in the Universe, after all: the one right in front of you.

5. Once again

And so I have been, once again, struggling to speak about an atrocity: this time in Gaza, this time against the Palestinian people. Like most people on the planet I have been aware of the Palestinian-Israeli "conflict" almost my whole life. I was four years old in 1948 when, after being subjected to unspeakable cruelty by the Germans, after a "holocaust" so many future disasters would resemble, thousands of European Jews were resettled in Palestine. They settled in a land that belonged to people already living there, which did not seem to bother the British who, as in India, had occupied Palestine and then, on leaving it, helped put in place a partitioning of the land they thought would work fine for the people, strangers, Palestinians, and European Jews, now forced to live together. When we witness the misery and brutality that is still a daily reality for millions of people in Pakistan and India, we are looking at the failure, and heartlessness, of the "partition" plan. Though it might be true that the partitioning of what became India and Pakistan came after the insistence of a Muslim leader, Muhammad Ali Jinnah, it is extremely doubtful that separating their millions of people into different countries would have occurred to the Indians, Hindu and Muslim, had England not spent centuries telling each group its misery was the other's fault.

6. Who would tell her?

I got to Gaza the way I have gotten to many places in my life: a sister called me. My friend, the writer Susan Griffin, with whom I was arrested protesting the start of the war against Iraq in 2003, sent an e-mail. Would I be interested in going to Gaza? With CODEPINK, the women's peace group that had gotten us into such soul-strengthening trouble six years before. She would go, she said, if she could sell the book she was currently writing. This is how so many of us live; I remember this when I look about the world and want more witnesses to the scenes of horror, brutality, chaos. We all have to work to feed ourselves, look after our families, keep our heads above water. I understand this completely, and wasn't sure I was free enough myself, to go.

However, it happened that, in the same week that the Israeli military began its twenty-two-day bombardment of Gaza, a refugee camp that became a city and is today a mere sliver of Palestine left to the Palestinians (a city and environs that Israel had laid siege to months before, keeping out food and medicine and building materials, among other necessities), my own sister had died after a long illness. Our relationship had been a good one for most of our lives, and then, toward the end of her life, it had become strained. So much so that when she died I had not expected to feel devastation.

Surprise. As I was grieving her loss, I learned of the dropping of bombs on the people of Palestine. Houses, hospitals, factories, police stations, parliament buildings, ministries, apartment buildings, schools went up in dust. The sight of one family in which five young daughters had been killed was seared into my consciousness. The mother, wounded and unconscious, was alive. Who would tell her? I waited to hear some word of regret, of grief, of compassion from our leaders in Washington, who had sent the money, the earnings of American taxpayers, to buy the bombs destroying her world. What little concern voiced from our "leaders" was faint, arrived late, was delivered without much feeling, and was soon overshadowed by an indifference to the value of

Palestinian life that has corrupted our children's sense of right and wrong for generations. Later our government would offer money, a promise to help "rebuild." As if money and rebuilding was the issue. If someone killed my children and offered me money for the privilege of having done so I would view them as monsters, not humanitarians.

I consulted my companion, who did not hesitate. We must go, he said. The sooner we reach the people of Gaza, the sooner they'll know not all Americans are uncaring, deaf and blind, or fooled by the media. He quoted Abraham Lincoln: You can fool some of the people all of the time, and all of the people some of the time, but you cannot fool all of the people all of the time. Americans have been deliberately misled by our government and by the media about the reality and meaning of events in the Middle East; this is especially true where Palestine and Israel are concerned. Our ignorance has cost us dearly. The feeling of having been taken, fooled, and of still being taken for a very expensive ride is quite galling, especially as we see our own society collapsing from lack of the same attention we give to Israel. Subsidized housing, for instance, and protection of our neighborhoods. There is actual puzzlement in most people's minds about why "the state of Israel" consumes far more interest and funding, and news coverage, than, say, my own former state, the state of Georgia, or the state where I live now, California. Americans are generally uninformed about the reality of this never-ending "conflict" that has puzzled us for decades and of which so many of us, if we are honest, are heartily sick. We began to pack.

7. A long way to Gaza

It's a long way to Gaza. Flying between San Francisco and Frankfurt, then from Frankfurt into Egypt, I kept my mind focused by meditating as much as possible, reading Aung San Suu Kyi and Alan Clement's book *The Voice of Hope*, thinking about Desmond Tutu and his courageous statement earlier in the month about the immorality of the walls Israel has built around Palestinian villages as well as the immorality of the siege itself. I had read President Jimmy Carter's book *Palestine: Peace Not Apartheid* before leaving home. I also ate a good bit of chocolate. And slept. Arriving in Cairo at three-thirty in the morning; my first task, assigned to me by the beautiful, indomitable, and well-loved co-founder of CODEPINK Medea Benjamin, was to meet with her and the U.S. ambassador to Egypt, Ambassador Scobey, at ten-thirty A.M. to ask for assistance in crossing the border into Gaza from Egypt. After a few hours' rest, I appeared early for the meeting (concerned that Medea had not arrived yet), which, though cordial, would yield no help. Even so, I was able to have an interesting talk with the ambassador about the use of nonviolence. She, a white woman with a Southern accent, mentioned the success of "our" civil rights movement and why couldn't the Palestinians be more like us. It was a remarkable comment from a perspective of unimaginable safety and privilege; I was moved to tell her of the effort it took, even for someone so inherently nonviolent as me, to contain myself during seven years in Mississippi when it often appeared there were only a handful of white Mississippians who could talk to a person of color without delivering injury or insult. That if we had not been able to change our situation through nonviolent suffering, we would most certainly, like the ANC, like the PLO, like Hamas, turn to violence. I told her how dishonest it seemed to me that people claim not to understand the desperate, last-ditch resistance involved in suicide bombings; blaming the oppressed for using their bodies where the Israeli army uses armored tanks.

I remembered aloud, us being Southerners, my own anger at the humiliations, bombings, assassinations that made weeping an endless activity for black people, for centuries, and how when we finally got to a courtroom which was supposed to offer justice, the judge was likely to blame us for the crime done against us and to call us chimpanzees for making a fuss. Medea arrived at this point, having been kept circling the building in a taxi that never landed, and pressed our case for entry into Gaza. While appearing sympathetic to our petition, our ambassador emphasized it was dangerous for us to go into Gaza and that her office would be powerless to help us if we arrived there and were injured or stranded. We were handed some papers telling us all the reasons we should not go.

8. Pastrami from "the butcher"

Next we were at a strange ministry whose name never registered, to fill out forms whose intent escaped me. Several CODEPINK women were already there, waiting their turn for the bit of paper we needed to move

PALESTINIAN LOSS OF LAND, 1946 TO 2000

a step closer to the Egyptian border crossing at Rafah, the only one available (maybe) to us. There I met a CODEPINKer who instantly made me happy to be with CODEPINK again. She'd been waiting for hours, felt she was growing into her chair, and we laughed at the absurdity of bureaucracy everywhere, which keeps you waiting interminably for some bit of paper that you feel sure is thrown into the trash or into a creaking file drawer as soon as you leave the room, never again to see the light of day.

I reconnected with Gael Murphy, who reminded me we had shared a paddy wagon after being arrested in front of the White House a few days before George Bush started his ill-fated war on the people and animals, rivers and dwellings, mosques and libraries of Iraq. She handed me an illustrated postcard that showed plainly what the situation between Israel and Palestine came down to: in 1946 the Palestinians owned Palestine, by their numbers, though Britain ruled it, with a few scattered Jewish villages (picture one); some years later, under a United Nations plan for partitioning, Palestine and Israel would each own roughly half of the land (picture two); from 1949 to 1967 the Israel "half" grew by about a third; after the 1967 war, Israel doubled its land mass by virtue of the land it took from Palestine at that time. The last picture shows the situation in 2000: Palestinian refugees (in their own country) live in camps in the West Bank and Gaza, and the whole land is now called Israel. On the back of this card are words from former Israeli president Ariel Sharon, known as the butcher of Sabra and Shatila (refugee camps in Lebanon where he led a massacre of the people), where he talks about making a pastrami sandwich of the Palestinian people, riddling their lands with Jewish settlements until no one will be able to imagine a whole Palestine. Or know Palestine ever existed.

9. Turtle Island

No one can imagine a whole Turtle Island, either, now known as North America, but formerly the land of indigenous peoples. The land of some of my Native ancestors, the Cherokee, whose homes and villages were obliterated from the landscape where they'd existed for millennia, the Cherokee who were forced—those who remained—to resettle, walking "the trail of tears," a thousand miles away. This is familiar territory. As is the treatment of the Palestinian people. On the bus ride through the Egyptian desert, toward the Rafah gate, which leads into Palestine, I think about this particular cycle of violence humans have made for themselves.

Hitler learned (partly) from the Americans how to "cleanse" Germany of the Jews. Even the use of Jewish hair to stuff mattresses. Indian hair had been mattress stuffing long before. Indian skin made into various objects. Indian children and families massacred. Not because they were "savages"—one glance at their art told anyone who they were—but because the European settlers who came to America wanted their land. Just as the Israelis have wanted, and have taken by force, Palestinian land. Like Americans they have attempted to hide their avarice and cruelty behind a mountain of myths: that no one lived in Palestine, that the Palestinians are savages, that there's no such thing as a Palestinian (Golda Meir's offering), that the Israelis are David and the Palestinians Goliath. Which is ridiculous, if you haven't been indoctrinated against the Palestinians for centuries from reading the Bible, where, as the Philistines (we are taught), they are forever causing trouble for God's children, the Hebrews. And then, there's Hollywood, which has a lot to answer for in its routine disregard for Arabs, generally, but which, where Palestine and Israel are concerned, projects

Israel as always in the right, no matter what it does, as American politicians, for the most part, have learned to do. This is not good for Israel, or the United States, just as always praising the regrettable behavior of one's child, or of anyone, can only lead to disaster. A disaster, where Israel is concerned, that is happening before our eyes, even if the media in America refuses to let Americans fully see it.

10. So many Jews

I had not been on a bus with so many Jews since traveling to the 1963 March on Washington by Greyhound when Martin Luther King Jr., John Lewis, and others spoke so passionately of black Americans' determination to be free. I went with a half-Jewish young man named, not so ironically when I later thought of it, David. He was not considered really Jewish because his mother was Irish Catholic, and you can only be a real Jew if your mother is Jewish. I didn't know that then. I had thought his behavior, coming to the side of the oppressed, very Jewish. It was fairly Irish, too, but at the time the Irish in Boston, except for the Kennedys, seemed far from their tradition in this area. They were regularly stoning and/or shouting obscenities at black children who tried to attend "their" schools. It was moving to hear the stories of why the Jews on our Gaza-bound bus were going to Palestine. Many of them simply said they couldn't bear the injustice, or the hypocrisy. Having spoken out against racism, terrorism, apartheid elsewhere, how could they be silent about Palestine and Israel? Someone said her friends claimed everyone who spoke out against Israeli treatment of Palestinians was a self-hating Jew (if Jewish) or anti-Semitic (though Palestinians are Semites, too). She said it never seemed to dawn on the persons making the anti-Semitic charge that it is Israel's behavior people are objecting to and not its religion. As for being self-hating? Well, she said, I actually love myself too much as a Jew to pretend to be ignorant about something so obvious. Ignorance is not held in high regard in Jewish culture.

One story that particularly moved me was this: A woman in her late fifties or early sixties stood at the front of the bus, as we passed donkey carts and Mercedes-Benzes, and spoke of traveling to Palestine without her husband, a Jewish man who was born in Palestine. Several times they had come back to Palestine, renamed Israel, to see family. To attend graduations, weddings, and funerals. Each time they were held for hours at the airport as her husband was stripped, searched, interrogated, and threatened when he spoke up for himself. In short, because his passport was stamped with the place of his birth, Palestine, he was treated like a Palestinian. This Jewish husband sent his best wishes, but he could no longer endure travel in so painful a part of the world. By now most of us are aware of the dehumanizing treatment anyone not Jewish receives on crossing a border into Israel. Especially brutal for Palestinians. I thought: even our new president, Barack Hussein Obama, were he just anybody, and not the president of the United States, would have a humiliating time getting into Israel. The poet, and rebel, in me instantly wanted him to try it. To don the clothing of an average person, as truth-seeking people do in Wisdom tales, and travel into Israel. To learn what is real and true, not by traveling through the air, but by walking on the ground.

11. Riding on the bus

Riding on the bus, listening to the stories of people drawn to the side of the Palestinian people, I leaned into the landscape. Mile after mile of barren desert went by, with scatterings of villages and towns. The farther into the Sinai we went the more poverty we saw. One sight in particular has stayed with me: the Bedouin, formerly the nomads of the desert, attempting to live alongside the road or on the barren hills, without their camels, without mobility. Sometimes in dwellings made of sticks and straw.

Occasionally lone women in flowing black robes walked along a ridge in the heat, going someplace not visible to the eye. Hundreds of tiny white-brick houses, most unfinished, studded the hills. I asked my friend: What do you think those small white buildings are? He said: Bunkers.* Mausoleums? But no, seeing them appear in all manner and stage of construction, over hundreds of miles, I saw they were poor peoples' attempts at building housing for themselves. They looked like bunkers and mausoleums because no one was around them, and because they were so small: some of them barely large enough to lie down in, and often with no windows, only a door. I realized people who worked far

*I have been informed that my companion was probably right. That these tiny white structures were not homes but bunkers and barracks erected by the Israeli military during its occupation of the Sinai.

away and were able to return to build only sporadically were building them. This is true in many places in the world, and I was moved by the tenacity of people trying to have a home, no matter how uprooted or displaced they have been. Creating and having a home is a primary instinct in all of nature as well as in humankind; seeing these tiny dwellings, with no water sources, no electricity, no anything but white mud bricks, made me remember my own childhood feelings of insecurity around housing, and the preciousness of having a home, as we were forced to move, year after year.

12. Rachel's parents, Cindy and Craig

I came out of this reverie to hear the story of Cindy and Craig Corrie, the parents of Rachel Corrie, who were traveling with us. Rachel Corrie was murdered when she tried to stop an Israeli tank from demolishing a Palestinian house. I was struck by her parents' beauty and dignity. Cindy's face radiates resolve and kindness. Craig's is a study in acceptance, humility, incredible strength, and perseverance. Rachel had been working in Palestine and witnessed the ruthlessness of the deliberate destruction of Palestinian homes by the Israeli army, most surrounded by gardens or small orchards of orange and olive trees, which the army consistently uprooted. No doubt believing the sight of a young American woman in a brightly colored jumpsuit would stop the soldier in the tank, she placed herself between the home of her Palestinian friends and the tank. It rolled over her, crushing her body and breaking her back. The Corries spoke of their continued friendship with the family who had lived in that house.

Everywhere we went, after arriving in Gaza, locals greeted the Corries with compassion and tenderness. This was particularly moving to me because of a connection I was able to make with another such sacrifice decades ago in Mississippi, in 1967, and how black people became aware that there were some white people who actually cared about what was happening to them. The "three civil rights workers," as they became known, were James Cheney, a young African American Christian man, and Andrew Goodman and Michael Schwerner, both white Jewish men from the North.

The Northerners had been called to the civil rights movement in the South by their consciences, having watched the racist and sadistic treatment of black people there. The three young men were riding through the backwoods of Neshoba County, Mississippi, when their car was firebombed. They were dragged from the car, bludgeoned, and shot to death; their bodies were buried in a dam that was under construction in the area and would not be found for months. While America waited for the bodies to be found, black and white people working for black liberation in the South discovered new ground. Who could not love these young men, all three of them, for risking their lives to change ours? And so, in every church, every Sunday, prayers went out for James, yes, but also for Michael and Andrew. They became ours, just as the Corries have become family to the Palestinian people.

This is one of the most beautiful passages for human beings. It is as if we enter a different door of our reality, when someone gives her or his life for us. Why this should be is a mystery, but it is the mystery, I think, behind all the great myths in which there is human sacrifice—not on an altar but on the road, in the street—for the common good. At a meeting of the Veterans of the Mississippi Civil Rights Movement held in Jackson, Mississippi, last year, I saw the widow of Michael Schwerner. There she was, over forty years later. There she was, still belonging to her own people, and still, also, one of us.

13. Mother force

We arrived in the Gaza Strip in the afternoon, after being kept at the border crossing for about five hours. Long enough to become accustomed to the bombing someone informed us is a constant just inside the Palestinian border, reminding the Palestinians of the Israeli presence during the cease-fire.

I had never been so close to bombs being dropped before, and I took the opportunity to interrogate my life. Had I lived it the best way I could? And so forth. A young Palestinian man, Abdullah X, a student of video at a school in Egypt, had joined us. He had managed to leave Palestine on scholarship to go to school in Cairo three years earlier. Because of the siege, and all borders being closed, he had not been able to see his family. He had not seen them for three years. Because of Israel's bombardment of Gaza he feared for the lives of his family and was determined to see them.

Abdullah might have stepped out of ancient Assyria. With large dark eyes, olive complexion, and hair in curly dark ringlets, he was a striking

young man. Between Cairo and the Gaza border, he had, without doing anything special, made many of us on the bus care about him. Sure
enough, the Egyptian border patrol gave Abdullah a hard time. When
I was told of this by a woman who had stood next to him until ordered
away by a patrolman, we decided to stand some distance from him, while
he seemed to be pleading to be allowed to visit his parents, and send the
Mother force, the Universal Parent force, to speed his liberation. We
stood together, closed our eyes, and sent every ounce of our combined
energy to Abdullah's back. When he was given his passport and allowed
to join us, we cheered. We could only imagine what going back into
Gaza meant for him. This was his home, and much of it had been obliterated. We could not know at the time that, coming out of Gaza, Abdullah would be kept at the border crossing, as he had feared, not permitted
back into Egypt. We would wait for him, but ultimately we would leave
him there. He had realized his education, and his future, were at risk.
But his love of his family, his home, and his land was very strong.

Later we would also have a glimpse of his father, and his relationship
with his father. We were moved by the love and affection expressed between them. For what could it mean to know from day to day that you
could easily lose each other to the madness of war? A war brought to
your door by people who claimed everything you had, no matter how
little was left, was theirs?

14. Rolling into Gaza

Rolling into Gaza City I had a feeling of homecoming. There is a flavor
to the ghetto. To the Bantustan. To the "rez." To the "colored section."
In some ways it is surprisingly comforting. Because consciousness is
comforting. Everyone you see has an awareness of struggle, of resistance,
just as you do. The man driving the donkey cart. The woman selling
vegetables. The young person arranging rugs on the sidewalk or flowers in a vase.

When I lived in segregated Eatonton, Georgia, I used to breathe
normally only in my own neighborhood, only in the black section of
town. Everywhere else was too dangerous.

A friend was beaten and thrown in prison for helping a white girl, in
broad daylight, fix her bicycle chain. But even this sliver of a neighborhood, so rightly named the Gaza Strip, was not safe. It had been bombed

for twenty-two days. I thought of how, in the United States, the first and perhaps only bombing on U.S. soil, prior to 9/11, was the bombing of a black community in Tulsa, Oklahoma, in the 1920s. The black people who created it were considered, by white racists, too prosperous and therefore "uppity." Everything they created was destroyed. This was followed by the charge already rampant in white American culture, that black people never tried to "better" themselves. There is ample evidence in Gaza that the Palestinians never stop trying to "better" themselves. What started as a refugee camp with tents has evolved into a city with buildings rivaling those in almost any other city in the "developing" world. There are houses, apartment buildings, schools, mosques, churches, libraries, hospitals. Driving along the streets, we could see right away that many of these were in ruins. I realized I had never understood the true meaning of "rubble." Such and such was "reduced to rubble" is a phrase we hear. It is different seeing what demolished buildings actually look like. Buildings in which people were living. Buildings from which hundreds of broken bodies have been removed; so thorough a job have the Palestinians done in removing the dead from squashed dwellings that no scent of death remains.

What this task must have been like, both physically and psychologically, staggers the mind. We pass police stations that were simply flattened, and all the young (most Palestinians are young) officers in them killed, hundreds of them. We pass ministries, bombed into fragments. We pass a hospital, bombed and gutted by fire. If one is not safe in a hospital, when one is already sick and afraid, where is one safe?

If children are not safe playing in their school yards, where are they safe?

Where are
The World Parents of All Children?
The World Caretakers of All the Sick?

15. Two Sisters

My companion and I are assigned to the home of two sisters who share their space with friends and relatives who come and go. One morning I get up early to find an aunt sleeping on the floor in the living room. Another time, a cousin. In the middle of the night I hear one of the sisters consoling her aged father, who sounds disoriented, and helping him back to bed. There is such respect, such tenderness in her voice. This is the same place that, just weeks earlier, was surrounded by rocket fire, a missile landing every twenty-seven seconds for twenty-two days. I can only imagine what the elderly residents must feel, as, even in their old age, they are subjected to so much fear. Each morning we are sent off to learn what we can in our four days in Gaza, well fed on falafel, hummus, olives, and dates, sometimes eggs, tomatoes, salad, and cheese. All of it simple, all of it delicious.

More delicious because we realize how difficult it is to find such food here; the blockade keeps out most of it. Delicious also because it is shared with such generosity and graciousness. Always the culinary student, I try to learn to make the especially tasty dish that consists mainly of tomatoes and eggs. I learn the tea I like so much is made out of sage! On International Women's Day we leave for the celebration for which we have come, a gathering with the women of Gaza.

16. Hatred and headscarves

Gael Murphy, Medea Benjamin, Susan Griffin, and I, along with twenty or so other women, had been arrested for protesting the war on Iraq on International Women's Day, 2003. If the world had paid attention we could have saved a lot of money, countless sons' and daughters' lives, as well as prevented a lot of war-generated pollution that hastens globe-threatening climate change. How doofus humans are going to look—we thought as we marched, sang, accepted our handcuffs—still firing rockets into apartment buildings full of families, and dropping bombs on school children and their pets, when the ice melts completely in the Arctic and puts an end to our regressive, greed-sourced rage forever. That had been a wonderful day; this International Women's Day, of 2009, was also. It was the kind of day that makes life, already accepted as a gift, a prize. Early in the morning of March 8, we were shuttled to a Women's Center in the north of Gaza City, to meet women who, like their compatriots, had survived the recent bombardment and, so far, the siege.

This center for women was opened under the auspices of the United Nations, which has been ministering to the Palestinian people since 1948, when thousands of Palestinians fleeing their homes under Israeli

attack became refugees. It is a modest building with a small library
whose shelves hold few books. It isn't clear whether most of the women
read. The idea, as it is explained to us, is to offer the women a place to
gather outside the home, since, in Palestinian culture, the mobility of
most women is limited by their work in the home as mothers and caretakers of their families. Many women rarely leave their compounds.
However, today, International Women's Day, is different. Many women
are out and about, and women who frequent this particular center are
on hand to welcome us. After arranging ourselves around a table in the
library, we, about thirty of us, sit in Council.

I learn something I'd heard but never experienced: Arabs introduce
themselves by telling you they are the mother or father of one of their
children, perhaps their eldest: then they tell you how many children
they have. They do this with a pride and joy I have never seen before.
Only one woman had one child. Everyone else had at least five. There
is a feeling of festivity as the women, beautifully dressed and wearing
elegant headscarves, laugh and joke among themselves. They are eager
to talk. Only the woman with one child has trouble speaking. When I
turn to her, I notice she is the only woman wearing black, and that her
eyes are tearing. Unable to speak, she hands me instead a photograph
that she has been holding in her lap. She is a brown-skinned woman,
of African descent, as some Palestinians (to my surprise) are; the photograph is of her daughter, who looks European. The child looks about
six years old. A student of ballet, she is dressed in a white tutu and is
dancing. Her mother tries to speak, but still cannot, as I sit, holding
her arm. It is another woman who explains: during the bombardment,
the child was hit in the arm, the leg, and the chest and bled to death in
her mother's arms. The mother and I embrace, and throughout our
meeting I hold the photograph of the child, while the mother draws
her chair closer to mine.

What do we talk about?

We talk about hatred.

But before we talk about hatred I want to know about headscarves.
What's the deal about wearing the scarf? Why do so many women wear
it? I am aware of some of the religious reasons for wearing the hijab,
and certainly no item of clothing has been more recently discussed, on
several continents. I had learned of the prophet Mohammed's demand
that his own wives be veiled, to protect them from the gaze of visitors

and strangers; and of course the ongoing discussions regarding hijab wear in England and France have been much in the news. There is also the brutal insistence in some Muslim countries that women cover themselves to demonstrate submission to religious (and male) authority. However, I was curious to know what grassroots Arab women thought about the scarf, assuming as I do that most items of clothing have a use before religion claims one for them. As was proved by what the women shared. I am told something I'd never considered: in desert countries most of one's hydration is lost at the back of the neck, which can quickly lead to heatstroke, so a headscarf that wraps around the neck is essential to block this loss. The top of the head is covered because if a woman is living a traditional life and is outside a lot, the sun beats down on it. This causes headache, dizziness, nausea, stroke, and other health problems. In Gaza, one of the women pointed out, there were many women who did not wear scarves, primarily because they worked in offices. This was true of the women in whose home we were sheltered. They seemed to own a lot of scarves that they draped about themselves casually, just as my friends and I might do in the United States.

Because I had shaved my head a week or so before going to Gaza, I understood exactly the importance of the headscarf. Without a covering on my head I could not bear the sun for more than a few minutes. And, indeed, one of the first gifts I received from an anonymous Palestinian woman was a thick black and red embroidered scarf, which I wore everywhere, gratefully.

Our host told us a story about the uglier side of the headscarf business: On the first day of bombing she was working downstairs in the basement and wasn't aware that her apartment building was next to one that was being shelled. When the policemen came to clear her building, and she stepped out of the elevator, one of them, a political and religious conservative, was taken aback at the sight of her bare head. So much so that instead of instantly helping her to a shelter, he called a colleague to come and witness her attire. Or lack thereof. He was angry with her for not wearing a headscarf, though Israeli rockets were tearing into buildings all around them. And what could we do but sigh along with her, as she related this experience with appropriate shrugs and grimaces of exasperation. Backwardness is backwardness, wherever it occurs, and explains lack of progressive movement in some afflicted societies, whether under siege or not.

17. It feels familiar

One of the triumphs of the civil rights movement is that when you travel through the South today you do not feel overwhelmed by a residue of grievance and hate. This is the legacy of people brought up in the Christian tradition, true believers of every word Jesus had to say on the issue of justice, loving kindness, and peace. This dovetailed nicely with what we learned of Gandhian nonviolence, brought into the movement by Bayard Rustin, a gay strategist for the civil rights movement. A lot of thought went into how to create "the beloved community," so that our country would not be stuck with violent hatred between black and white, and the continuous spectacle, and suffering, of communities going up in flames. The progress is astonishing and I will always love Southerners, black and white, for the way we have all grown. Ironically, though there was so much suffering and despair as the struggle for justice tested us, it is in this very "backward" part of our country today that one is most likely to find simple human helpfulness, thoughtfulness, and disinterested courtesy.

I speak a little about this American history, but it isn't history that these women know. They're too young. They've never been taught it. It feels irrelevant. Following their example of speaking of their families, I talk about my Southern parents' teachings during our experience of America's apartheid years, when white people owned and controlled all the resources and the land, in addition to the political, legal, and military apparatus, and used their power to intimidate black people in the most barbaric and merciless ways. These whites who tormented us daily were like Israelis who have cut down millions of trees planted by Arab Palestinians, stolen Palestinian water, even topsoil. They have bulldozed innumerable villages, houses, mosques, and in their place built settlements for strangers who have no connection whatsoever with Palestine, settlers who have been the most rabid anti-Palestinian of all, attacking the children, the women, everyone, old and young alike, viciously, and forcing Palestinians to use separate roads from those they use themselves.

What is happening here feels very familiar, I tell them. When something similar was happening to us, in Mississippi, Georgia, Alabama, and Louisiana, I say, our parents taught us to think of the racists as we thought of any other disaster. To deal with that disaster as best we could, but not to attach to it by allowing ourselves to hate. This was a tall order, and as I'm talking, I begin to understand, as if for the first time, why some of our parents' prayers were so long and fervent as they stayed there on their knees in church. And why people often wept, and fainted, and why there was so much tenderness as people deliberately silenced themselves, or camouflaged atrocities done to or witnessed by them, using representative figures from the Bible.

At the end of the table across from me is a woman who looks like Oprah's twin. In fact, earlier she had said to me: Alice, tell Oprah to come see us. We will take good care of her. I promised I would e-mail Oprah, and, on returning home, did so. She laughs, this handsome woman, then speaks earnestly. We don't hate Israelis, Alice, she says, quietly. What we hate is being bombed, watching our little ones live in fear, burying them, being starved to death, and being driven from our land. We hate this eternal crying out to the world to open its eyes and ears to the truth of what is happening, and being ignored. Israelis, no.

If they stopped humiliating and torturing us, if they stopped taking everything we have, including our lives, we would hardly think about them at all. Why would we?

18. Overwhelm

There is a sense of overwhelm, trying to bring comfort to someone whose sleeping child has been killed and buried, a few weeks ago, up to her neck in rubble. Or to a mother who has lost fifteen members of her family, all her children, grandchildren, brothers and sisters, her husband. What does one say to people whose families came out of their shelled houses waving white flags of surrender only to be shot down anyway? To mothers whose children are, at this moment, playing in the white phosphorous–laden rubble that, after twenty-two days of bombing, is everywhere in Gaza? White phosphorus, once on the skin, never stops burning. There is really nothing to say. Nothing to say to those who, back home in America, don't want to hear the news.

Nothing to do, finally, but dance.

19. Dance

The women and I and everyone with us from CODEPINK went across the hall to a big common room where music was turned up full volume.

At first I sat exchanging smiles and murmurs with an ancient grand-mother who was knitting booties, and who gave me two pairs, for my own grandchildren. Sitting didn't last. Without preamble I was pulled to my feet by several women at once, and the dance was on. Sorrow, loss, pain, suffering, all pounded into the floor for over an hour. Sweat flowing, wails and tears around the room. And then, the rising that always comes from such dancing; the sense of joy, unity, solidarity, and gratitude to be in the best place one could be on earth; with sisters who have experienced the full measure of disaster and have the heart to rise above it. The feeling of love is immense. The ecstasy, sublime. I was conscious of exchanging and receiving Spirit in the dance. I also knew that this Spirit, which I have encountered in Mississippi, Georgia, the Congo, Cuba, Rwanda, and Burma, among other places, this Spirit that knows how to dance in the face of disaster, will never be crushed. It is as timeless as the wind. We think it is only inside our bodies, but we also inhabit it. Even when we are unaware of its presence internally, it wears us like a cloak.

20. They broke my house

I could have gone home then. I had learned what I came to know: that humans are an amazing lot. That to willfully harm any one of us is to damage us all. That hatred of ourselves is the root cause of any harm done to others, others so like us! And that we are lucky to live at a time when all lies will be exposed, along with the relief of not having to serve them any longer. But I did not go home. I went instead to visit the homeless.

Coming out of a small grouping of tents, with absolutely nothing inside them, no bedding, no food, no water, were middle-aged and el-derly people who looked as if their sky had fallen. It had. An old, old man, leaning on a stick, met me as I trudged up a hill so I might see the extent of the devastation. Vast. Look, look! He said to me in English, come look at my house! He was wearing dusty cotton trousers and an old army greatcoat. I felt dragged along by the look in his eyes. He led me to what had been his house. It had obviously, from the remains, been a large and spacious dwelling; now he and his wife lived between two of the fallen walls that made a haphazard upside-down V. She looked as stunned and as lost as he did. There was not a single useable item visible.

Near what must have been the front entrance, the old man placed me directly in front of the remains of bulldozed trees. They broke my house, he said, by bombing it, and then they came with bulldozers and they broke my lemon and olives trees. The Israeli military has destroyed over two and a half million olive and fruit trees alone since 1948. Having planted many trees myself, I shared his sorrow about the fate of these ones. I imagined them alive and sparkling with life, offering olives and lemons, the old man and his wife able to sit in the shade of the trees in the afternoons, and have a cup of tea there in the evenings.

You speak English, I observed. Yes, he said, I was once in the British army. I supposed this was during the time Britain controlled Palestine, before 1948. We walked along in silence, as I did what I had come to do: witness. CODEPINK members and my companion and I walked through the rubble of demolished homes, schools, medical centers, and factories. After the bombing the Israelis had indeed bulldozed everything so that I was able to find just one piece of evidence that beauty had flourished on this hillside, a shard from a piece of colorful tile, about the size of my hand. Someone in our group wanted it, and I gave it to her. They had taken pains to pulverize what they had destroyed.

Coming upon another grouping of tents, I encountered an old woman sitting on the ground in what would have been, perhaps, the doorway of her demolished, pulverized home. She was clean and impeccably dressed, the kind of old woman who is known and loved and respected by everyone in the community, as my own mother had been. Her eyes were dark and full of life. She talked to us freely.

I gave her a gift I had brought, and she thanked me. Looking into my eyes she said: May God protect you from the Jews. When the young Palestinian interpreter told me what she'd said, I responded: It's too late, I already married one. I said this partly because, like so many Jews in America, my former husband could not tolerate criticism of Israel's behavior toward the Palestinians. Our very different positions on what is happening now in Palestine/Israel and what has been happening for over fifty years has been perhaps our most severe disagreement. It is a subject we have never been able to rationally discuss. He does not see the racist treatment of Palestinians as the same racist treatment of blacks and some Jews that he fought against so nobly in Mississippi. And that he objected to in his own Brooklyn-based family. When his younger brother knew he was seeing me, a black person, he bought and nailed over an entire side of his bedroom the largest Confederate flag either of us had ever seen. His brother, a young Jewish man who had never traveled to the South, and had perhaps learned most of what he knew about black history from *Gone With the Wind*, expressed his contempt for black people in this way. His mother, when told of our marriage, sat shiva, which declared my husband dead.

These were people who knew how to hate, and how to severely punish others, even those beloved, as he was. This is one reason I understand the courage it takes for some Jews to speak out against Israeli brutality and against what they know are crimes against humanity. Most Jews who know their own history see how relentlessly the Israeli government is attempting to turn Palestinians into the "new Jews," patterned on Jews of the Holocaust era, as if someone must hold that place, in order for Jews to avoid it.

21. Jewish friends of the planet

Lucky for me, my husband's family were not the only Jews I knew, having met Howard Zinn, my history teacher at Spelman College in 1961, as my very first (secular) Jew, and later poet Muriel Rukeyser, at Sarah Lawrence College, who, like Grace Paley, the short-story writer, raised her voice against the Israeli occupation of Palestine and the horrible mistreatment of the Palestinian people. There are my Jewish friends of the planet: Amy Goodman, Jack Kornfield, Noam Chomsky, Medea Benjamin, and Barbara Lubin, who are as piercing in their assessments of Israeli behavior as they have been of African or African American, or Indian, or Chinese, or Burmese behavior. I place my faith in them, and others like us, who see how greed and brutality are not limited to any segment of humanity but will grow wherever it is unchecked, in any society. The people of Israel have not been helped by America's blind loyalty to their survival as a Jewish state, by any means necessary. The very settlers they've used American taxpayer money to install on Palestinian land turn out to be a scary lot, fighting not only against Palestinians, but also against Israelis, when they do not get their way.

Israelis stand now exposed, the warmongers and peacemakers alike, as people who are ruled by leaders that the world considers irrational, vengeful, scornful of international law, and utterly frightening. There are differing opinions about this, of course, but my belief is that when a country primarily instills fear in the minds and hearts of the people of the world, it is no longer useful in joining the dialogue we need for saving the planet. There is no hiding what Israel has done or what it does on a daily basis to protect and extend its power. It uses weapons that cut off limbs without bleeding; it drops bombs into people's homes that never stop detonating in the bodies of anyone who is hit; it causes pollution so severe it is probable that Gaza may be uninhabitable for years to come, though Palestinians, having nowhere else to go, will have to live there.

This is a chilling use of power, supported by the United States of America, no small foe, if one stands up to it. No wonder that most people prefer to look the other way during this genocide, hoping their disagreement with Israeli policies will not be noted.

Good Germans, good Americans, good Jews.

But, as our sister Audre Lorde liked to warn us: our silence will not protect us. In the ongoing global climate devastation that is worsened by war activities, we will all suffer, and we will also be afraid.

22. The world knows

The world knows it is too late for a two-state solution. This old idea, bandied about since at least the eighties, denounced by Israel for decades, isn't likely to become reality with the massive build-up of settlements all over what remains of Palestinian land. Ariel Sharon is having the last word: Jewish settlements exactly like a pastrami sandwich; Palestinian life erased, as if it never existed, or crushed under the weight of a superior Israeli military presence and a teaching of Jewish supremacy sure to stunt Palestinian identity among Arabs living in Israel.

What is to be done?

What is to be done? Our revered Tolstoy asked this question, speaking also of *War and Peace*. I believe there must be a one-state settlement. Palestinians and Jews, who have lived together in peace in the past, must work together to make this a reality once again. This land (so soaked in Jewish and Palestinian blood, and with America's taxpayer dollars wasted on violence the majority of us would never, if we knew, support) must become, like South Africa, the secure and peaceful home of everyone who lives there. This will require that Palestinians, like Jews, have the right of return to their homes and their lands. Which will mean what Israelis most fear: Jews will be outnumbered and, instead of a Jewish state, there will be a Jewish, Muslim, Christian country, which is how Palestine functioned before the Europeans arrived. What is so awful about that?

The Tribunals, the generals will no doubt say. But both South Africa and Rwanda present a model of restorative justice in their Truth and Reconciliation Councils. Some crimes against humanity are so heinous nothing will ever rectify them. All we can do is attempt to understand their causes and do everything in our power to prevent them happening, to anyone, ever again. Human beings are intelligent and very often, compassionate. We can learn to heal ourselves without inflicting fresh wounds.

23. Liberation for the tyrant

Watching a video recently about Cuba's role in the ending of apartheid in South Africa, I was moved by the testimony of Pik Botha, once a high-ranking official of white South Africa. He talked about how liberating it had been when South Africa was forced to attend talks prior to negotiating Nelson Mandela's release from prison and a change from a fascist white-supremacist regime to a democratic society. He said the feeling of not being hated and feared and treated like a leper everywhere he went was wonderful. The talks were held in Egypt and for the first time he felt welcomed by the Egyptians and took the opportunity to visit the pyramids and the Sphinx and to ride on a camel! As a white-supremacist representative of a repressive, much-hated government, he'd never felt relaxed enough to do that. His words demonstrate what we all know in our hearts to be true: allowing freedom to others brings freedom to ourselves. It is true that what one reads in the papers sometimes about the birthing pains of the New South Africa can bring sadness, alarm, and near-despair. But I doubt that anyone in South Africa wishes to return to the old days of injustice and violence that scarred whites and blacks and coloreds so badly. Not just citizens of South Africa were demoralized, oppressed, and discouraged by white South Africa's behavior, but citizens of the world. Israel helped keep the racist regime in power in South Africa, giving it arms and expertise, and still the people of the world, in our outrage at the damage done to defenseless people, rose to the challenge of setting them free. That is what is happening today in Palestine.

24. The world is finding its voice

The world is, at last, finding its voice about everything that harms it. In this sense the twin teachers of catastrophic climate change (some of it caused by war) and the Internet have arrived to awaken the voice of even the most silenced. Though the horror of what we are witnessing in places like Rwanda and Congo and Burma and Israel/Palestine threatens our very ability to speak, we will speak. And, because almost everyone on the planet now acknowledges our collective slide into global disaster unless we profoundly change our ways, we will be heard.

Suggested reading, listening, viewing:

- "A Letter to the Editors of *Ms.* magazine," in my book *In Search of Our Mothers' Gardens, Womanist Prose,* 1983. This is an essay/memo written a few weeks prior to the Israeli invasion of Lebanon and a few months before the Beirut massacres, in response to an article by Letty Cottin Pogrebin: "Anti-Semitism in the Women's Movement" which appeared in the June issue, 1982. I am writing about my refusal, as a woman of color, to be silenced. And how black history supports this stance.

- My April 2010 interview in Gaza with reporters from *Democracy Now!* on YouTube: www.democracynow.org/blog/2010/4/13/poet_and_author_alice_walker_speaking_in_gaza

- "Sisterloss," an essay about the bombing of Gaza that appears in this book

- alicewalkersgarden.com

- *Palestine: Peace Not Apartheid,* by President Jimmy Carter, 2006

- *One Country: A Bold Proposal to End the Israeli-Palestinian Impasse*, by Ali Abunimah, 2006 (probably the most important book to read on Israeli/Palestinian issues at this time). Abunimah gives a remarkably balanced account of the Palestine/Israeli history, as well as a convincing argument for choosing a one-state settlement.

- *Palestine Inside Out: An Everyday Occupation*, by Saree Makdisi (2010) is a must-read, though on a day when the reader is feeling strong. The day-to-day oppression of Palestinians brought this reader almost too close to memories of growing up in the American South when any white person could demand that you get off the sidewalk.

- *A People's History of the United States,* by Howard Zinn (1980). Israel learned a lot of its behavior from America; this vital resource illustrates this.

- On YouTube: a wide selection of Noam Chomsky's teachings on Israel and Palestine

- The writings and taped lectures of Edward Said

- Interviews with Israeli soldiers on YouTube, Alternate Focus, AlterNet, and World Focus; also on *Democracy Now!* and the BBC

- Movies: *The Battle of Algiers,* 1966, and *Waltz with Bashir,* 2009

EMPATHY IS A WAVE

*The Banning of Palestinian Children's Art
(from the Museum of Children's Art in Oakland)*

I WAS INJURED AS A CHILD; my brother shot me in the eye with a pellet gun, causing disfigurement and loss of sight. The incident itself, as well as the trauma surrounding it—my father was unable to flag down a white driver (cars among black people were rare) to take me to a doctor—left me despairing and contributed to severe depressions that lasted for many years. What helped? I was able to get my hands on paper and pencil and began to write—not about what had happened to me, but about whatever arose from my melancholy, death-leaning imagination. These early "poems" I was encouraged to share; so I showed them, albeit with head hanging low, to members of my family and to anyone I trusted who came to visit. I am convinced this process of creating and sharing saved my life.

There was no museum in the tiny, segregated Georgia town closest to where we lived; though I could be wrong. I was fifty before I understood there was, somewhere hidden in the white part of town, a public library. I do remember that the art of Jimmy Lee Brundidge, a young black folk artist, was shown on the walls of the local shoe shop.

The decision by the Museum of Children's Art in Oakland not to show the work of Palestinian children from Gaza makes me sad. But not discouraged. The art will be shown. The walls of a shoe shop will be found. We will all—those of us who care about these children, whose pain our tax dollars assured—go to see it. Furthermore, we will write to the children to let them know we've seen their work and what we think of it. This is the least we can do.

Such banning as this usually backfires. I don't think I was born yet, but I "remember" that, in 1939, Marian Anderson, the great black contralto, was refused venue at Constitution Hall in Washington, D.C., by the Daughters of the American Revolution because (gasp) the audience would be integrated! Anderson supporters, including president Franklin Roosevelt and Eleanor Roosevelt, rallied to the cause and Anderson sang to a crowd in the tens of thousands while standing on the steps of the Lincoln Memorial.

We will find a Lincoln Memorial. We will eventually, on this issue of freeing the Palestinians, find a Lincoln.

I personally have never trusted museums. And I welcome this opportunity to explain what my classmates at Sarah Lawrence considered a really peculiar mind-set. It is because museums, broadly speaking, live off of the art and artifacts of others, often art and artifacts that have been obtained by dubious means. But they also manipulate whatever it is they present to the public: hence, until Judy Chicago, in the 1970s, busted open the art scene wider than it had ever stretched, few women artists were hung in any major museum. Indian artists? Artifacts only, please. Black artists? Something musical, maybe? And so forth.

Do we really need them? Or should we make more of an attempt to teach our young that art is everywhere around them: that every leaf and pebble is art? Or, that the spirit that infuses so much folk art, spirit not often encountered in "museum-quality pieces" of art, is that expression of the soul that joins human creative endeavor with the Divine.

Ah, well.

I was in Gaza a few weeks after the twenty-two days of nonstop bombing by the Israeli military. I spent an afternoon with several social workers and psychiatrists talking about the damage done to the children who survived. Hundreds of them died. I realize it's hard for grown-ups to accept that we've had a hand in making a small child armless, legless, eyeless. We want to keep thinking Americans are generous, fun-loving, baseball-crazed folks who draw the line, collectively, at child abuse. At child murder.

That image was never true, and it certainly isn't now, if we dare to acknowledge our complicity in the atrocities committed against the

Palestinian people in Gaza, and, of course, the ongoing destruction of Palestinians in the Occupied West Bank.

What will help us, now that we find ourselves standing, with Marian Anderson and countless others, in this unfair place, again?

Each child who sees the art should be given some background about war. Any war. For it is war that humanity must outgrow, wherever it arises. Most modern children have seen on television more tanks and helicopters and missiles and guns of all kinds than I could have imagined as a child. And, in fact, as a child I never had any war images in my imagination at all, since we had no television and the Civil War had ended over a century before. (I did, unfortunately, because of movies, have images of cowboys and Indians.)

I love the Bay Area for the diversity and creativity of its people. We frequently exhibit an energy of inclusivity and sharing that is a delight. We can educate and increase the capacity for compassion among our children with this art. We can make something magical, even of the present disappointing dilemma. We can encourage ourselves, and our children, never to be afraid to feel. *No one dies from compassion* is a mantra they might like.

Empathy is a wave that need never be stopped. If our children can catch this wave, from the ocean of tears shed by Palestinian children, they might have a future in a more stable and saner world.

TO THE FREEDOM RIDERS
OF PALESTINE

NOVEMBER 13, 2011

BLACK AND INDIGENOUS PEOPLE in the American South had suffered humiliation and brutality for hundreds of years (including literal enslavement) before our Freedom Riders (with the support of the civil rights movement) arrived in the 1960s to challenge the status quo. They risked everything: their reputations, their connections to families that didn't understand the sacred nature of their mission, their bodies, and their lives. They were beaten, firebombed, jailed. Misrepresented in the media and misunderstood by some of their dearest friends.

Their hunger for freedom, and justice for all, was strong.

In my own life, I have come to understand, and cherish, the hunger for what is right: it is the absolute certainty that there is no "other" who suffers, leaving me in peace. There is only each and every one of us, together creating a world where justice might bring peace to all.

Board the buses to Everywhere. Sit freely. Go into Jerusalem with my blessing. Like many of my countrypeople, I have witnessed this scenario before and know where it can lead. To a straightening of the back and a full breath taken by the soul.

Some of us have shed blood, others have shed tears. Some have shed both. All sacred to the cause of the dignity we deserve as beautifully fashioned citizens and Beings of this Universe.

Onward through the Myth!

Namasté,
Alice Walker

On November 15, 2011, Palestinians boarded settler-only buses and attempted to ride on settler-only roads (built on Palestinian land) in the "territories" occupied by Israel.

THE SANITY OF
FRIENDSHIP

A Foreword to Miko Peled's book
The General's Son

THERE ARE FEW BOOKS on the Palestine/Israel issue that seem as hopeful to me as this one. First of all, we find ourselves in the hands of a formerly Zionist Israeli who honors his people, loves his homeland, respects and cherishes his parents, other family members, and friends, and is, to boot, the son of a famous general whose activities during Israel's wars against the Palestinian people helped cause much of their dislocation and suffering. Added to this, long after Miko Peled, the writer, has left the Special Forces of the Israeli army and moved to Southern California to teach karate, a beloved niece, his sister's daughter, Smadar, a young citizen of Jerusalem, is killed by Palestinians in a suicide bombing. Right away we think: Goodness. How is he ever going to get anywhere sane with this history? He does.

I don't remember when I heard Miko Peled talk about the Israeli/Palestinian "conflict" but I was moved by a story he was telling (probably on YouTube) about his mother. I am sensitive to mothers, who never, it seems to me, get enough credit for their impact on society and the world, and so I was eager to hear what this Israeli peace activist, karate master, and writer had to say about his. He was telling the story of the Nakba from his mother's point of view. Nakba is Arabic for the "Catastrophe" that happened to Palestinians when the Israeli army, in lethal force, invaded their communities in 1947–48 and drove them, in the hundreds of thousands, out of their homes, frequently looting and/or blowing up homes, but if the houses were beautiful and/or well situated, taking them for themselves. As the invaders moved in, the coffee, Peled was informed, was sometimes still on the table, still hot, as the inhabitants were forced to flee. His mother, Zika, was offered one of these confiscated houses. She refused it. It was unbearable to her that she might be sitting sipping coffee in the home of another woman who was now, with her frightened or wounded family, sitting, hungry and miserable, in a refugee camp.

Miko Peled's father, General Matti Peled, also rises to full and compassionate dignity in his son's narrative, though somewhat later, and, one feels, with considerably more of a struggle than his wife. He was, after all, a staunch Zionist and a general in the Israeli army, richly praised for his acumen and courage in battle, both in Israel's "War of Independence" in 1947–48 (the Palestinians' "Catastrophe") and in the 1967 war in which Israel preemptively attacked its neighbor, Egypt, and proceeded, illegally, to take huge parts of what was until then Palestine.

Although the generals knew that the Egyptian army was too weak at the time to pose a military threat to Israel, Peled and his fellow officers carried out their plan to attack and destroy Egypt as a military power. However, even before this event, Peled had begun experiencing a change of outlook. The aftermath of a massacre of Palestinian civilians by Israeli soldiers made a deep impression on him, and caused him to believe that an army of occupation kept in place indefinitely would ultimately lead to the most hideous violence, and demoralization not only of the Palestinian oppressed but of the Israeli oppressors as well.

After many decades of service to his country, General Peled left the army to become a professor of Arabic literature at Tel Aviv and Haifa Universities. He learned Arabic and spoke it fluently. He became, as well, a peace activist. He worked with and made friends among Palestinian peace activists and leaders, as his son Miko Peled would do decades later. One such friend was the controversial head of the Palestine Liberation Organization, Yasser Arafat.

What is the prevailing feeling, having read this moving book, given how determined our testosterone-driven world seems to be to make continuous, endless war, and, perhaps, to blow all of us up in one—possibly soon? I feel immense relief, and gratitude. Someone(s) must take responsibility for being the grown-ups of our human Universe. There must be people, in all walks of life, who decide: *enough's enough; there are children here.* That even if, in your derangement and pain, or your greed and covetousness, you do me grievous harm, even the taking of the life of my child, I still choose to see you and your people as human, though perhaps distorted, warped and tortured almost beyond human recognition. I refuse to turn away from the effort to talk to you, frightened though I might be. Whenever possible, I will not refuse to make friends.

Miko Peled, at first terrified of reaching out to Palestinians because of the false reports he was, since childhood, given of them, realizes the insanity of remaining enemies of a people he has had no opportunity to truly know. What he discovers energizes and encourages him. He begins to understand the danger inherent in living in ignorance of the so-called "other" and begins to realize he would be a far different, a far less open and loving person, had he not, despite his fears, freed himself in this way. His freedom to be at ease with the very people he was taught to hate is, of course, a bonus for his own children and for the next generation of Israelis and Palestinians.

The extreme volatility of the Middle East, with Israel's lengthy list of human rights abuses and contempt for international opinion and law at the center of everybody's fear, is a threat to us all. It is senseless to believe anyone on the planet can afford to ignore or dismiss it.

Miko Peled is a credit to both his parents. As he tries to raise funds for and then to ship 1,280 wheelchairs to those maimed and made invalids in Palestine and Israel, I see his mother's compassion for others who have lost what he still has; in his tireless teaching of martial arts to children, especially those in Palestine, I see his father, the general, spreading the faith among the troops that being outnumbered and out-armed is no reason not to win.

A shared homeland, the dream of growing numbers of Israelis and Palestinians, in which each person feels free to be herself or himself, is, or might be, the prize of friendship. In fact, it is only by choosing friendship over enmity that winning makes any sense in a world as on the brink as the one we are living in, where being enemies and attempting to disappear each other has played out, leaving destruction, ugliness, cynicism, and fear. Not to mention a ruined planet, disease, and death.

We will share the Earth, and care for it together, as friends of each other and to Her, or we will lose it. I look to the examples of "enemies"

becoming friends everywhere in this book to help us continue to carefully choose our way.

THE FOLLOWING POEM was inspired by watching, on video, home demolitions and house grabbing by Israeli settlers in Palestine. It was a
shock to witness the jubilation of the "conquerors" while installing
the Israeli flag on the roof of a house whose just-evicted inhabitants
huddled in the street below.

I dedicate it to Smadar, the Israeli, and to the two unknown Palestinian suicide bombers who died with her, perhaps also teenagers, as
she was. I wish with all my heart that they might have been friends,
playing together rather than dying together, to the grief of all of us
who honor the young.

HOPE
©2011 by Alice Walker

Hope never
to covet
the neighbors' house
with the fragrant
garden
from which a family
has been
driven by your soldiers;
mother, father,
grandparents,
the toddler and
the dog
now homeless:
huddled, holding on
to each other,
stunned
and friendless
beneath you
in the street:

sitting on
cobblestones
as if on the sofas
inside
that you have decided
to clean, re-cover and
keep.

Hope never
to say yes
to their misery.

Hope never to gaze
down into their faces
from what used to be
their rooftop.

Hope never to believe
this robbery
will make you a better
citizen of your new
country
as you unfurl and wave
its recent
flag
that has been given
to assure you
of this impossibility.

SOLIDARITY
Onward

ENCOUNTERING THE
UNKNOWN BRAZIL

APRIL 25, 2012

IT IS ONLY FAIR, I BELIEVE, to state plainly: I know very little about Brazil. But this should not be discouraging to contemplate. Since my college years I have first visited places I knew little about in preparation for finding out a lot. The primary incentive to make a trip to Brazil was a documentary called *Waste Land* made by the Brazilian artist Vik Muniz. It seemed, serendipitously, to drop into my lap, just when I was thinking I knew nothing whatsoever about Brazil, and it opened a very important window. Vik Muniz, in his work with the garbage pickers (i.e., dedicated recyclers of society's waste) in a dump in Rio De Janeiro shows us what it means to be an artist who truly cares about the world he is depicting. I was able to see something of the spirit and soul of the people considered "lowest down" in Brazilian society. I admired, and even loved them.

There for the world to see, and to respect, is their willingness to work hard, their beautiful dignity, their appreciation of beauty: even at the garbage dump the women wear their earrings (long!) and their determination to make a better life for their comrades and their children. It is a remarkable documentary, and of course the art that Vik Muniz creates out of the "garbage" of society is spectacular. I loved his very simple way of making each person who would become "art" someone deeply involved in his or her own growth. Here is an artist who doesn't "steal" the people's image (and bits of their soul) but rather nourishes and enlarges it.

What a marvelous introduction to Brazil was this documentary!

Serendipitously also I read, shortly before arriving here, an article in the *New York Times* that you have—that is to say, your country, Brazil, has—managed to figure out and implement a way of supporting your artists; that their income is somehow tied to the Gross National Product. They need never, as artists so often do, even in so called "developed" countries, beg for sustenance, as they prepare the work that feeds the spirit and soul of the entire people.

I must emphasize that hearing that you are wise enough to take care of the arts in your country made a great impression on me. In fact, I was moved to tears. Any country that cares enough to truly support art will be a strong country; for it is inevitable that the spiritual life of every citizen will be enriched and empowered.

It was suggested to me by the very kind people who invited me to speak today that I take a stab at sharing my thoughts about the African/Amerindian presence in the United States and the ways in which, through the arts, especially literature (and perhaps music), political activism, and, I must add, suffering, we have managed to carve out a positive presence in our deeply racist country. A country that is changing, but one in which it is impossible to claim that people of color exhibit radiant physical, mental, or spiritual health. Even though our president is a person of color, black people as a whole are perhaps worse off, economically, and spiritually, than we've been in many generations. Many of us have lost optimism. As you can imagine, this is a great shock and sadness for millions of us.

We are intrinsically a hopeful people, however; we earned this attitude the same way many Brazilians did: we survived hundreds of years of brutal enslavement, exploitation, apartheid, and general soul and body assault. I like to point out that our suffering, like some of yours, under what amounted to Nazi rule, continued for centuries. Because we understand ourselves to be extensions of our ancestors, who had lives of much greater stress and cruelty than ours, we feel ourselves blessed, even when times are bleak, as they are today.

We are a people who have become racially and culturally mixed (and here I will offer my own composition of: African, Native American, and European) to become beautifully and/or oddly a blend and, partly because of this blending, we have brought many gifts to North American culture. In music, in dance, in poetry, in literature and in spirituality, though these gifts have often been insulted, stolen, or ignored. This was our lot for centuries. In the past seventy or so years, as the world has witnessed and sometimes cheered, we have made changes.

I would like to use my own life as an example of some of those changes.

Many of you know of me because of my novel *The Color Purple*, which was made into a film by Steven Spielberg. I am grateful for this film, especially if you have seen it, because it represents a period in the lives of people of color in the United States you might not know anything about, otherwise. This is one reason I love films and especially documentaries. We are able to educate ourselves about each other so that there's less of the ignorance about "the other" that can cause wars.

Many viewers of this film, and readers of the novel, have assumed it is autobiographical. It isn't. Though it does have more than a little of the life force of the community my parents and grandparents lived in, and to a degree, shaped, years before I was born. I wrote the novel out of a passion to spend time with these family members who became "characters" and the result has been what I had hoped it would be: their humanity would be witnessed, their story would have meaning for others, and their life experiences would be a lesson for anyone in need of one.

The Color Purple was my tenth book.

My first novel, *The Third Life of Grange Copeland*, is also set in the South and explores the practice of sharecropping, which was a system of exploitation of former slaves that in all respects was still enslavement, though there was the "freedom" to work for several different white land owners instead of one.

My second novel, *Meridian*, is set in the South, in Mississippi, and explores the civil rights movement as it impacted the mostly young people who were drawn to it. This is a movement in which I was involved. Before this movement began there was very little visible evidence of black achievement in mainstream society; this lack was even more blatant in the South. So much so that it was expected, if one had any ambition at all to become an artist, a musician, or a surgeon, for instance, that one would move immediately to the North, where one's ambitions might have a chance.

Our schoolbooks, when I was a child, were the used books from the white schools and these books were entirely racist. The few images of black people in them were horrible. Red people, the Indians, fared a bit better. But only because it was assumed they were all "vanishing." Yellow and brown people were practically nonexistent. Our parents did their best to enrich our education by reading to us at home—from catalogs and magazines—and by telling stories, at which they were masters.

I admired both my parents, for their ingenuity in keeping a household that contained ten people going, but I especially adored my mother, who was, it seemed to me, probably the best human being on the planet. However, nowhere in the literature, either in grade school, high school, or college, did I encounter anyone who resembled her: not in the literature, nor in the actual buildings of these institutions themselves. I set out to correct this failing. And wrote about my mother. In fact, there is a book, *In Search of Our Mothers' Gardens*, that is dedicated to my mother, the missing Goddess in the North American landscape.

Only late in my development, in the work of the poet Langston Hughes, did I sometimes find a reflection of people that I knew; and at the time Hughes and I met, when I was in college, I had not read any of his work. He very kindly gave me a stack of his books and became my champion and friend.

I also studied on my own such writers as Richard Wright, Jean Toomer, Gwendolyn Brooks, and Nella Larsen. I discovered the amazing writings of the author of *Their Eyes Were Watching God*, Zora Neale Hurston.

Central also to my growth as a human being and as a writer was the great writer James Baldwin, who seemed to be, and I think was, entirely fearless, his fierce intelligence and incisive speech a gift he offered to those of us in North America who called our country on its racist behavior and championed the courage and determination of our own folks. Struggling as we were to win the vote, to put an end to the wanton murder of black people, to become citizens second to none.

This was to be the beginning of my lecture at the huge international festival of the book in Brasilia that I was invited to address. I never gave it, because I realized, at the point that I stopped writing it, that I am bored with addressing audiences in this way.

As Life would have it, days before we left for Brasilia, Brazil, I was invited to appear (on my return) at Pop-Up Magazine, a yearly event in San Francisco at which writers and poets and musicians and activists of all stripes present an idea, a thought, a memory, an action, that can be no more than five minutes long. The event is ephemeral. Nothing is recorded. Nothing is taped. This appealed to me, as it apparently appeals to the people of San Francisco. The event occurred days after I returned from Brazil; tickets for it, at the several-thousand-seat symphony hall in downtown San Francisco, sold out in hours.

I invited a wonderful band of friends to what was a lively, joyful, vibrant affair. They very much enjoyed the novelty of the experience, and this is what I read.

So there I was, on my way to a huge book festival in Brasilia and only then realizing, because friends casually mentioned it, Brasilia isn't actually Brazil. It is a man-made city, only fifty-two years old, created to be the center of Brazilian government and plunked down in the middle of a desert, with 1950s-style buildings and surrounded by miles of scrub vegetation.

Yikes! What to do?

My partner Kaleo and I went anyway. And we made a fascinating discovery. Perhaps the same discovery we make everywhere we go.

In this world of war, where peace seems elusive and the war machine grinds relentlessly, how does one extend the integrity of peace?

By giving one's self over to the experience of being genuine with the humans one meets, without a single false smile or bit of pretension, and by being present to each encounter in one's true character.

Does this sound easy? It actually is.

Jet-lagged, I still found myself the first evening of the festival flying out the door of the hotel to hear the great Vandana Shiva, whom I had not known would be there! She was, of course, amazing, and talked with her usual strength about the corruption of the planet's seeds, soil, and water, and her heroic battles in India against the evil corporate giant Monsanto. Like Vandana Shiva, I believe unless Monsanto is stopped and the damage done by its attacks on biodiversity undone, the very ground under our feet will eventually become sterile and uninhabitable. The practices of the corporate giant are emblematic of ignorance, heartlessness, and greed; the impact on the world's farmers, who are killing themselves by the hundreds of thousands, enough to keep all of us tossing and turning in our beds.

And that was just the first night!

The night of my "lecture," and after a restful sleep, I talked about Some of Everything, to one of the most affectionate audiences I have ever experienced. Overwhelmingly Afro-Brazilian women, all luscious colors of the human rainbow, they were so vibrantly alive the huge tent in which we gathered seemed to hum! They called out that they loved me. I responded that I adored them. At the signing later I was kissed and hugged, and I kissed and hugged back, until it felt as if our mutually enslaved and separated ancestors were, after four hundred years, reuniting. We were. Ah, the magic of experiencing at least this one bright outcome of collective suffering!

I talked about some of the things I wrote in my not-to-be-delivered "lecture." Though because I wasn't "lecturing," someone (probably an academic) in the audience complained. Which gave me the opportunity to talk about the gracefulness of accepting what is offered rather than what is desired. And so on.

The following day Kaleo and I were taken on a tour of Brasilia by someone connected with the festival whom we only knew as Pablo. In the heat, in a white van that had seen better days. With a driver we'd never seen before. Reassured somewhat by the fact that we were joined by "the other Alice" who had translated one of my several interviews. Off we went rolling around Brasilia, looking at the incredible, to us, flatness of everything. Northern California, our own stomping ground, seeming at times to be one big hill composed of slightly smaller ones.

And here is where we came around to our realization of peace. For half the ride I was not inclined to talk, or even to look at the others in the van. I let my partner do the talking, which, luckily, he is inclined to do, no matter his exhaustion. We felt dragged along, at first, and longed to be done. I felt I could never live in a place like Brasilia. Too flat. Not enough hills. No ocean. No real views. The land seemed red and depressed. The trees stunted. There were no horses, cows, pigs, or goats, which, in my view, would greatly improve everything: the soil would be fertilized, for instance, and gardens might be planted. Food grown.

No gardens. No fields of growing food. *At all!* Shocking to the farmer in me.

So. No smiling. No anything on my part but stoic endurance.

The first shift came when Pablo sent the driver off to buy gas and we were left at a huge apartment block (heavy and lifeless-looking as anything) where we stood among a few sickly trees with yellow flowers and Pablo began to talk about how beautiful everything was. It was so strange. As was our realization that a man was sitting near us with his dog—the only dog we'd seen—and that the dog was objectively "ugly," all pug nose and scrunched jowls, but that, subjectively, it was sweet and lovely. It sniffed all of us gently and with benign interest. Dog lovers, we began to revive in spirit.

And then a single bird dashed through the flowering trees.

And again, Pablo thought this one bird was fabulous. We all admired its long tail and graceful way of hopping about in the dirt.

And then, because my partner (who mixes his own tobacco) had lost his pipe and wanted to buy a new one, we found ourselves at the local head shop. And there, haggling over the prices of a couple of cool pipes, a haggling that eventually drew us all in—the two young women selling the pipes adamant about their price—Alice, the translator, called into the fray. Me, called in to give my opinion that haggling over anything is absurd in hot weather. . . . The other Alice smoking a cigarette and not knowing there was a time women were beaten for doing so in public. . . . Me noticing her quiet kindness and sweetness and not just the coolness of her onyx-gray eyes. The two saleswomen following us out of the shop with kisses and hugs. Pablo suddenly, back in the van, talking about how he'd rather have schools and hospitals built rather than the huge stadium we were passing that is being constructed for the World Cup coming to Brasilia in 2014. Then saying, out of the blue, that he plays the piano—and at this point giving me a video of a beloved musician he wants us to hear and later meet when we (he's sure it will happen) travel someday to Bahia.

He decides to take us to what he calls "the real Brazil." It is on the outskirts of Brasilia. It is the Third World. A place like others everywhere in Mexico, Africa, Latin America. Indian reservations in America. Backroads in some American mountains. No running water or paved streets. No sanitation. No fifties-style buildings and no sterility. Only poverty. Where poor people have squatted, settled, begun to build their shanties, and over time have made a community. Drugs make it a scary place to be at night, Pablo tells us, but I see that a few of the inhabitants have taken what excess of money they have and painted the walls of their dwellings blue, orange, yellow, green; the bright, clear colors of the hopeful heart. I begin spontaneously to clap my hands, to applaud.

And I keep finding things to applaud all the way back to the hotel. Not the flatness, not the grandiose and unfortunate statue of the founder of the city of Brasilia, not the president's strange house that looks like a library, or the congress that looks suspiciously uninviting, but the spirit that lives beneath all of this. The "real" Brazil. Pablo caring enough about two strangers to hire a van and take us to experience his environment. The other Alice offering her assistance and presence; the driver good-naturedly helping to turn our "tour" of Brasilia into an exploration. An event.

The four of us are happy and peaceful as we turn toward our hotel. Arriving there we exchange e-mail addresses and phone numbers. We hug and kiss good-bye. Friends, though we may never see each other again.

What makes any place truly beautiful? Even the flat places, the deserts. Even Brasilia. The courage and patience to encounter the unknown Other simply as one's self. Whether it is other humans, animals, or land. To see that self reflected back at you. *Namaste*.

Only this.

PERMISSIONS

CELEBRATING
INDEPENDENT PUBLISHING

Thank you for reading this book published by The New Press. The New Press is a nonprofit, public interest publisher. New Press books and authors play a crucial role in sparking conversations about the key political and social issues of our day.

We hope you enjoyed this book and that you will stay in touch with The New Press. Here are a few ways to stay up to date with our books, events, and the issues we cover:

- Sign up at www.thenewpress.com/subscribe to receive updates on New Press authors and issues and to be notified about local events
- Like us on Facebook: www.facebook.com/newpressbooks
- Follow us on Twitter: www.twitter.com/thenewpress

Please consider buying New Press books for yourself; for friends and family; or to donate to schools, libraries, community centers, prison libraries, and other organizations involved with the issues our authors write about.

The New Press is a 501(c)(3) nonprofit organization. You can also support our work with a tax-deductible gift by visiting www .thenewpress.com/donate.